Fit for Fertility

Michael Dooley, FRCOG

Fit for Fertility

Overcoming infertility and preparing for pregnancy

HODDER

MOBIUS

Copyright 2006 by Michael Dooley, FRCOG

First published in Great Britain in 2006 by Hodder & Stoughton
A division of Hodder Headline

This paperback edition published in 2007

The right of Michael Dooley, FRCOG to be identified as the Author of the Work has been asserted by him in accordance with the Copyright, Designs and Patents Act 1988.

A Mobius paperback

1

A CIP catalogue record for this title is available from the British Library

ISBN 978 0 340 89633 4
ISBN 0 340 89633 7

Typeset in Sabon by Hewer Text UK Ltd, Edinburgh
Printed and bound by Clays Ltd, St Ives plc

Hodder Headline's policy is to use papers that are natural, renewable and recyclable products and made from wood grown in sustainable forests. The logging and manufacturing processes are expected to conform to the environmental regulations of the country of origin.

Hodder & Stoughton Ltd
A division of Hodder Headline
338 Euston Road
London NW1 3BH

Contents

Acknowledgements

This book is dedicated to all my patients, who, having put their trust in me, inspire me to keep going.

There are many individuals whom I would like to thank for their professional guidance and friendship throughout my career looking after couples with infertility. To all those I have forgotten to thank personally – please forgive me!

Mr Sam Abdalla, Mary Power and all the team at The Lister Hospital really secured my knowledge and have been a fantastic support to me ever since. Working with the British Olympic teams has been inspirational and I would like to thank Dr Richard Budgett and all the team at The Olympic Medical Institute for their kindness. The staff at The Poundbury Clinic, which is developing into an excellent women's integrated health centre, have been fantastic. Working at Westover House has allowed me to continue my work with different practitioners and I would like to thank Dr Tim Evans for his faith in me to work with his team. All the staff at The Winterbourne Hospital fertility clinic and the fertility clinic at Dorset County Hospital need a big thank you for their hard work and dedication to the patients that come under our care. Dr Mosaraf Ali, Dr Wendy Denning and Vicki Vlachonis deserve particular thanks for teaching me about the integrated approach to healthcare. Annette Wilkinson from The Doctors' Laboratory has encouraged me throughout the project and I would also like to thank her for her true professional approach to healthcare.

This whole project could not have been accomplished without the superb administrative care provided by Pat McAuley, Louise

Pounds, Paula Eastwell and Jane Marsh. Others that I would like to thank include Sarah Stacey for her help, kindness and guidance. Kay McCauley for being such a fabulous agent – without her drive this book would never have evolved. All the staff at Hodder Mobius – a big thank you and special thanks to Rowena Webb, Helen Coyle and Karen Geary. A huge thank you must go to Hannah Black for her total dedication to the project and her unending patience, motivation and good humour.

Finally, I would like to thank Barbara my wife and our children, Denis, William and Rebecca for putting up with me during the long hours working on this book.

INTRODUCTION

Understanding My Approach

I f you have bought this book, it is likely that you are either planning to get pregnant in the near future or you and your partner have been trying to have a baby for some time without success. Whatever your situation, this book is designed to prepare your body and your mind for conception and pregnancy and, if appropriate, help you and your partner navigate your way through the various treatments that you may encounter in the future.

Planning for pregnancy and infertility have an effect on both partners. For simplicity's sake, I have made the assumption that this book is being read by the female partner, but I cannot stress enough that the male partner should be equally involved.

Every day in my working life, as a consultant obstetrician and gynaecologist, I encounter couples who are longing for a baby but are full of anxiety, frustration and sadness because they have so far been unable to fulfil their dream. But happily – in most cases – those same couples do eventually go on to have a healthy baby. It is my firm and honest belief that most problems of infertility can be overcome, and in this book I will show you how, with the right preparation, communication and positive approach, you and your partner can have the best possible chance of having your own baby. At the very least, you will be able to say, 'We have done our best.'

The decision to have a baby is a wonderful thing, and just as you would make preparations for any other major life change, it is vital that both you and your partner take time to prepare for this new adventure. If you have been experiencing problems with fertility, it is all the more important that you are equipped with the best information available. Along with this, it is crucial to try to stay positive – whatever setbacks you may have experienced in the past or may encounter in the future. We'll be seeing again and again throughout this book just how important it is to maintain a determined and positive outlook.

Fit for Fertility is divided into four main parts. Part 1 looks at the basics of reproduction and conception – you may already have a general idea about this, but it is really important to familiarise yourself thoroughly; Part 2 covers my Fit for Fertility Programme, which aims to get you in the best shape for conception. Part 3 deals with initial medical consultations and investigations; while the final section, Part 4, covers specific fertility problems and treatment options. The philosophy behind my treatment, as you're about to discover for yourself, is based on partnership with patients, so I have included tools to enable you to tailor the different options to your own unique situation. More than anything, I hope you will find this book a useful and inspiring resource.

Before we go any further, I would like to explain to you the three key elements in my approach to the treatment of infertility. These three elements will help guide you through any treatment or changes you may make to your lifestyle in preparation for having a baby. They are:

1. an integrated approach
2. the Dooley equation
3. a positive approach

AN INTEGRATED APPROACH

The development of an integrated approach (by which I mean the combination of orthodox and complementary medicine) to health and fertility has long been my dream. Having worked with couples experiencing infertility for over 25 years and treated many thousands of individuals, I have witnessed first-hand the efficacy and importance of a holistic and multi-disciplinary approach to healthcare. I am a passionate believer in integrated healthcare and have established The Poundbury Clinic in Dorset in order to develop a women's integrated healthcare programme and helped coordinate the integrated infertility treatment programme at Westover House, London. In this book one of my main aims will be to guide and assist you in creating for yourself a tailor-made, bespoke package of care that is right for you. We hear a lot these days about complementary and alternative healthcare, but it has not always been something that patients were encouraged to consider alongside conventional medicine. Happily, this is starting to change, and more and more GPs and other clinicians snow recognise the benefits of combining different approaches to healthcare. In fact, half of the GP practices in the UK now provide access to complementary therapies in some shape or form.[1] For many couples, it can take only a very simple change in diet or lifestyle in order for them to finally be able to conceive – even after years of trying. That is why it is so important to get a balanced view of the whole picture.

As you probably already know from your own past experiences, different treatments and methods from conventional healthcare and alternative medicine work for different people. We are all unique and have our own specific needs and preferences, and my treatment plan is designed to accommodate everyone. Because what works for you may not necessarily work for others, and vice versa, this book will encourage you to consider the various routes open to you, while making sure that they feel right for you and your particular circumstances. I use the acronym DR AID to describe this integrated approach. This stands for:

D – Diagnose
R – Review the treatment options
A – Agree the plan of treatment for you
I – Implement the plan
D – Demonstrate that it is working

Diagnose

Before starting any treatment journey, it is essential to get an appropriate diagnosis. With time, the diagnosis will evolve and treatment may change. In some ways, the management of fertility is an evolutionary process.

CASE STUDY

Mr and Mrs T. J., aged 25 and 27 respectively, approached me about their fertility after only trying to conceive for six months. Following a careful history and examination, I discovered that Mrs T. J. was three stone overweight and Mr T. J. smoked 20 cigarettes a day and drank 40 units of alcohol a week. At this initial stage, the diagnosis was lifestyle issues. Due to their age and the duration of time they had been trying to conceive, I felt it was inappropriate for them to have further investigations.

With this diagnosis, I started them on our Fit for Fertility Programme (more on that in Part 2). Six months later, they had made a dramatic improvement to their lifestyle but had still failed to conceive. I felt it was then appropriate to do further investigations. Mrs T. J. was diagnosed with blocked tubes. They went on to have successful IVF (in vitro fertilisation) treatment.

In this case, the diagnosis evolved, but I am sure the benefit of the Fit for Fertility Programme encouraged the positive result with IVF.

Review the Treatment Options

Once the diagnosis has been made, you need to review the treatment options with the appropriately trained and qualified health professionals. These options should be linked up and integrated. Here, I use another acronym to describe how the stages of treatment work, and that is FAMSAM. This means:

F – Fit for fertility options
A – Alternative treatment
M – Medical treatment
S – Surgical treatment
A – Assisted conception
M – Moving on

None of these work in isolation; they all work together. It is important that we talk through each option and mix and match.

Agree the Plan of Treatment

Once you have reviewed your options, agree a plan between yourself and your partner. This is a key part of my DR AID concept. I look at the management of an infertile couple like planning the programme of training and care for an Olympic athlete – the journey is to gain gold. At an early stage in the journey, time is spent putting together a journey plan. The same should be true when managing your journey for infertility. Take time in reviewing all the options. Remember, you must be happy with your plan. It is, in some ways, like going to buy a pair of shoes. Initially, the shop assistant will go through what type of shoes you need – walking, work, dancing, colour, etc. He or she will then give you a selection to try on. Once you have found shoes that are comfortable for you, you make the decision as to which ones you want.

JOHNNY THE HORSE DEALER

I have a great friend called Johnny who is a horse dealer in Ireland. Whenever he goes to a horse sale, he receives and listens to lots of different people's advice about which horse to buy.

At one stage, he will vanish and return a few hours later having purchased several horses. On one occasion, I asked him why he did not buy the horses with his advisors present. He said he wanted to get everybody's opinion, but eventually the decision was his and he wanted to make the decision and live with it.

In some ways, this is true of fertility: listen to people's advice, but eventually make your *own* decision.

Implement the Plan

Once you have agreed your plan, the next step is to implement it and link all the professionals together. This is another core aspect of DR AID. Once you have started the implementation, do not start tinkering and changing the plan at whim with this new diet and this new supplement. You need good evidence to make changes, otherwise you will get confused and concerned. Imagine if Steve Redgrave kept on changing his training programme; he would not remain focused, and I am sure he would not have won five gold medals. Obviously, there will be time to regroup and readjust. Pick your team of advisors, have confidence in their professional ability and every so often audit their progress.

Demonstrate That it Is Working

After implementation, demonstration that your plan works is important. Have regular review sessions with your health professional to confirm you are on the right track. You may make changes to your agreed plan if any new information has come to light.

In entrepreneurial speech, they say, 'Conceive a dream; believe in your dream; achieve your dream.' The same idea should be applied to your fertility: 'Conceive your fertility plan; believe in your plan; achieve your dream.'

As you read, you will see that I have tried to give as detailed and broad a view of the various different approaches and treatments that may be available to you without overloading you with unhelpful information. It is important that together with your partner – and also, in some cases, family and friends – you make positive and informed decisions, that you know what questions you might need to ask, what to expect from different procedures and what alternative options you have. By reading this book and arming yourself with the right information and guidance, you are giving yourself the best possible chance of success.

THE DOOLEY EQUATION

Simply put, fertility treatment is made up of consultations, investigations, coming up with an appropriate diagnosis and then deciding on a course of treatment or treatments. This may sound quite straightforward, but there are also a number of other very important elements that play a significant role in the successful treatment of fertility problems and infertility. In order to make decisions regarding investigation and treatment options, it is important that you take a bit of time – with your partner – to talk over those other equally significant factors that may not immediately occur to you or that may not come up during consultation with your GP.

Over the years, in treating many couples from very different backgrounds and circumstances, I have come up with what I call the Dooley equation. Don't worry, I'm not asking you to understand a complicated mathematical formula; this is simply a way of breaking down what I think are the key elements to your fertility treatment. It seems to get longer as times goes on, but simply put, it is made up of the following:

Medical + Ethical + Emotional + Financial + Legal + Complementary and Alternative Medicine + Family and Friends = Treatment

Not quite A + B!

For any couple wanting to have a child but facing difficulties in conceiving, there may be times when it feels as though you would do just about anything to make your dream come true. That is why I think it's important to look at each factor in the Dooley equation before you do anything else. This equation asks you to look at more than just the obvious factors, like health, and instead shows how your support systems, beliefs, financial situation and legal position all contribute in their own ways to your choice of treatment. By considering all the factors, you will be better equipped to make the best decision for you and your partner – and for your baby. As with any decision, there are long-term consequences and implications that should be taken into account, and that is why this equation is so important. There'll be a chance for you to have another look at the different parts of the equation later on in the book, but for now let's have a brief look at each factor in turn.

Medical

Before embarking on any course of treatment, it is important that your GP and/or consultant is able to provide you with a good diagnosis. In order to conceive, we need a healthy egg, a healthy sperm and for the two to get together in a healthy body. The diagnosis of these three prerequisites is key to future plans. This will involve finding out about both you and your partner's health histories, which we'll cover in greater detail in Part 3. Diagnosis can also involve examination and investigation. It is important to have choices when it comes to treatment, which is why a good diagnosis is so crucial. I'll talk more later about finding the right 'team' for you – be it in your local surgery or hospital unit. You need to feel you are in safe and understanding hands, and I would always support seeking a second opinion if you feel you are not being given adequate care. Once the diagnosis has been made, a treatment plan is made, as in the DR AID format.

Ethical

Questions of fertility and infertility can – understandably, I think – easily become moral and ethical questions. While this may not apply to you and your partner, for many, the idea of having a baby – perhaps by assisted means – can bring up issues concerning religious, cultural and moral beliefs. It is important that you discuss with your partner – and perhaps also with your families – any fears or concerns that you have regarding likely examinations or treatment as well as the overall implications of fertility treatment. Not everyone will view the idea of assisted conception in the same way. It may be that you have made the decision to undergo a course of IVF, but your family strongly disapproves. It's important to weigh up the effects of this kind of opposition and to make sure that you feel adequately supported – even if not by everyone.

In Hong Kong, there is a marked negative attitude towards IVF. The stigma surrounding it is such that many who undergo treatment keep it secret – even from their immediate families.[2]

I often encounter the same kinds of attitude in my own practice here in the UK. There are different religious reasons for why people can feel uncertain about some of the fertility treatments that they may be offered. Again, it's important that you take time to talk these over with those closest to you. In most cultures, infertility is undesirable and many people consider that having children is the main purpose of marriage. In Jewish culture and under Islamic law the family is central and assisted conception without a donor is acceptable. The Roman Catholic Church, on the other hand, has a strict view that procreation should not be separated from the act of intercourse. If religious questions are important to you, discuss matters with your pastor or religious leader.

RUMPELSTILTSKIN

In the introduction to their book, *Inconceivable Conceptions*, Jane Haines and Juliet Miller discuss the Grimms' fairy tale 'Rumpelstiltskin'. In the story, the miller's daughter is locked away by the king and told to spin straw into gold. The girl doesn't know what to do, but then a little man appears and says that, in return for a gift, he will spin her straw into gold. Over the course of several days, the girl gives the little man everything she has, and each time he spins straw into gold for her. Eventually, she has nothing left to give, and so he agrees to complete the task for her on condition that when she falls pregnant she will give him her firstborn child. The miller's daughter, being naïve, acquiesces. The tragic consequences of her uninformed actions earn her an awful experience when, having fallen in love with her baby, Rumpelstiltskin returns to demand his reward. Haines and Miller go on to state that in the course of assisted reproductive technology many women or couples will go to any length to spin straw into gold and achieve their golden fantasy of a baby, but they do not always take heed of the long-term consequences or implications of their decisions.

Some couples will change consultant or even country to obtain a baby, regardless of ethical, medical and financial implications. It is only retrospectively that they may be confronted with the Rumpelstiltskin consequences of their actions.

Emotional

Anyone who has had difficulty in conceiving will naturally experience lots of emotions. These can range from frustration and anger to depression, sadness and even despair. Of course, the upside is that embarking on a course of treatment or trying new therapies or exercises can be a very positive move. When looking at the options that are available to you, be honest with yourself and your partner about the lengths to which you feel you are prepared to go. I will be talking more about the importance of setting goals later on because this is a key factor in choosing treatment. Know exactly what your ultimate goal is and really go for it.

As I said earlier, it's very important that you feel happy with your doctor or consultant and their team. After all, medical treatment can often come with its own emotional implications, so it's right to do what you can now to minimise any additional worry.

Financial

As with most things, issues and decisions surrounding fertility treatment will undoubtedly involve money. In the UK, availability of treatment on the NHS is still very much a postcode lottery. The NICE (National Institute for Health and Clinical Excellence) guidelines indicate that funding should be available for couples who fulfil certain criteria; however, it is not yet clear exactly what those criteria are. Some health authorities will offer two courses of IVF or ICSI (intra-cytoplasmic sperm injection) treatment for couples who have been together for three years or more, have no living children from either side and who are aged 38 or under. Other health authorities have more restrictive criteria, so there is still no universal decision about what forms of fertility treatment are available on the NHS.[3]

If you've decided to use your own private funds, it is very important that you find out *exactly* what you are likely to be paying for. This includes checking out whether costs cover initial consultations, examinations and investigations as well as the different forms of treatment. It can be extremely easy to run up huge bills, so do make sure you are aware of any hidden costs from the very start. Do not forget to include the cost of medication.

Legal

Legal issues are becoming an increasingly important factor to consider in the treatment of infertility, particularly as units now not only have to take into consideration the couple's welfare but also the welfare of any child that may result from that treatment and the welfare of any children already in the family.

You may well have heard of the HFEA (Human Fertilisation and Embryology Authority). The HFEA is a UK non-departmental public body set up under the Human Fertilisation and Embryology Act 1990 that regulates and inspects all UK clinics that provide IVF, donor insemination or the storage of human eggs, sperm or embryos. The HFEA also licenses and monitors all human embryo research being conducted in the UK.

The guidelines that they provide clinics are often the source of news stories and debates. It is the job of the HFEA to ensure the welfare of any child born as a result of treatment, as well as looking into the needs of particular groups of patients – particularly in areas such as donor conception treatment.[4] New laws have just been passed lifting the anonymity for sperm and egg donors, which will give children born from a donated egg or sperm the right to trace their biological parents when they turn 18. For understandable reasons, many potential donors have been put off by this new legislation, which has had a knock-on effect on sperm stocks and waiting lists.

It's important to illustrate just how much legislation surrounding the broad area of infertility treatment has been put in place over recent years. Any unit or practice that you join should be able to give you all the necessary information and guidance covering this topic. More often than not, they will also offer some sort of counselling, which you may choose to accept.

Complementary and Alternative Medicine (CAM)

The role of complementary and alternative medicine in the treatment of infertility is crucial and is something I will come back to again and again throughout this book.

Complementary medicine is just that: a diagnosis, treatment and/or prevention that *complements* mainstream medicine. An estimated 5.75 million people in the UK see a complementary practitioner for some form of treatment each year.[5] A review of my personal practice found 60% of couples used some form of CAM, and this number is on the increase. CAM comes in a wide variety of forms, from acupuncture and Ayurvedic medicine to nutritional therapy, many of which are now available on the NHS. The best treatment for any kind of condition is one that treats the individual, and this means looking at a variety of treatments and finding out which one – or which combination of treatments – will best suit that person. Just as one 'orthodox' approach to a health problem may not work, neither should you assume that a particular therapy will single-handedly cure a condition. By integrating a cross section of approaches – both conventional and alternative – you will increase your chances of finding the right package of treatment for your own needs. The aim of an integrated approach to health is to promote optimum health levels and a consistently high standard of overall wellbeing. By providing you with as much sound information on all the available treatments as possible, you will be able to devise your own bespoke package of healthcare, which in turn will give you the best chance of success.

I can't stress enough just how important it is to consider all your treatment options, as by doing this, you are maximising your chance of giving birth to a healthy baby. So do take time with your partner to look at all the approaches available before deciding on a course of action.

Be careful of fad treatments. Infertility is very exposed to this.

The chance of a spontaneous conception is always there, and this allows for claims of success that may not be substantiated.

Family and Friends

Many people have a deep-seated, instinctive desire to have children, and families with children are very much what we in the West have come to expect for ourselves and our loved ones. The inability to have children can cause desperate heartache and grief and can dramatically change people's lives and outlooks. The emotional effects of infertility are all too often overlooked. Because it is such a private issue, many couples suffer their grief in silence, not wishing to share their pain with family and friends.

For some couples, the role of the family will be a crucial part of the equation. This won't apply to all, of course, but for many, the views, attitudes and support that family members can provide may help to determine decisions relating to treatment, as well as influencing some of the emotions surrounding the sensitive issues of fertility.

CASE STUDY

Moira and Alan came to see me after trying for three years, without success, to have a baby. After some searching questioning, it came to light that when Moira was nine years old her mother had given birth to a stillborn baby. This obviously had had a profound effect on Moira, so much so that she admitted that for the first year of trying she was really concerned about getting pregnant in case the same thing happened to her.

All routine medical investigations were carried out and proved clear. After looking at the options open to them, Moira decided to try a course of hypnotherapy and, after five sessions, conceived naturally.

Family and friends can be a tremendous support, whether in terms of their emotional or practical help – providing transport to the unit for instance. But often family and friends can be responsible for putting pressure on their loved ones. Comments like 'When are you going to make me a grandparent?' or 'You shouldn't leave too long a gap between children' can – unwittingly or not – cause stress for you and your partner, particularly if you have been trying to have a baby for a while without success. If you feel it is appropriate, it can sometimes help to tell your closest family or friends about any problems you might be encountering in trying to have a baby. This way, they can avoid behaving in ways that may put you under more stress. It may be a relief to share your concerns with someone other than just your partner.

If you are trying for a baby and already have a child, it is important that you take into account their feelings and views. Existing children can often feel overlooked or 'forgotten' in some way, particularly if their mother is undergoing IVF treatment, which can take up a lot of time and energy, leaving little left over for the child.

Planning a second child can cause as much, if not more, emotional stress. A common question you will be asked is 'When are you having another child?' There can also be a guilt spiral. It goes something like this: you have what you want in a child. You want more of what you've got in the form of another child. You cannot easily get more of what you have and so you get emotionally low. You get annoyed because you already have what you want . . .

Do take time to factor in your family and friends as they play a vital role – now, when embarking on any form of treatment and once your baby is born.

> 'Wherever there is a human being, there is an opportunity for kindness.'
>
> *Lucius Annaeus Seneca*

So that is the Dooley equation! Each of the above factors will play an important role as you embark on your journey towards having your baby, so it's a good idea to take time to look at each in turn and think about how it relates to your own circumstances. Some will have more relevance to you than others. The case study below illustrates just how decisions regarding treatment can be influenced by the different elements in this equation.

CASE STUDY

John and Sue have been married for five years. John is a 36-year-old carpenter; he has three children from a previous marriage and had a vasectomy seven years ago. Sue is a healthy 39-year-old and has not conceived before. Because of John's vasectomy, there is no way that the couple will be able to conceive naturally. This leaves them with the following options:

1. Give up trying for a baby altogether.
2. Try for donor insemination (DI).
3. Try for ICSI treatment using sperm from John.
4. Try for adoption.

For emotional reasons, the couple are not prepared to give up on their hopes for a child, so they immediately rule out option one. The second option, donor insemination, is a strong contender for many couples, and John and Sue consider it carefully. The success rate for donor insemination is in the region of 10–15% per treatment cycle, depending on age group. (The average cost that a unit will charge is around £300–500 at the time of writing, although for certain couples, it may be available on the NHS.) John and Sue realise that the success rate is good, and they do have the funds necessary. However, although legally any child born by donor insemination would be theirs, for emotional and ethical reasons, they both want to have a baby that is genetically their own. Option three is to consider extracting John's sperm from his testes and then undergo ICSI treatment. Before doing this, John would have to have a blood test to check that his testicles are working and then a surgical procedure would follow to aspirate (which means to draw out) the sperm from his testicle followed by ICSI treatment (which I'll cover in more detail in Chapter 24). Initially, this sounds very exciting – it would mean the chance of having their own child, but when they discover that the cost will be considerably over their budget and that the success rate can be as low as 20% per treatment cycle for people of their age, option three no longer seems quite so attractive – even though emotionally and ethically it remains very appealing. The last option, adoption, for the same reasons given for option two, is not yet something they feel they can consider.

So, having carefully weighed up the options available to them and taken into account the various factors in our equation, they decide to go for option two after all – donor insemination. And happily, after three attempts, John and Sue are now the very proud parents of a healthy baby boy. At the time of conception, they sensibly chose to store sperm from the same donor and have since gone on to have a second son.

You can see from this real-life example just how much the decisions that this couple made were influenced by a number of factors and that once they had considered the options available to them, they found that their original viewpoint had changed. This is the role of the Dooley equation.

If you are in the position of making similar kinds of decisions, remember that medical issues are just one of the factors to consider. Try to keep an eye on the whole picture. Yours is a very personal journey, and it makes good sense to only take steps that you and your partner feel happy and comfortable with. The more relaxed and positive you are feeling, the greater the likelihood of a successful outcome.

A POSITIVE APPROACH

We have looked at the importance of creating a bespoke, integrated package of wellbeing and healthcare and have outlined the key factors to consider in relation to treatment. In this last section I'd like to say something about the importance of your attitude and approach to your fertility.

During my eight years as Director of Sports Science and Medicine for the British Equestrian Federation, I travelled to two Olympic Games – Atlanta and Sydney. I also work at the Olympic Medical Institute seeing female athletes with gynaecological problems. From this background, I have realised the importance of sports psychology in enabling athletes to win gold.

My experience in this area let me witness first-hand the extraordinary power of positive thinking and goal setting. When observing world-class athletes who have dedicated their lives to honing and refining their strength and skills, it is interesting to see that there may be almost nothing to separate them from their competitors in terms of speed, length of training, fitness or agility; it is their *attitude* that sets them apart as winners. You may be wondering what exactly this all has to do with the treatment of fertility problems! What I learnt from my work with sportsmen and women was that a positive approach leads to a positive outcome, and this is as relevant to your health and wellbeing as it is to the result of a race.

Throughout this book I will be showing you the importance of approaching this journey with the right spirit and attitude. As most know only too well, a positive outlook is not something that can be acquired instantly in any area of life, and this is particularly true of something as emotionally charged as trying for a baby. Any change in outlook requires commitment. This means taking time to plan ahead, to consider your goals and make the necessary adjustments to achieve them. By learning to develop positive ways of thinking, you will also be far better equipped to deal with any setbacks or challenges along the way.

For some, a positive approach may sound like an unlikely and perhaps rather vague solution to what is a complex problem, but research carried out in the US among groups of women being treated for infertility showed how behavioural treatment used to help tackle feelings of negativity, anxiety and depression led to increased rates of conception.[6] And from my own experience of working with couples trying to conceive, there is much to suggest that adopting a positive approach to treatment plays a significant role in its success.

Whatever course of action you and your partner are considering – be it making changes to your diet, giving up smoking and alcohol, having a series of acupuncture treatments or starting a cycle of IVF – the more focused you are on your goals and what you hope to achieve, the more likely you are to succeed. So, for instance, your goals may include reducing your weight, clearing any infections or getting on to an IVF waiting list. You might have a series of mini goals or a number of back-up options in case your first plan of action doesn't work out. What is important is that you know where you are heading and what steps you need to take in order to get there. By working out a realistic plan, you are less likely to feel overwhelmed or pressurised and more likely to obtain and maintain a happy, optimistic and upbeat sense of purpose and focus. It is also important to avoid thinking from month to month. Work out a plan that covers a number of months. If your focus is only on the short term, you are likely to feel disappointed.

Here's something I often remind my patients: the chance of conception for a healthy couple through one single act of intercourse is in the order of 1–3%! If I were to suggest a fertility treatment with those odds, no one would ever try! Make sure your package of treatment is clear, realistic and includes a number of options.

In my work, I have noticed that even when a couple has tried various courses of treatment but still not conceived, the very fact that they tried all that they set out to try has given them a vital sense of reassurance.

Do not underestimate the power of your thoughts and objectives! Chapter 14 will look at how you can promote a positive approach and outlook that will stand you and your partner in good stead and give you a clear vision of what it is you can achieve. Just as an athlete must have absolute faith in the training programme that they are following and in the team with which they are working, so it is important that you maintain your own strong and focused team and agenda.

THE IMPORTANCE OF PREPARATION

In order to get the very best from any treatment or therapies you may receive, it's a good idea to take time to prepare. This means looking at the positive-thinking exercises that I suggest in Chapter 14 and really preparing yourself mentally and emotionally – and your partner too, of course.

It also makes good sense for you and your partner to positively prepare your *health* and *body*. I've noticed how often a couple will overlook their own general fitness and wellbeing as they try for a baby. Just as in the animal kingdom a farmer or horse breeder will spend an average of three months preparing their stock for conception, so it makes absolute sense to ensure you are at your optimum level of health before you even begin to try for a baby.

Finally, do bear in mind that 10% of *fertile* couples fail to conceive during their first year of trying,[7] so it is important to appreciate the chance nature of fertility.

If you are experiencing difficulty conceiving, take heart: the majority of infertility problems can now be overcome, thanks to a very wide choice of treatments.

PART 1

UNDERSTANDING FERTILITY AND INFERTILITY

We will start by looking at what actually happens at conception. Don't be tempted to skip Chapter 1 – you'd be surprised by just how few people really know about the different processes that take place in the body to enable this miraculous event to occur. Or perhaps you might be one of those who are still a little hazy on the details!

Much has been written about calculating the 'right' time for conception, from temperature charts to urine tests. I hope to dispel some of the myths that abound – rarely is there a perfect situation for conception! Instead, I will outline a sensible approach to finding *your* best time for conception and tell you how to create the optimum conditions for this.

Increasingly, women are choosing to start a family later in life, and so for some reading this book, you may be concerned that your age is affecting your chances of conception. In Chapter 2 I'll be looking at how age plays its part in fertility and how long you should reasonably wait before deciding to seek further help.

Chapter 3 concentrates on the most common causes of problems with fertility. Some are more straightforward than others, but it is important that you and your partner familiarise yourselves with the possible causes so that you can take the most appropriate steps to tackle them effectively. You may find that all that is required are a few simple lifestyle changes. For many, the cause of infertility is unknown, which can feel like a depressing conclusion. However, my experience with couples with unexplained infertility has taught me that, in most cases, there really is no such thing as infertility! Time and again I have seen a couple decide to give up trying for their own genetic baby and take the decision to adopt, only to then immediately fall pregnant. The body is a most mysterious machine, and with the right encouragement and care, it really can perform miracles!

Chapter 1

Understanding Conception

WHAT HAPPENS DURING CONCEPTION?

As I said earlier, in simplistic terms, all you need is the egg and the sperm to get together in a healthy body. While that is true, conception relies on various complex processes all happening in the right way at the right time. It's really no wonder that it can take a bit of time to occur. In order to understand conception, we need to look at the different stages that take place within the female and male bodies and what chemical or hormonal changes are involved in these processes.

Conception is basically a story of transport. The sperm has to travel from the man's testicles into the vagina via the penis. Once the sperm have been placed in the vagina, they have to move up through the cervix, across the uterus and down the fallopian tube to meet an egg. The egg has travelled from the ovary across to the tube. Once the egg is fertilised, the embryo is now developed and moves back down the tube to implant into the uterus. There are eight essential stages involved in reproduction. These are:

1. reproduction in women: the production of eggs
2. reproduction in men: the production of sperm
3. the sperm meeting the egg
4. fertilisation of the egg by the sperm

5. movement of the embryo back down the fallopian tube
6. implantation of the embryo
7. development of the embryo inside the womb
8. birth

Below, I will describe the first six of these stages in more detail, but for the purposes of the remainder of this book, we are going to be concentrating only on those first three crucial stages.

1. Reproduction in Women

Human eggs – otherwise known as ova or oocytes – are produced by the two ovaries that sit either side of the lower abdomen. Unlike the male sperm, women are born with their full quota of eggs – about one million – which by the time the female carrying them is born have already stopped being produced and have begun to die off. By the time a girl reaches puberty, around the age of 13, this number will have fallen to around half a million. Throughout a woman's reproductive life, the eggs will continue to die off, and as she gets older, the percentage of 'abnormal' eggs will start to increase because the normal ones have died.

On the first day of a woman's menstrual cycle (i.e. the first day of bleeding), the hypothalamus region of the brain signals the pituitary gland to release a hormone called follicle-stimulating hormone (FSH), which causes a number of egg-containing follicles in the ovaries to start to develop. Usually around 20 immature eggs will begin to develop within these sac-like follicles. As these follicles develop, they start to produce the hormone oestrogen. This release of hormone tells the pituitary gland to reduce the amount of FSH being produced so that only enough is made to allow just one egg to continue maturing, while the remaining follicles simply shrivel up; thus multiple pregnancy is not common. The oestrogen also signals to the pituitary gland to produce another hormone called luteinising hormone (LH). In a normal 28-day cycle, the sudden surge in LH around day 12 causes the follicle to grow rapidly, and by day 14 the follicle ruptures, releasing the matured egg. The exact days vary from month to month and individual to individual. This is called ovulation. The egg is then wafted into the opening of one of two fallopian tubes. The fallopian tubes run from beside the ovaries to the uterus, and it is the job of microscopic hairs, called cilia, that line these tubes to gently move the egg down towards the uterus. Of course, if there is no sperm in the fallopian tube to meet the egg, then fertilisation does not take place, and the egg won't reach its destination.

Following the release of the mature egg, the ruptured follicle that had previously contained the egg now forms what is called the corpus luteum. This structure produces the hormone progesterone, which, along with the oestrogen, works to stimulate the thickening of the womb (or uterus) lining, called the endometrium. This is where a developing embryo will get its nutrients from. If the released egg is not fertilised, however, the progesterone levels will fall, the thickened lining is shed (and so menstruation begins), and the unfertilised egg disintegrates.

2. Reproduction in Men

Unlike women, from the age of puberty (around 13), men will remain fertile for the rest of their lives, continuing to produce sperm every day. Sperm are being constantly made inside the two testes or testicles. Each testicle is, on average, approximately 5cm long. The testes are contained within a sac called the scrotum. Within each testis are partitions dividing the interior into about 250 separate lobes. In turn, each of these is filled by a series of long, convoluted tubes called seminiferous tubules, and it is here that sperm are made.

The hormonal processes in men are not dissimilar from those in women. Sperm production is stimulated by the pituitary gland, which produces the hormones we saw earlier: FSH (follicle-stimulating hormone) and LH (luteinising hormone). FSH causes sperm production, while LH stimulates the production of that other more well-known hormone, testosterone. Testosterone is responsible for a number of processes, including the development of male physical characteristics, the production of seminal fluid and for enhancing the production of sperm.

The long, coiled seminiferous tubules eventually open out into a wider convoluted tube called the epididymis. Here, the sperm spend around 90 days maturing and gaining motility (the sperm's ability to use its 'tail' to move them forward). Then, over the next 14 days or so, the epididymis carries the now fully matured sperm to another thick-walled channel called the vas deferens. Here, the sperm may be stored for several months. It is via this tube that the sperm will eventually leave the scrotum, passing first through the urethra, at ejaculation. (It can take up to 30 ejaculations to completely empty the vas deferens of sperm. This explains why in some cases men who have had a vasectomy can still, for a period immediately after the procedure, fertilise a woman's egg.) During intercourse, the secretions of the seminal vesicles and the prostate gland are added to the sperm as they enter the urethra. These secretions form the seminal fluid in which the sperm are suspended. (Sperm actually forms less than 20% of the total volume of a man's ejaculate, but it is not unusual for there to be around 300 million sperm in 3–5ml of ejaculate. If each sperm could find an egg, this would be enough to populate most of North America!)

3. The Sperm Meeting the Egg

In order for fertilisation to occur, the sperm will need to meet the egg within around 24 hours of ovulation, after which the unfertilised egg will disintegrate. At ejaculation, roughly 300 million sperm are released into the woman's vagina. The vagina is acidic in order to protect against infection, and this acidity will also kill off many of the sperm. Those sperm that manage to reach the cervix, found at the top of the vagina, then need to find their way through the cervical mucus. This serves to prevent any abnormal sperm from continuing along the cervical canal into the uterus. Contractions of the uterine wall help to propel the healthy sperm up into the fallopian tubes. The distance from the entrance of the vagina to the fallopian tubes is only about 10cm, and this journey will take approximately half an hour; yet only around 300 sperm make it this far.

Once the sperm reaches the fallopian tube, it moves along it in order to reach the egg. Because most healthy sperm can live in the uterus and fallopian tube for several days, if intercourse takes place prior to ovulation, the released egg can still be fertilised for up to three days after intercourse.

4. Fertilisation of the Egg by the Sperm

The egg is covered with a protective coating called the zona pellucida. This will only allow one sperm to penetrate it. This is no easy task! The zona pellucida is much thicker than the head of the sperm and so most will fail to attach themselves, simply bouncing off. It is only the most healthy and strong sperm that will succeed in penetrating the egg's surface. Then, once a sperm has successfully implanted its head into the surface of the egg, it will shed its tail, releasing the contents of its head into the egg's nucleus. The egg is now fertilised and will contain all the genetic material needed to grow into a baby.

5. Movement of the Embryo Down the Fallopian Tube

The fertilised egg must now move along the fallopian tube towards the uterus, aided by the contractions of the tube. The fertilised egg, now called an embryo, will take around three to four days to reach and enter the uterus.

As we saw in the section on reproduction in women, since ovulation the lining of the uterus – the endometrium – has begun to grow thicker, creating a nice 'bed' in preparation for the embryo's arrival. The endometrium will also produce proteins that will help to attach the embryo. As the embryo reaches the uterus, it breaks out of its protective coating, the zona pellucida.

6. Implantation of the Embryo

Once inside the uterus, the embryo becomes embedded in the now thick endometrium. This implantation triggers the release of a hormone called human chorionic gonadotropin (hCG), which serves to maintain the pregnancy for the first 12 weeks by increasing the production of progesterone. It is the hCG hormone that you would look for in a urine sample or when you do a pregnancy test to confirm pregnancy.

CREATING THE OPTIMUM CONDITIONS FOR CONCEPTION

You may have been trying for a baby for some time or perhaps you are just now planning to get pregnant. Whatever your particular set of circumstances might be, try to remember the following: unlike other areas of your life (such as work or planning your summer holiday), having a baby will not always go according to plan; neither will it be always be in your control. Accepting this will help to take off some of the pressure you might be experiencing.

Of course, you can take many steps to increase your chances of conception, such as making sure that you and your partner are fit and well, but try not to let your desire for a baby dictate your every move or decision. Planning for a baby shouldn't become an obsession; it must be fun − a journey.

Often when couples come to see me, they will argue that they have done everything they can to ensure conception − they have timed intercourse down to the very last minute, with carefully plotted temperature charts, daily urine checks and the man on call with his mobile phone at the ready should his partner start to ovulate. Now, of course, timing is important, and I strongly believe in increasing your overall fertility awareness, but I am not a great advocate of excessive bodily monitoring or indeed having sex on the Cerne Giant during a full moon! By becoming overly preoccupied with trying to find the perfect time for conception, you risk putting pressure on your relationship – hardly a recipe for romance and spontaneity! Turning a problem into an obsession is not the best way of preparing your body and mind for conception. Get the passion back into your sex lives, enjoy it, and do not worry!

Winnie the Pooh said, 'A problem is a problem because it has a solution,' and I say, we must be careful not to let that problem become an obsession. If you have a problem, it will have a solution, but do not change a problem into an obsession.

The Ten Rules of Sex

1. Enjoy it.
2. Have enough; this means two to three times a week across the week.
3. If it hurts, ask for help.
4. Do not make it stressful.
5. Do not become obsessive.
6. Do not get worried about having sex at the 'right' time of the month.
7. Inject some passion into your sex lives, in whatever way suits you.
8. Talk about it.
9. Do not worry.
10. Enjoy again!

Regular sex means at least two to three times a week, and this doesn't mean two to three times on a Saturday night and nothing for the rest of the week!

Timing

Bearing what I have said in mind, there *are* a number of bodily changes that will indicate when you are likely to be at your most fertile. Many of these bodily changes are used to detect fertility timeframes by complementary practitioners, so do discuss the benefits with them. These include:

1. temperature
2. cervical mucus
3. salivary ferning
4. urine

Temperature

Around the middle of your menstrual cycle, your temperature rises, indicating that ovulation has occurred. This method of monitoring your fertility won't tell you in *advance* when you are going to ovulate, but by checking and recording your temperature daily, you should be able to work out when you are likely to ovulate in future months.

If you have a regular cycle, that is 28 days, you will notice a rise in temperature between days 14 and 16. So, on the days just *before* this point, you are probably at your most fertile. You should plan to have sex every other day from about day 11 to day 16, thus covering the time from just before to just after ovulation.

Because our normal basal body temperature fluctuates throughout the day, you will need to check your temperature first thing in the morning – preferably at the same time each morning – before you even get up. You'll need to record your temperatures on a chart. You can get temperature charts from the website, www.thepoundburyclinic.co.uk or www.fitforfertility.co.uk.

Use a different graph for each monthly cycle. (Remember to count the first day of your period as day 1.) You should also bear in mind that there are a number of other factors that can affect your temperature, including illness, alcohol, long-haul flights and medication.

Cervical Mucus

The bottom part of the uterus, the cervix, goes through quite dramatic changes during your menstrual cycle, depending on which hormones are being produced. Learning to detect and identify these changes is one way of figuring out when you are likely to be at your most fertile.

The cervical canal is lined with glands that are continually producing mucus. However, as you go through your cycle, this fluid changes. For the first 14 days of the cycle, the mucus is thick and pasty; this is so that it can form a kind of protective barrier over the cervix to stop sperm getting in. As the levels of the hormone oestrogen increase, around three to four days before ovulation, the mucus becomes clear and more stretchy and more of it is produced. Sperm can live in this kind of mucus for longer and are more able to swim through it. Then, once ovulation is over, the mucus will again return to its thick consistency.

This was described by John Billings, an Australian neurologist. There is information about this on the website, www.naturalfamilyplanning.org. Women are able to test their cervical mucus to see how stretchy or thick it is and so determine when they are most likely to be ovulating. The clearer and more watery the mucus, the more likely you are to be in your fertile time.

Salivary Ferning

I spent two years doing my thesis on the role and use of salivary steroids in fertility. Just as you may be able to detect changes in your cervical mucus as you approach ovulation, so your saliva will undergo similar changes. The term 'ferning' refers to the fern-leaf patterns that have been detected in both cervical mucus and saliva, due to the increase in salt in the fluid that occurs just before and around ovulation. It is possible to buy fern testing kits, which will detect when salivary ferning is taking place and so identify when ovulation is about to occur.

Urine

Even with regular periods, monitoring your basal body temperature or checking your cervical mucus may not be very reliable. Some women prefer to use ovulation kits, which test the urine to predict ovulation. These kits work to predict ovulation 24–36 hours in advance by detecting the increase, or surge, of luteinising hormone (LH) that occurs naturally one to two days before ovulation. LH is the triggering process for ovulation and therefore becomes a signal that your 'fertility window' has arrived.

A small amount of LH is always present in your blood and urine, but during the days before ovulation, the amount increases by about two to five times. Therefore, the 12–36 hours between the beginning of the LH surge and the time when your egg is actually released is considered the most fertile part of your cycle and the most likely time for conception.

Depending on the kit, you'll either collect your urine in a cup or hold a stick in your urine stream. Coloured bands will appear on the test card to indicate whether or not the LH surge is occurring. In general, you should try to collect your urine between 10 a.m. and 8 p.m. – the best time is supposed to fall between 2 p.m. and 2.30 p.m., but be sure to read the instructions on your kit. Try to collect your urine at about the same time every day.

You should try to reduce the amount of liquids you drink for about two hours before you collect your urine. Too much liquid could dilute your urine, which could cause you to miss a surge result. These tests can be bought without prescription and usually include seven days of tests.

As I said before, I don't generally advocate anything that

involves obsessing about time. These tests are not always reliable, and the strict planning of intercourse can be quite stressful and have detrimental effects on the couple's relationship. But, having said that, it may work for some.

The Perfect Position?

I think it's true that there are more myths surrounding fertility than any other area of medicine. I personally am not convinced that different sexual positions are better for conceiving than others; however, some experts involved in studies looking at just this have concluded that certain positions are more likely to help with conception.

Studies found that the best positions for conception should aim to expose the woman's cervix to as much sperm as possible while reducing the amount of sperm that leaks out (by positioning the woman's hips so that sperm stays inside), allowing enough time for it to travel towards the cervix.

Therefore, they recommend that you avoid having sex in positions that defy gravity, as this lessens the likelihood of your partner's sperm reaching your cervix. That would include avoiding sex while sitting, standing or with the woman on top of her partner. Positions believed to be good for conceiving include the missionary position (with the male partner on top), since this allows for deep penetration; you can also try elevating your hips using a pillow or cushion in order to expose the cervix further. Rear entry may also be effective, as it enables sperm to be deposited close to the cervix, and is thought to be particularly good for women with a tipped or tilted uterus.[1]

One question often asked is 'Do women need to have an orgasm to conceive?' The simple answer is no. We've seen this in artificial insemination by donor and intrauterine insemination. But while it is not necessary, it may help if a woman climaxes, as the contractions of her womb and vagina help to create a sort of partial vacuum, which draws the sperm into the cervix.

> Traditional Chinese medicine teaches that simultaneous orgasm will pull more of the man's sexual essence into the partner's womb.

A HEALTHY BODY AND A HEALTHY MIND

Temperature charts, saliva tests and finding the right position may all help to contribute to your chances of conception, but a general good level of health and wellbeing is really crucial if you are trying to conceive. This doesn't just mean ensuring you and your partner are eating the right foods or taking the right supplements, it also means adopting a positive and mutually supportive mindset. The stronger and more loving your relationship is with your partner, the better you will both feel. If stress levels are minimised, your health will also benefit. We will be looking at the importance of your preparations for trying to have a baby in my Fit For Fertility Programme in Part 2, but for now it is worth remembering what all these preparations are really for. You are making plans for a baby! Although this may seem a rather silly or obvious reminder, it is important that you have the emotional, physical and mental space for a baby in your lives. This may mean finding a more suitable, baby-friendly place to live, making more time in your daily life to spend with your partner and doing what you can to limit the amount of stress in your lives. For some couples, the preoccupation with getting pregnant can eclipse the very point of it! It's important to try to visualise yourselves as parents.

Chapter 2

How Long Should It Take to Get Pregnant?

There is no set answer to this question. My advice would always be 'If in doubt, shout!' There is no point in quietly worrying, even if you perhaps have only just begun trying to get pregnant. There really is nothing to be said against seeking a little reassurance and advice. There is no harm having a general review even before you have started. At The Poundbury Clinic and Westover House, we have established a pre-conceptual checklist, which is included below.

In general, I would suggest that if you have been having regular unprotected sex for a year with no sign of pregnancy, it is worthwhile making an appointment to see your GP to make sure there are no obvious problems. Equally, you may choose to see your GP as soon as you decide you want to become pregnant so that he or she can check you are in good health and, if appropriate, arrange for you to be screened for infections. (I will come to screening in Chapter 8.)

TIME TO GO TO THE DOCTOR?

If you're wondering whether or not to seek help, have a look at the checklist below. If you answer 'yes' to any of the questions, then it is probably worth making the time to see your doctor. Of course, answering 'yes' to any of the statements doesn't necessarily mean anything is wrong; it just makes sense to save yourself some time and worry.

Pre-conceptual Checklist

- Are you or your partner worried that you have not yet conceived?
- Have you been trying to get pregnant for over a year without success?
- Do you have irregular periods? (This means, is your cycle variable in length, shorter than 24 days or longer than 35 days?)
- Are your periods painful?
- Have you or your partner been in a prior relationship in which attempted conception did not occur?
- Has your partner suffered from any testicular injury in the past?
- Have you had any major abdominal surgery?
- Are you over 35?
- Has your partner had any testicular surgery?
- Have you ever had an ectopic pregnancy?
- Have you noticed any milk being discharged from your breasts?
- Do you have diabetes, Cushing's disease or a thyroid disorder?
- Are you overweight or underweight? (See Chapter 6 for weight guidelines.)
- Are you and your partner unable to have regular intercourse?
- Do you experience any pain during intercourse?
- Have you had pelvic inflammatory disease?
- Has your partner ever had mumps?
- Does your partner have difficulty getting an erection?
- Does your partner have problems ejaculating?

DOES AGE MAKE A DIFFERENCE?

More women are choosing to have their first child later in life. In the UK, the average age of a woman at the birth of her first child has risen from 25 in 1980 to 29.[1] Research shows that one in every five American women is having her first child after the age of 35 – a 50% increase on the last decade.[2] This is one of the reasons why infertility as a medical complaint appears to be on the increase.

While I have no intention of sounding alarmist or negative, it is true that the single most important determinant of a couple's fertility is the age of the female partner. For women up to the age of 25, the average *monthly* chance of conceiving in couples with normal fertility is only 20–25%,[3] with a cumulative conception rate of 60% at six months and 85% over a year.[4] For couples where the female partner is aged 35 or over, the conception rate over a year falls to 60%, and over two years will be 85%, so halving the rate of a woman's fertility.[5]

Remember, these statistics are based on *averages* taken from research studies carried out with groups of women. Every woman is different, and although a woman's fertility will start to decline from the age of 30, this does not mean you will automatically find it difficult to conceive. And there is much that you can do to increase your fertility – we will look at these steps in detail in Part 2. It is important to be aware of these kinds of statistics, but it is equally important to keep a positive outlook. Always assume the best, and work towards making it happen. The more optimistic and upbeat you are, the more relaxed you will feel and so the better your chances of a successful outcome.

> Women aged 20–25 have the best chance of conceiving naturally. The average time it takes for a woman aged 25 to get pregnant is two to three months. For a 35-year-old woman, it takes on average six months to conceive.[6]

The Age of the Male Partner

Contrary to popular understanding, the age of the male partner is also a factor. A UK study based on research shows that the older a man is, the longer it may take his partner to conceive, regardless of her age. Women with partners five or more years older have less chance of conceiving within a year of trying than those whose partners are the same age or younger. For every year after a man passes the age of 24, the odds of conceiving within six months of trying drop by 2%. This seems to be the first clear evidence that the age of the male – as well as that of the female – is an important factor.[7]

The decrease in a man's fertility can be due to hormonal changes, poor blood supply to the testicles or impotence. Most men over the age of 50 will also begin to undergo some degree of testicular failure. What is perhaps less commonly known is that sperm are more likely to display abnormalities than eggs. The reason for this is that, unlike the egg, which goes through fewer cell divisions in order to mature, the maturing sperm must divide an estimated 380 times before they become 'adult' sperm. The greater the number of cell divisions, the greater the chance for errors to occur.[8]

However, as we know, men can continue to father children throughout their lives. Pablo Picasso and Charlie Chaplin are two examples of men who became fathers again in their seventies!

Chapter 3

Understanding Infertility

It is not uncommon for couples to seek help at some point in their lives because of difficulty in conceiving. Population studies in the US, France and the UK show that around one in six couples will look for specialist help in dealing with problems with fertility.[1] It's a little known fact that humans are one of the least fertile creatures,[2] with only a short time during the menstrual cycle when conception is possible. Simply becoming pregnant is not that easy – even when there are no obvious fertility problems.

THE DEFINITION OF INFERTILITY

Infertility is defined as the inability to conceive after 12 months of regular unprotected sex.[3] But I do believe that if you think you have a problem, even if you haven't been trying for 12 months, then you should ask for help. Primary infertility refers to couples who have never been pregnant. Secondary infertility means at least one conception has taken place previously. This definition sounds depressingly final, and of course it's not! The term 'infertility' doesn't mean the complete inability to have children, and neither should it ever be confused with sterility, which means – due to hysterectomy, for example – conception will never be possible.

Although the prevalence of infertility has remained constant, the number of visits to GPs by couples having problems conceiving has tripled over the past 20 years.[4] This increase can be attributed to couples postponing starting a family until later and to a greater public awareness of the many fertility treatments now widely available.

COMMON CAUSES OF INFERTILITY

There are many different reasons why you may be finding it hard to conceive, some of which are not directly related to the male or female reproductive systems, and we will look at those in detail later in the book. The table below will show you how GPs and units tend to break down the most likely causes.

Do not forget that there can be multiple factors at work in infertility – there may be several problems involving either the male or female, or equally both partners.

Causes of Infertility of Patients Presenting to GPs	Incidence (%)
Male fertility problems (infections, testicular injury, sperm defects, damage to the penis, etc.)	35
Tubal (tubal damage due to pelvic adhesions, endometriosis, ectopic pregnancy, etc.)	20
Ovulatory (polycystic ovarian syndrome, premature ovulation failure, lack of ovulation, etc.)	20
Unexplained infertility (specialist help has failed to uncover an obvious reason for their infertility)	15 (varies from from clinic to clinic, depending on the categories used)
Cervical (infections, previous cervical surgery, etc.)	10

However, causes of infertility in patients presenting to their general practitioner may be different to the causes of infertility in those patients having IVF and ICSI treatment in clinics. Looking at *The HFEA Guide to Infertility and Directory of Clinics* (2005/06), the causes of infertility in patients having IVF and ICSI treatment in the UK are as follows:

Causes of Infertility of Patients Presenting to Clinics for IVF/ICSI	Incidence (%)
Male factor	32
Unexplained infertility	18.7
Multiple factors female and male	17
Tubal disease	16.7
Ovulatory disorders	4.9
Multiple factors female only	4.6
Endometriosis	3
Other causes	2.9
Uterine factor	0.3

Parts 3 and 4 will look closely at the main causes of infertility, the tests for them and their treatment, but below is a brief outline of what these terms actually mean.

Male Fertility Problems

Fertility has often been thought of as a 'women's issue' when, in fact, infertility is just as likely to be related to male factors as female factors.

I have had patients, even doctors, concerned about testing the male as it may upset them. It must be remembered that this whole journey is a team approach and the male is as equally involved as the female.

There are a number of causes of male infertility, but the major cause is failure to produce enough healthy sperm. The term 'azoospermia' refers to a complete absence of sperm in the semen, and 'oligozoospermia' refers to too few sperm being produced. Sperm can also be damaged in a number of ways or may be immotile (see page 217). Semen analysis will help to identify where the problem may lie.

Other causes of male fertility include testicular injury, which can affect the release of the hormones the testes produce as well as the quality and quantity of sperm produced. Damage caused by accidents can sometimes block the blood supply to the testes and should always be treated quickly. Such injuries can occur on the rugby field, a fight or even as a result of an infection such as mumps.

Hormonal imbalances caused by medical conditions unrelated to fertility (for instance diabetes) can nevertheless affect the reproductive system. Your doctor will be able to test for any imbalances.

Other physiological disorders, including retrograde ejaculation (where the muscles responsible for pumping the semen through the penis are not working) or obstructions within the male reproductive system (often caused by infections), can also lead to problems with fertility and should be discussed with your GP. We will look at the specific investigations and treatments for male infertility in Parts 3 and 4.

Whatever the cause, coping with fertility problems is never easy, and many men may feel robbed of their virility when they find they have a fertility problem. They may struggle with feelings of low self-esteem and inadequacy. As ever, the key to coping with these kinds of emotions is to give each other plenty of support and share your feelings and concerns. Whether difficulty in having a baby is related to male or female factors – or both – infertility is a couple's shared challenge, and it is important that neither one of you feels you are in any way to blame.

Tubal

The fallopian tubes are delicate structures about the same thickness as the lead of a pencil. Because of this, they can easily become blocked and so prevent the progress of the egg or sperm along the tube or give rise to problems of implantation of the fertilised egg. Blocks in the fallopian tubes can often result from scarring due to infection (such as pelvic inflammatory disease, see page 247) or previous abdominal surgery, or from pelvic adhesions caused by endometriosis (see page 249).

Surgery may be needed to treat the blockages, and we will look more closely at this procedure in Chapter 23. The difficulty is that you not only need the tubes to be open but also functional. Tubal surgery can open up tubes, but they are not always functional.

Ovulatory

If you are not ovulating, it needs to be investigated to see if there is a treatable cause. Sometimes all that is needed is lifestyle advice. That is why my Fit for Fertility Programme is so essential, whatever your problem. On other occasions, medication is used that either helps to balance your hormones or drive your ovaries to produce eggs. Rarely, it may be found that you have run out of eggs and reached the menopause prematurely.

Ovulation relates to the hormones that are necessary for the healthy functioning of a woman's reproductive system. Your hormones are continually fluctuating, which makes your body's balancing of these different hormones a delicate and complex process. As we saw in Chapter 1, for ovulation to occur, certain hormones need to be triggered at different times during your cycle.

Regular periods (24–35 days) usually indicate ovulation, but not always. If you suffer from irregular periods or an absence of periods, then you are probably not ovulating. If this is the case, your doctor will either be able to correct the hormonal imbalance that is preventing ovulation with medication or refer you for ovulation-stimulating treatment. He or she may also suggest dietary and lifestyle changes, which can all help to rebalance your hormones.

Polycystic ovarian syndrome (PCOS) is also a hormone-related ovulatory condition (see page 242). Again, your doctor can test for this by checking for raised levels of male hormones in your blood. All women produce male hormones, but in some cases, a large concentration of the luteinising hormone (LH) are released, causing an increase in testosterone levels. In mild cases of PCOS, women may have no menstrual irregularities at all and may ovulate normally but it may take longer than usual to conceive. However, in more severe cases, ovulation can stop altogether. In these cases, the Fit for Fertility Programme is essential. Medication to stimulate the ovaries may also be used.

Unexplained Infertility

This refers to any couple who have failed to conceive and for which no cause has been found after full investigation of both partners. Many cases of unexplained fertility are probably the result of minor degrees of ovulatory disorders or sperm dysfunction for which there may not yet be adequate tests.

As I said in Chapter 1, conception is a story of transport and so an upset here will upset fertility. None of the tests we do ever really assess transport. I have often wondered if the worst thing for the progress of fertility investigations (*not* treatment) has been IVF. We can now bypass the causes of infertility and look towards treatment. This may explain why couples are diagnosed with unexplained infertility. It may be 'we just don't know', and it demonstrates the inadequacy of the investigations that we are able to do.

CHOOSING A CAR TO DRIVE ABROAD

To demonstrate the limitations of some of our investigations, I have often explained to patients that looking at semen analysis is like looking in a car park and choosing which car to drive abroad. We obviously would pick the best-looking car; hopefully, this will have an adequate engine. However, whatever the car looks like, it does not give us a true idea of what the engine is like. This is the same for semen analysis; looking at the sperm does not actually tell us whether the sperm has a functional ability to fertilise an egg.

A diagnosis of unexplained fertility is particularly frustrating and stressful for couples. When there seems to be no obvious cause, it is hard to know what best to do in terms of treatment. Often, however, doctors will suggest trying to improve the quality of ovulation through courses of medication. And, of course, a change in diet and lifestyle can also make a dramatic difference.

Research does show that couples with unexplained fertility of less than three years are mostly 'normal' and have just been unlucky so far, and most will conceive within two years.[5]

Cervical

The cervical mucus secreted by the glands lining the cervix can sometimes be found to be 'hostile' to sperm. It may contain antibodies that interfere with the sperm's usual motility and so prevent their journey into the cervical canal. A cervical mucus penetration test can ascertain if this is the case – although the value of this test is debatable.

We've looked at the *main* causes of infertility, but there are other reasons why you and your partner may be experiencing some problems in getting pregnant. For many people, improving their diet or learning to manage their stress levels a little better can make all the difference. There are many factors that come into play – in all aspects of our health – so by making some adjustments here and there, you are immediately giving yourselves a head start. In Part 2 we'll be looking at the importance of 'controlling the controllables' and taking responsibility for your overall wellbeing. Even if you eventually decide to go along the IVF route, by being in good health, you give yourself a much better chance of successful conception, a healthy pregnancy and a strong and healthy baby.

AGE AND INFERTILITY

We saw in Chapter 2 how a woman's age will affect the rate at which she is likely to conceive. A woman's fecundity – that is the likelihood of conceiving during a single monthly cycle – will have reached its peak by the time she is 30, and from there it starts to gradually decline. By the age of 35, fertility starts to decline more steeply. This *does not* mean that after the age of 30 you are automatically going to find it hard to conceive, only that the rate of conception will begin to slow down in most women.

You can see from the table below how the rates of infertility start to increase as a woman gets older.[6] (Remember, this refers to couples unable to conceive after one year of regular unprotected sex.)

Woman's Age	Incidence of Infertility (%)
20–24	7
25–29	8.9
30–34	14
35–39	21.9
40–44	28.7

You can see from this that after the age of 35 the rise in infertility rates becomes steeper. There are a number of reasons for this. In the 10–15 years before menopause, there is a gradual decline in the number and quality of eggs. As we saw in Chapter 1, you were born with all the eggs you will ever have, just under one million. The number of eggs drops rapidly even before a female baby is born, from an initial figure of about three million, and will carry on dropping throughout your life. Each month, during your reproductive years, usually only a single egg matures and although ovulation will contribute to the decrease in eggs, the majority of them are simply being slowly absorbed by the body over the years. At the same time, the follicles that contain the developing eggs will also begin to die off. The menstrual cycle then gradually starts to shorten in length, by an average of three to four days compared to the cycle length you had in your twenties.

AGE AND MISCARRIAGE

In addition to being less fertile, your age also increases your chance of miscarriage.

Miscarriage is the most common complication during pregnancy, occurring during approximately 15% of all pregnancies. A quarter of women who become pregnant will experience at least one miscarriage. Of these, the majority – around 95% – occur in the first trimester. In many cases, though, a woman will miscarry without even knowing that she was pregnant.

The table below shows how a woman's age can affect the incidence of miscarriage.

Woman's Age	Incidence of Miscarriage (%)
15–35	12
35–39	18
40–44	33
45+	50+

The reason for the increased incidence of miscarriage in older women is that there are more likely to be genetic abnormalities – the most common known cause of miscarriage. Miscarriage can also be related to an abnormality such as a distortion of the uterine cavity or scarring caused by surgery or infection. An inadequate production of progesterone necessary for maintaining the pregnancy can result in miscarriage, as can a poor immune system, blood clotting abnormalities, infections within the reproductive tract and defective sperm.

In many cases, the cause of miscarriage is unknown, but by making sure you take care of your health, through cutting out smoking and reducing your alcohol and caffeine intake, you can reduce the risk of miscarrying.

Despite the statistics, which can often seem a bit daunting, there is much that you and your partner can do for yourselves to improve your fertility, however old you are. It's important to ensure you take responsibility for your health. A poor diet, hectic lifestyle and unhealthy habits immediately put you at a disadvantage. By taking charge now, you are likely to feel more confident and more positive about your chances of conception. This is the key to the Fit for Fertility Programme, which we will look at in Part 2.

It is important that you learn to listen to your body. Familiarise yourself with the different changes that occur physically and emotionally over each month. Every woman is unique, and by paying attention to your own subtle signals, you will be better equipped to make good and positive decisions regarding self-help and professional treatments.

PART 2

THE FIT FOR FERTILITY PROGRAMME

Planning to start a family or to increase the one you already have is one of the most important decisions you are ever likely to make. That's a good reason to make sure you and your partner are fit for conception. Just as you would prepare the way for implementing other major life choices, so it is important that you do what you can to ensure you are in good health. After all, the healthier you both are, the healthier your eggs and your partner's sperm will be. By taking the time to look at your health and general lifestyle and make a few positive changes now, you will giving yourself the best chance for conception, and because you are improving the environment for your developing baby, you are more likely to conceive earlier on. If you're embarking on fertility treatment, then it's equally important that you are in good health and feeling emotionally and mentally positive. Whatever your circumstances, you will not only be creating the optimum conditions for conception, but you will be more likely to enjoy a healthy pregnancy, reduce the risk of miscarriage and have a happy, healthy baby at the end!

By following the advice in this section, I can also guarantee that you will feel better for it. Your energy levels will increase; you may find you lose those excess pounds; you'll feel more rested and may notice an improvement in your sleep quality; and most importantly, you'll feel more positive with an increased self-esteem, which can only benefit your relationship. Not a bad payoff for making just a few changes to your current routine!

'It is hard to fail, but it is worse never to have tried to succeed.'

Theodore Roosevelt

Chapter 4

What Is Fit for Fertility?

The Fit for Fertility Programme aims to get your body in shape for conception and pregnancy. It is designed to give you the best chance for conception and to give your baby the best possible start – this is vitally important in those first four weeks after conception. That's why you need to start making changes now, rather than when you are undergoing treatment or once you have become pregnant. I recommend starting the Fit for Fertility Programme three months before you start trying to conceive.

Don't let your partner think that he's off the hook either! It's just as important for men to be in good health prior to conception. As we saw, it takes around three months for sperm to fully mature and make their journey into the testes. Three months is long enough for these sperm to become damaged irreparably. A man who is fit and in good health is much more likely to produce healthy sperm, so increasing the chances of conception and of a healthy baby.

THE CORE THEMES

There are ten core themes to my Fit for Fertility Programme. These are:

1. Diet
2. Exercise
3. Stress reduction
4. Lifestyle
5. Positive approach
6. Team approach
7. Goal setting
8. DR AID
9. Planning the journey
10. Education

The following chapters will look at these core themes.

Patients I see are often genuinely amazed by what an enormous difference relatively simple steps can make. I think it's so important to remind yourself from time to time just what extraordinary, complex and finely balanced creatures we humans are. Everything we put into our bodies – whether it's a headache pill or an apple – has its effect, impacting on the millions of cells that make us what we are. That's why when we take care of our bodies, cells, tissues and even organs can begin to repair themselves more swiftly, and our different body systems can start to work together easily and harmoniously.

We are all unique, and as I said at the start of this book, we all have slightly different needs and preferences. What might work for one person may not work for you – and this doesn't just apply to treatments but also working conditions, your choice of exercise, how you like to relax or what lengths you will go to to have a child.

By implementing some or all of the changes suggested in this book you are – in most cases – significantly increasing your chances of conceiving. Knowing that there is so much that you and your partner can do for yourselves can be a source of great confidence and optimism.

Often when couples come to see me, they can at first be quite dismissive of the idea that their fertility is something that they can control, that, for example, by increasing their intake of zinc or by cutting back on drinking, they will be making all the difference to their chances of conceiving in the near future.

From diet to supplements to stress management to general good health, there is an enormous amount that you can be doing to help yourself that is within your own control. You may need to give it a little time, but in so many cases the outcome is a successful and happy one.

KEEP IT SIMPLE

Having spent over a decade working with elite athletes and watching their trainers, I have come up with one key piece of advice: keep things simple. World-class trainers pay attention to detail but at the same time do not allow their training techniques to become complicated. Often they only give one bit of advice in each session. The less experienced trainers give lots of advice and make things complicated. In some ways, they create a mystique about the subject, and this is something they should not do. The same is true of fertility and infertility. It really worries me that couples can come along from other infertility clinics or advisors with a hundred and one things to do or not to do – an impossible task. The result is that if success does not come their way, they can only blame themselves. Try to avoid this trap. Please only make one little change at a time, but, most of all, keep positive. Do not set yourselves unrealistic goals, and try to apply the SMART technique – goals must be:

S – Specific
M – Measurable
A – Achievable
R – Realistic
T – Time-related

This means that, for example, rather than saying, 'I want to lose weight', you should say, 'I want to lose a stone and I will do it within six months'.

It's important to take stock of your lifestyle and do what you can to minimise stress levels – both for yourself and for your partner. There are lots of ways that you can do this, and the benefits are immeasurable, as I hope you'll discover for yourself. I'll be suggesting some different techniques to help you overcome any pressures or anxiety you may be experiencing and looking at how there might be ways to strengthen and improve your relationship with your partner. Trying for a baby can often seem like a military operation rather than a romantic and loving adventure, but by encouraging each other and being as supportive and positive as you can, this can be a very rewarding and bonding experience for you both.

You can make small and informed changes that will go some way to improving your overall fertility fitness, but this doesn't mean you will immediately become pregnant. Don't get hung up about factors you feel you can't control – not everyone is going to be able to see a nutritionist or persuade their partner to take zinc each day.

What I hope I am providing here is useful, well-researched advice, not a list of rules that you must abide by if you are ever to become pregnant. Fertility is a complex and often mysterious area, and no one is ever to blame when difficulties emerge. We can all make changes to our lifestyle or try out different foods or treatments, but there is no absolute guarantee that these changes will result in a baby.

Do what you can, but don't give yourself a hard time about not doing *everything* – it's simply not possible, nor is it a good idea. When trying for a baby, it's important that you go at your own pace, in your own way, supporting and encouraging each other as you go.

Chapter 5

The Fit for Fertility Checklist

Before you and your partner start to address the factors discussed over the following chapters, take a look at the checklist that follows. This is something I use when couples who perhaps have been trying to conceive for a year without success first come to me. By looking at the Fit for Fertility Checklist together, you and your partner may quickly be able to pinpoint the areas in your health and lifestyle that could be affecting your chances of becoming pregnant. Often, of course, it is a combination of factors that together are causing problems. But it can sometimes be a surprisingly innocent-looking culprit, like a prescribed medicine you've been taking for years, that is the key.

> **CASE STUDY**
>
> *I saw a couple recently who presented with a two-year history of primary subfertility. They both appeared extremely healthy and fit. The male partner went to the gym on a regular basis to work out but on questioning denied any use of recreational drugs. We did a semen analysis, and to my surprise, I found that the male partner had no sperm at all.*
>
> *Having had a quiet discussion with him in private, it became apparent that he was taking anabolic steroids in order to help his weightlifting, which he was trying to do competitively. Sadly, the anabolic steroids were having a negative effect on*

> *his fertility. I discussed this at length with him, and it obviously caused significant upset between the couple.*
>
> *He agreed to stop his anabolic steroids and see if this would improve his semen analysis, but sadly, they did not return for any future appointments.*

By considering each of the factors listed below and seeing whether or not they seem to be relevant to *your* lifestyle, you are arming yourself with information that could make all the difference. Once you have identified the changes that you need to make, you'll then be able to move forward. This is not a diagnosis, but it is an important way of helping yourself before, or in tandem with, seeking further specialist help. Some of the questions are for the male partner and some are for the female partner, but it would be a good idea to do the checklist together.

Couples who have sought specialist help and have been diagnosed with 'unexplained fertility' may find that making certain lifestyle changes can assist in conception, so the following checklist might be of particular use to them.

The Fit for Fertility Checklist is made up of four individual checklists, which are designed to assess your fertility fitness. The four checklists look at:

1. the egg
2. the sperm
3. can the two get together?
4. general male and female

1. The Egg (Female)

1. *Are you having irregular, short (less than 21 days) or long (greater than 34 days) periods?*   Yes/No
2. *Do you bleed between your periods?*   Yes/No
3. *Are you overweight (with a body mass index greater than 25)?*   Yes/No

4. Are you underweight (with a body mass index under 18.5)? Yes/No
5. Do you do exercise excessively? Yes/No
6. Have you had treatment for cancer? Yes/No
7. Are you being treated for depression? Yes/No
8. Do you have diabetes? Yes/No
9. Have you ever had thyroid problems? Yes/No
10. Have you stopped having periods? Yes/No

2. The Sperm (Male)

1. Have you had an operation on your testicles? Yes/No
2. Have you had a hernia repair? Yes/No
3. Is there blood in your ejaculate? Yes/No
4. Have you had mumps? Yes/No
5. Have you had an injury to your testicle/s? Yes/No
6. Have you got/had any relations with cystic fibrosis? Yes/No
7. Have you had a vasectomy? Yes/No
8. Are you overweight (with a body mass index greater than 25)? Yes/No
9. Are you taking medication for a peptic ulcer? Yes/No
10. Do you have diabetes? Yes/No

3. Can the Two Get Together (Female)?

1. Do you have intercourse less than twice a week? Yes/No
2. Do you have a problem with intercourse? Yes/No
3. Do you bleed after intercourse? Yes/No
4. Do you have pain with intercourse? Yes/No
5. Does your partner have problems with erection? Yes/No
6. Does your partner have premature ejaculation? Yes/No
7. Have you had pelvic inflammatory disease? Yes/No
8. Have you had an operation on your abdomen (e.g. a burst appendix?) Yes/No

| 9. *Do you have discharge?* | Yes/No |
| 10. *Have you had an ectopic pregnancy?* | Yes/No |

4. General Health (Male and Female)

1. *Do you have a good, healthy diet?*	Yes/No
2. *Do either of you smoke or drink excessive amounts of alcohol? (For men, this is more than 21 units per week, and for women, it is more than 14 units per week.)*	Yes/No
3. *Have either of you been exposed to environmental hazards?*	Yes/No
4. *Have either of you tried to conceive before without success?*	Yes/No
5. *Are either of you under significant stress?*	Yes/No
6. *Do you spend a lot of time apart?*	Yes/No
7. *Do either of you drink excessive amounts of caffeine?*	Yes/No
8. *Do either of you take regular medications?*	Yes/No
9. *Do either of you use recreational drugs?*	Yes/No
10. *On either side, is there a history of a genetic problem?*	Yes/No

If you have answered 'yes' to one or more of these questions, then it is possible that this factor/s may be affecting your chances of conceiving. Make an appointment to see your GP so that you can discuss things further. By looking out for and avoiding those influences that could be compromising your fertility until you have conceived and given birth (for women), you will automatically be improving your chance of a successful conception.

Chapter 6

How Does My Lifestyle Affect My Fertility?

In this chapter we will look at the key lifestyle factors that have a negative impact on fertility. Then, in Chapter 7, we'll look at how making positive changes to these factors will increase your fertility. Remember, small changes to your lifestyle can have a big impact on your health and fertility.

ALCOHOL

We are a nation of great drinkers, and for many of us, alcohol plays a big role in our social lives and is a way of de-stressing after a hard day at work, but if you are trying to become pregnant, it is important that you are not letting your enjoyment of a glass of wine each evening get in the way of your chances of conceiving.

Alcohol and Female Fertility

Studies have shown that drinking even as little as two units of alcohol a week can increase your levels of the hormone prolactin, adversely affecting your hormonal balance.[1] Heavy drinking can lead to amenorrhea (an absence of periods) and ovulatory disorders. If you're trying to conceive, the odd glass of wine here and there is unlikely to do much harm, but do be aware of the amount you're consuming and keep it to a minimum. The consumption of alcohol also causes an increase in the excretion, via urine, of folic acid – which can lead to neural-tube defects[2] and the occurrence of spina bifida.

Drinking when pregnant can increase the risk of miscarriage and can lead to severe developmental abnormalities in the baby.[3] Alcohol is a low-molecular substance, which means it is capable of crossing the placental barrier and entering the foetus, causing the level of alcohol in the foetus to be roughly that of the mother.[4] In the first 21 days of foetal development, the preliminary cell organisation of the embryo starts to take place. If an excessive amount of alcohol is consumed before the blastocyst (the developing embryo) is embedded in the uterus, there is an increased chance of miscarriage.[5] Please do remember, though, that this is only in the case of *excessive* drinking, by which I mean more than 14 units of alcohol per week.

Alcohol and Male Fertility

Men don't get off lightly either. It's thought that up to 40% of male subfertility is caused by alcohol intake. Some studies suggest that men would be as well to give up alcohol altogether while trying for a baby. Alcohol interferes with the secretion of testosterone, speeds up the conversion of testosterone into oestrogen and lowers sperm count and sex drive, while the breakdown product of alcohol in the body – acetaldehyde – is toxic to sperm.[6]

If your partner is reluctant to give up drinking while you try for a baby, here are some very convincing reasons for why he should. Alcohol is one of the most common causes of male impotence, and 80% of male alcoholics are sterile.[7] Furthermore, alcohol is a direct testicular toxin,[8] causing atrophy of the seminiferous tubules (the tubes that carry sperm), loss of sperm cells and an increase in abnormal sperm.[9] Alcohol can cause a significant decrease in sperm concentration, sperm output and motility.[10] Testosterone production and secretion is also affected by drinking and can lead to a build-up of female hormones.[11]

However, the effect is reparable. Of 67 men monitored in the course of one study, 30% had a low sperm count. When they gave up alcohol, the sperm counts of half of them returned to normal and, of these, 78% went on to have children.[12]

Unlike you, your partner need only give up for the months preceding conception – not such a great sacrifice really! For advice on giving up drinking, see page 74.

CASE STUDY – BINGE BONKING

Recently, while taking a couple's patient history, the couple indicated that they didn't drink at all during the week but at the weekends drank quite a lot – in the order of 21 units for the man and 15 units for the woman.

I spent a lot of time talking to them about the impact of alcohol on infertility and told them that not only should they reduce the amount of drinking that they do but also it would be better to spread it across the week rather than binge drinking just at the weekends.

Later on in the consultation we discussed intercourse, and I indicated to them that in order to conceive it is best to have intercourse two to three times a week across the week and not necessarily two to three times on a Saturday night and nothing else for the rest of the week. The husband duly commented, 'Oh, so that's not only the end of my binge drinking but my binge bonking, too!'

SMOKING

Smoking has a serious detrimental effect on your fertility, as well as that of your unborn baby. It has a toxic effect on the body, robbing it of vital nutrients. There's information on giving up smoking on page 73.

Smoking and Female Fertility

There has been much in the news recently about the effect smoking can have on a woman's fertility. Research has found that women smokers who have experienced difficulties in getting pregnant are adding *ten years* to their reproductive age, and those who do conceive are more likely to miscarry if they smoke. A 30-year-old non-smoker therefore has the same chance of conceiving as a 20-year-old smoker.[13]

The impact of tobacco use on successful IVF treatment has also been highlighted, with only 13% of smokers having a live birth compared with 20% of non-smokers.[14] Even smoking on the day of egg collection can reduce results.

The chemicals found in cigarettes are believed to have a toxic effect on the endometrium and can cause a thickening and hardening of the zona pellucida (the sac surrounding the egg, which the sperm must penetrate).

In 2001, just over one in four women smoked.[15] This is an alarming figure, particularly since we are learning of more and more research that shows that women who smoke are putting their fertility at risk. Smoking also significantly increases the time it takes to conceive. Among smokers, the chances of conceiving fall by 10–40% per cycle. The greater the quantity of cigarettes smoked, the longer a woman is likely to take to achieve pregnancy.[16] Even comparatively low levels of smoking can have a significant impact. An investigation involving almost 11,000 women in Denmark revealed that women who smoked between five and nine cigarettes a day were 1.8 times more likely than non-smokers to wait longer than 12 months to conceive.[17] A British study found that both active and passive smoking was associated with delayed conception.[18] In fact, such is the effect of smoking on a woman's fertility that women born to mothers who smoked are less likely to conceive than those women whose mothers were non-smokers.[19]

Smoking increases the chances of complications during pregnancy and labour, which can include bleeding during pregnancy, premature detachment of the placenta and premature rupture of the membrane.[20] Studies indicate that women who smoke are 1.5–2.5 times more at risk of an ectopic pregnancy than those who don't.[21]

Studies also show that women who smoke more than 14 cigarettes a day are almost twice as likely to miscarry, regardless of their age or consumption of alcoholic beverages. The risk of losing a pregnancy increases with the number of cigarettes a woman smokes.[22]

And, of course, smoking can harm the health of your child. Children born to maternal smokers are known to have weakened immune systems and be more susceptible to illness than children of non-smokers.[23] Research has also found that a child's mental development and behaviour is detrimentally affected by maternal cigarette consumption.[24]

Smoking and Male Fertility

If your partner smokes, it is just as important that he gives up now – not once the baby is born, or even once you become pregnant, but preferably a good three months before you start trying to conceive.

Smoking can seriously jeopardise a man's fertility. Research studies show that men who smoke have a decreased sperm count,[25] reduced testosterone secretion,[26] decreased sperm density[27] and a lower proportion of motile sperm.[28] A study carried out in Finland found 41.9% of infertility among men who smoked compared to 27.8% among non-smokers.[29] The chemicals in cigarette smoke dramatically deplete the amount of vitamin E and zinc in the body, which is particularly important for protecting sperm. Studies show that smoking ten cigarettes a day can lower the male sperm count by 15%, while children of fathers who smoked 20 cigarettes a day are twice as likely to be born with a heart defect.[30]

Recent studies also show that the chances of a woman miscarrying rise sharply if her partner smokes heavily during her pregnancy. In the study, nearly one-third of women whose partners smoked more than 20 cigarettes a day lost their babies within six weeks of conceiving. The rate among those whose partners didn't smoke was one-fifth.[31]

If all of the above isn't enough to make you want to give up instantly, consider the health of your much-wanted baby. Research has shown that men who smoke but have non-smoking partners run a greater risk of fathering children who develop cancer. Smoking between one and nine cigarettes a day increased the risk by 3%, with an increased risk of 42% for those men smoking 20 or more a day.[32]

CAFFEINE

There are mixed views within the medical community as to whether or not the consumption of caffeine significantly affects fertility. Numerous studies have examined the effects of caffeine intake on fertility and pregnancy. Most studies found that moderate caffeine intake does not affect fertility or increase the chance of having a miscarriage or a baby with birth defects; some studies did find a relationship between caffeine intake and fertility or miscarriages. However, most of those studies were judged to be inadequate because they did not consider other lifestyle factors that could contribute to infertility or miscarriages.[33]

Caffeine can impair your body's absorption of iron and calcium, upset your stomach, lead to anxiety and keep you from getting the sleep you need. So, as a rule of thumb, men and women who are trying to conceive should limit their individual caffeine consumption to about 300mg per day, the equivalent of three mugs of instant coffee or three cups of brewed coffee of the type used in cappuccinos or espressos.

Remember that caffeine doesn't just mean normal coffee; it's also an ingredient in tea, dark and milk chocolate, chocolate milk, regular and diet colas. Remember also that 'decaffeinated' doesn't necessarily mean 'caffeine free'. A cup of decaffeinated coffee contains about 5mg of caffeine. For example, if you eat a small bar of plain chocolate and drink three cups of tea, a can of cola and a cup of instant coffee in a day, you'll have reached your 300mg limit

BEING OVERWEIGHT OR UNDERWEIGHT

Weight is important when it comes to fertility. Having said that, being either slightly over- or underweight isn't something you should get too hung up about. If you really do have a problem with your weight, this may be something you should discuss with your GP, or if you have issues about food, you may prefer to speak with a counsellor. So long as you are within a sensible weight range for your build and height and eat a balanced diet, you shouldn't have to worry. The chart on page 67 gives you an idea of what your 'normal' weight should be.

It is true that women who have a normal body mass index (BMI) are more likely to conceive and have a normal pregnancy than those who aren't the recommended weight (either over- or under-weight). Women who are underweight (with a BMI of less than 18.5) can stop ovulating. Too little fat can cause the levels of the hormone oestrogen to fall, so that periods become irregular or stop altogether. On the other side of the spectrum, women who are overweight (with a BMI of more than 25) can have raised levels of oestrogen, which can also prevent ovulation. Obesity is often linked with polycystic ovarian syndrome (PCOS – see page 242), in which an imbalance of hormones prevents eggs from maturing properly. Women who are overweight are more at risk of having PCOS, and weight gain itself is a symptom of the condition. There are a number of ways of treating PCOS, which we'll discuss in Chapter 20, but losing weight is one recommendation.

Research has found that being either too thin or too heavy may lower a man's sperm count, in some cases enough to impair fertility. In a study of 1,600 men, those with a high or low body mass index were more likely than men of normal weight to have a sperm count below 20 million/ml of semen – an abnormally low count. Also, men's testosterone levels decreased as the BMI increased, again affecting sperm quality.[34]

Body Mass Index (BMI)

There is no such thing as an ideal body weight – at best, there is only a healthy weight range. To determine this healthy weight range, and whether you are a normal weight, overweight or obese, doctors use a height–weight system called body mass index. Body mass index is a measure that takes into account a person's weight and height to gauge the weight status in adults.

It is calculated by dividing your weight in kilograms by your height in metres squared. If your BMI is in the range of 19–24.9, you have a healthy weight. If your BMI is in the range of 25–29.9, you are considered to be overweight and may be at greater risk of developing heart disease, diabetes and high blood pressure. A BMI of more than 30 is considered obese and can present all kinds of serious health problems. A BMI of less than 18.5 means you are underweight.

NARCOTICS

Using narcotics, such as methadone, heroin or marijuana, even very occasionally, can have a profound effect on your fertility. Hormone levels are upset, causing irregular periods in women and sometimes lack of ovulation altogether. In men, sperm motility may be reduced, and all narcotics can affect libido. Smoking just one joint can lower testosterone levels and libido for up to 36 hours.[35]

Studies have shown that 85% of opiate-dependent women have major menstrual dysfunction, while 80% are infertile.

	1,50	1,55	1,60	1,65	1,70	1,75	1,80	1,85	1,90	1,95	2,00	BMI
	Height (in metres)											
kg	32	34	36	38	40	43	45	48	51	53	56	14
kg	36	38	41	44	46	49	52	55	58	61	64	16
kg	41	43	46	49	52	55	58	62	65	68	72	18
kg	45	48	51	54	58	61	65	68	72	76	80	20
kg	50	53	56	60	64	67	71	75	79	84	88	22
	54	58	61	65	69	74	78	82	87	91	96	24
Weight (in kilograms)	59	62	67	71	75	80	84	89	94	99	104	26
	63	67	72	76	81	86	91	96	101	106	102	28
	68	72	77	82	87	92	97	103	108	114	120	30
kg	72	77	82	87	92	98	104	110	116	122	128	32
kg	77	82	87	93	98	104	110	116	123	129	136	34
kg	81	86	92	98	104	110	117	123	130	137	144	36
kg	86	91	97	103	110	116	123	130	137	144	152	38
kg	90	96	102	109	116	123	130	137	144	152	160	40

ENVIRONMENTAL HAZARDS

Media reports, from time to time, highlight research studies showing that sperm counts are falling and that male fertility is declining, possibly because of environmental pollution. A similar number of studies have shown no change whatsoever, but these do not make such good headlines and often fail to be reported in the media. What is clear, however, is that many more environmental toxins that might affect fertility exist now than 50 years ago.

While couples who are trying to conceive cannot control every factor that might impact fertility – though they may well try to! – researchers believe that limiting contact with environmental toxins may improve your chances of conceiving. Exactly how some environmental toxins impact fertility is still unclear, and experts say fertility is more likely to be affected by a combination of factors (including cigarette smoke, excessive alcohol and poor diet) than by a single toxic exposure or multiple trace exposures.

Studies on humans have long indicated that exposure to the metal lead may decrease fertility. That means you should limit your exposure to lead-based paints and varnishes. Most new house paints are lead free, but it's always best to protect yourself from noxious fumes when you're trying to conceive.

Professionals whose work includes daily contact with chemicals should consult their GP about the safety of the chemicals they use. Artists, chemical workers, metal workers, those who work in electronics manufacturing and people whose work is related to printing, nuclear power and other power plants, or medical technology typically use toxic chemicals and processes. For more information on chemicals that may affect male fertility, see page 148.

It is always very difficult to prove the relationship between environmental hazards and infertility. However, one particular case does spring to mind that I think is worth mentioning.

CASE STUDY

Mr and Mrs F. G. came to a colleague with two years' subfertility. Mrs F. G. was a 26-year-old schoolteacher who, with preliminary investigations, was found to have no abnormality. Mr F. G.'s two semen analyses demonstrated a low count, a low motility and a high number of abnormal forms.

After a long discussion about his lifestyle, and it so happened that he had a busy job working for an open-air-show production agency. This required him to carry two mobile phones for most of the day. These were kept in his left and right trouser pockets (i.e. very close to his testicles). I indicated to him the possible relationship between mobile phones and subfertility, and in view of this, we agreed that he should try to use only one mobile phone and move it to different parts of his body.

This was duly done, and I am delighted to say that, six months later, the couple conceived naturally. Whether this was the effect of the mobile phones, I will never know, but it made me realise how important it is to address the role of the environment.

Recent research has raised the possibility that men who regularly carry and use mobile phones may have a significantly reduced sperm count. The researchers studied 221 men for 13 months, comparing the sperm of those who used their phones heavily with others who did not. They found that heavy users of mobile phones – those who carried their phone around with them most of the time – had a 30% lower sperm count. Many of the sperm that did survive showed abnormal movements, further reducing fertility. Other experts in this field have, however, argued that different factors also need to be taken into account, so this remains an uncertain area. In my view, it would seem to be good sense for men to avoid carrying their phone in their pocket or belt holster.[36]

Chapter 7

Making Lifestyle Changes to Boost Fertility

EXERCISE

As a nation, we are guilty of not getting enough exercise, and this is compounded by the fact that many of us lead sedentary lifestyles, stuck at a desk for most of our working day.

It is important that you make time to exercise – at least three 20-minute sessions a week if you can. You needn't go the gym: brisk walking, swimming or cycling are also very effective. Try to incorporate a little more activity into your daily routine; you'll feel so much better for it, and your body will thank you, too!

But, as always, exercise in moderation. Too much exercise can lead to upsets in the menstrual cycle, low body weight and even osteoporosis, all of which can compromise your fertility.

Ten Simple Ways to Increase Exercise

1. Use stairs rather than lifts.
2. Use stairs rather than escalators.
3. Park further away from your destination.
4. Run upstairs.
5. Do not use the remote control on the television – get up and change it.
6. Consider housework as exercise – it is.

7. Walk more to work.
8. Try to do some gardening.
9. Think positively about exercise.
10. Enjoy your exercise.

THE FROG IN WATER

This is a story about a frog. If a frog is in a bowl of water, it will swim around and be happy. If the water is heated up at a gradual rate, the frog will adapt to the changes in temperature. The frog's pores will open more, and its heart rate and respiratory rate will increase.

Gradually, as the temperature is increased, the frog makes more and more adaptations to the temperature of the water that he is in. Eventually, the temperature will get to such a stage that the frog's adaptation process will cease and he will die.

If you get another frog and put it in the water at the temperature at which the first frog died, it will jump out.

The moral of this story? We can be very good at adapting to little changes in our life, not realising that these changes will eventually kill us. We must pay attention to detail because the little things add up to make a big difference.

MINIMISE THE RISK FACTORS

We all know that smoking is bad for our health and that overindulging in alcohol can also cause serious health issues. But for many of us, drinking – and to a lesser extent smoking – form an integral part of our daily lives. Whether smoking socially with friends, having a quick drink with colleagues after work or simply coming home and enjoying a glass or two of wine after a long day, the use of cigarettes and alcohol has long been considered an acceptable way of unwinding or spending time with others. And they are easy habits to form.

In Chapter 6 we looked at the negative impact of these big vices. The dangers of drinking and smoking while pregnant are well publicised these days, but sadly far less emphasis is placed on the problems that smoking and drinking *before* pregnancy can create. If you are planning to start a family – whether you have been trying for some time or are just starting out now – it is terribly important that you are aware of how your drinking or smoking habits will affect your chances of successful conception. This does not just apply to women but also to men. Often when I see couples, the male partner is reluctant to give up his favourite tipple and can't see how the pints of beer he has in the evening at the pub are really going to make all that much difference to his partner's chances of conceiving. It's very important that you *both* take responsibility for your pre-conception health – it is going to play a vital role in your chances of getting pregnant.

Smoking

As we saw in Chapter 6, smoking robs the body of vitamin C, zinc and selenium, thereby greatly weakening the immune system. Besides nicotine (the addictive substance of tobacco), cigarette smoke contains thousands of other toxic, carcinogenic, mutagenic, growth-retardative and immunosuppressive compounds, including cyanide, carbon monoxide, lead and cadmium.[1] I'm sure that even hardened smokers would agree that this is not the most appealing-sounding of concoctions. These chemicals and toxins all take their toll on male and female fertility – not to mention overall health.

Not only is giving up smoking one of the best things you and your partner can possibly do for your own health, it will also increase your fertility fitness dramatically *and* help protect the health of your baby.

Giving Up Smoking

Try to make sure you give up smoking a good three months *before* you start trying to conceive. This will give each of your bodies the chance to eliminate the toxins caused by cigarette smoking and for the levels of zinc and vitamin E to reach a healthy level.

It's not easy giving up something that your body has formed an addiction to and that has become a habit – particularly if it is triggered by social activities. But it is a small sacrifice given the benefits of giving up. You will give your health and longevity an enormous boost and increase your chances of becoming parents.

There are many different aids now available to help you to give up, including over-the-counter patches and gum, acupuncture, hypnosis techniques and herbal remedies. Whatever works best for you – it is most certainly worth it! Call the NHS Stop Smoking Programme Helpline or visit their website (see Useful Contacts and Websites).

Alcohol

For centuries, observations all over the world have shown that drinking can have serious adverse effects on the health of the newborn. In ancient Carthage and Sparta there were even laws prohibiting the use of alcohol by newly married couples in order to prevent conception during intoxication![2]

Alcohol has become such an integral part of most of our lives. It is something we associate with stress relief, celebration, socialising, eating out, eating in . . . and although most women do give up drinking once they become pregnant, there are also a good many reasons for you both to give up alcohol while trying to conceive as well.

In Chapter 6 we saw the negative impact of alcohol on both male and female fertility. As with smoking, alcohol robs the body of essential nutrients, including zinc and vitamin B6, which are vital for your fertility fitness. By cutting out alcohol, you are also more likely to enjoy better sleep, more energy and feel more focused.

Giving Up Alcohol

If you and/or your partner are drinking more than five units of alcohol a week, it's a good idea to cut right back to no more than two units a week – or you might think of stopping drinking altogether. Men should try reducing their alcohol intake up to three months before trying for a baby, as this is the length of time it takes for sperm to fully mature. Of course, once a man's partner is pregnant, then he may choose to resume drinking, though the benefits felt from *not* drinking may encourage him to stick to it, and his partner might appreciate the support while she's pregnant.

Because drinking alcohol is so much part of the fabric of our everyday lives, it may be a good idea to let those close to you know that you plan to cut alcohol out for a time. That way, there will be less pressure to drink in social situations, and you won't feel the need to avoid such events altogether.

And remember, it's not forever – and it's really not such a high price to pay for good fertility fitness and, ultimately, a healthy baby.

Chapter 8

How Does My Health Affect My Fertility?

In addition to making sure you and your partner follow my lifestyle advice, it's a good idea to see your GP about having a general health check. Whether or not you've been experiencing difficulty in conceiving, it always makes good sense to check for any infections or underlying health problems that could compromise your fertility. It could be that you know of an existing problem already.

By doing your bit to ensure good fertility fitness, you are 'controlling the controllables' and thus limiting the factors you cannot control. It makes sense to eliminate as many of the possible causes of fertility problems as you can. In taking responsibility for your health, you are giving yourselves a head start and creating a positive attitude that will stand you in good stead. In this chapter, we will look at the health factors you need to address in order to increase your fertility.

HIGH BLOOD PRESSURE

There is evidence that high blood pressure in women needs to be controlled before embarking on a pregnancy. For some, it can be associated with an increase in the chance of developing fibroids, which, in turn, can affect fertility. For men, high blood pressure, caused by stress, diet or certain medication, can lead to impotence.

It's important for you both to get your blood pressure checked out, and if it is high, to make the necessary changes to get it back to a healthier level.

DIABETES

Both type I and type II diabetes are associated with disturbed ovarian function. If you are not controlling your diabetes properly, ovulation may stop altogether. Women with type II diabetes may suffer from polycystic ovarian syndrome due to the increase in insulin resistance (often linked with excess weight). So if you are diabetic, it's important that you keep a tight control over your blood sugar concentration and take care to maintain a healthy weight. Problems with your blood sugar level can lead to babies with abnormalities.

Studies show that 25% of men with longstanding diabetes (ten years or more) experience some impotence, and the chances of this increase with age.[1] Ejaculation may also be affected as the nerve and circulatory processes are linked to diabetes.

THYROID DISEASE

Thyroid disease is common in young women and both hypo- and hyperthyroidism can affect fertility by upsetting the menstrual cycle and inhibiting ovulation. If you are being treated for a thyroid disorder and planning to get pregnant, make an appointment to discuss the levels of medication you're on and how this may be affecting your fertility. It's important that your thyroid function is closely monitored during pregnancy – and after the birth.

Thyroid disease is less common in men, but it can affect libido, and hypothyroidism may be linked to sperm production, so it's important to get a proper diagnosis and correct treatment.[2]

PEPTIC ULCERS

Medication prescribed to treat peptic ulcers (such as ranitidine and cimetidine) can inhibit sperm production, affect libido and cause impotence. For women, the drug omeprazole should be avoided during pregnancy.

So for both men and women, it's vital that you seek advice *before* trying to conceive to ensure that the medication you're receiving is not going to jeopardise your fertility – or the health of your unborn baby.[3]

INFLAMMATORY BOWEL DISEASE (IBD)

Inflammatory bowel disease is the general term for Crohn's disease and ulcerative colitis. Men with Crohn's disease may produce fewer sperm when the disease is very severe, and the sperm they do produce may be damaged or function less well than normal. These problems are thought to be temporary, and treatment to improve Crohn's should restore your fertility to its natural level. The same effects on sperm may be caused by the medication sulfasalazine, which is commonly used to treat IBD. For the majority of men, these side effects, if they do occur, are also temporary, and fertility returns to its natural level two to three months after stopping sulfasalazine. Very rarely, men with IBD who have had their colon, including the rectum, removed may be unable to have an erection. This is usually temporary and, with more sophisticated surgical techniques that are less likely to damage nerves, is much less likely to occur nowadays.

Women who have IBD that is well controlled by medication should have no more difficulty in becoming pregnant than those without IBD. However, if you have active Crohn's disease and you're underweight or eating poorly, this can affect fertility. Also, if there is severe inflammation in the small intestine, the normal functioning of the ovaries can be affected. Complications such as abscesses in the vaginal area are likely to put a halt temporarily to having sex. It is best not to try to get pregnant when IBD is very active, as the symptoms can then be more problematic throughout the pregnancy. The likelihood of miscarriage is also higher. However, numerous women have had uneventful and successful pregnancies even when they have conceived during active phases of IBD. But, as ever, it is important to talk this over with your GP first.[4]

CHRONIC RENAL FAILURE

In men, renal disease may cause erectile dysfunction and a decreased libido. In women, pregnancy may negatively affect renal function, so it is essential that specialist advice is sought before trying to conceive. Men and women who have had renal transplants and who have been in good health for two years subsequently may find that previous fertility problems are lessened.[5]

DEPRESSION

Infertility can understandably cause enormous psychological distress and anxiety, and in Chapter 10 I'll be looking at ways in which some degree of stress may be overcome or controlled. Depression and other mental-health problems may also, of course, be a pre-existing condition.

Women with a diagnosed psychiatric illness, such as schizophrenia, may have menstrual disturbances. This can be as a result of the illness itself but can also be due to the medication prescribed to treat the illness.

For men, some antidepressants can lead to impotence, delayed ejaculation, a decreased sperm count and raised prolactin levels, so men should discuss with their GP the alternative treatments and therapies available.

Many antidepressants can interfere with hormone levels, which can impact on your chances of conceiving, and they may also lead to a loss of libido, so it's important to consult your doctor before trying to conceive. If you are being treated for depression, it might be a good idea to speak with a counsellor, your psychologist or your psychiatrist about the implications of having a child.[6]

PRESCRIPTION AND NON-PRESCRIPTION MEDICATION

So many of us regularly take prescription and over-the-counter medication without even giving a thought to how it might be affecting our fertility. Of course, just because a medication is commonly prescribed doesn't automatically insure you against side effects. Many drugs are known to affect a woman's cervical mucus and the production and motility of sperm in men – all essential for fertilisation. If you regularly take any of the following, it's possible they may be compromising your fertility, so it would be a good idea to discuss them with your doctor: antibiotics, antihistamines, inhalers, sleeping pills, antidepressants, antihypertensives, antimalarial pills, diuretics and pain-killers.[7]

Any fertility concerns related to prescribed medication should be discussed with your GP – do not just stop taking them yourself.

CHEMOTHERAPY AND RADIATION TREATMENT

Chemotherapy treatment can severely affect the production of sperm and the seminiferous tubules. Nowadays, men are advised to freeze their sperm before starting treatment.

For women, the effect of chemotherapy may mean premature ovarian failure. This does depend on your age and the dose of treatment, so of course should be discussed with your GP. Egg storage may be possible, but it is still in a research stage (see Chapter 26). There are several units in the UK that do offer egg storage; this list can be obtained from the HFEA. Most chemotherapy now allows for the preservation of ovarian function once the cancer has been treated.[8]

GENITOURINARY INFECTIONS (GUI)

It's important that you get yourself screened for possible genitourinary infections that can either prevent you from becoming pregnant or increase the chances of miscarriage. What's more, these infections can be particularly problematic once you are pregnant, which is why it's important to be screened now. Many of these infections can be sexually transmitted, so it's *just as important* that your partner gets himself checked out, too.

Chlamydia

How to detect chlamydia:

- blood tests
- sperm tests
- swabs
- PCR (polymerase chain reaction)

Chlamydia is now the most common sexually transmitted disease in the Western world.[9] Unfortunately, it is almost completely without symptoms, which is why it is know as the 'silent illness'. Some countries, including Sweden, routinely screen for chlamydia; however, Britain is not among them. This is why it is so important to take the initiative yourself and get screened, *before* you start trying to conceive. Although chlamydia is easy to treat with antibiotics when detected early on, if it is left untreated, it can cause serious problems.

For women, the infection can spread upwards from the cervix to the womb, fallopian tubes and pelvis. This is called pelvic inflammatory disease (PID). If not treated promptly, PID can cause scarring or blocking of the fallopian tubes, which can lead to infertility or an ectopic pregnancy (pregnancy in the fallopian tube instead of the womb). If a woman has a chlamydial infection when she is pregnant, it may be passed on to her baby, causing miscarriage, premature birth or severe eye or lung infections after birth. Very few women experience symptoms, which can include a change in their menstrual bleeding – with periods becoming more heavy or painful than usual or with bleeding between periods. Vaginal discharge may change, becoming discoloured, excessive or offensive-smelling. Passing urine may be painful. There may be some lower abdominal pain or pain felt during or after sex. To test for chlamydia, a doctor or nurse will take some swabs from the cervix and vagina.

For men, the infection can spread upwards into one or both testicles, causing pain and swelling. Evidence suggests that an undiagnosed or untreated infection can cause scarring of the seminiferous tubules and associated ducts, which may impair or inhibit the passage of sperm and can result in infertility.[10] Symptoms of chlamydia in men may include discharge from the penis and a burning sensation when they pass urine. Chlamydia in men can generally be diagnosed from a urine sample.

Because not all tests for chlamydia are conclusive, often a doctor will take the decision to treat for it, even if the test is negative. This is usually in cases where symptoms are present or the patient's partner is infected. For both men and women, chlamydia is treated with a course of antibiotics, either for a week or, with more complicated infections such as PID, three weeks.

As chlamydia is sexually transmitted, if you suspect you have the infection, it's terribly important that your partner is also checked and treated and that you refrain from having unprotected sex until you are both over the infection.

Trichomoniasis

Trichomoniasis is a sexually transmitted infection caused by the organism *Trichomoniasis vaginalis*. In women, this causes a greenish vaginal discharge and may be accompanied by burning and itching. Unlike chlamydia, this doesn't cause PID, but it may compromise your fertility by altering the cervical mucus, making it more difficult or, in some cases, impossible, for sperm to swim through.[11] In men, the bacteria can cause infections in the urethra or under the foreskin of the penis. Symptoms may include discharge from the penis and pain when urinating.

Trichomoniasis can be cleared up with a course of antibiotics.

Mycoplasmosis and Ureaplasmosis

Mycoplasma and ureaplasma are small organisms commonly found in the genitourinary tracts of both men and women. However, in couples who are having trouble conceiving, these organisms are often found in higher quantities, and this bacterial infection, often without symptoms, can be sexually transmitted between partners. The bacteria can survive in the reproductive tract for a number of years, undetected, until a patient is specifically tested for the infection.

In women, the presence of these bacteria has been linked with miscarriage,[12] while in men, the mycoplasma may increase the percentage of abnormal sperm and affect sperm by lowering the levels of zinc and fructose in semen. Zinc is very important for good fertility in men, while the absence of fructose can cause a blocking of the seminal vesicles, preventing sperm from getting through.[13]

These infections are not routinely tested for on the NHS as they can be costly, so if you have experienced a miscarriage in the past and/or are having difficulty conceiving, you may choose to go for tests privately.

Cytomegalovirus (CMV)

This is a relatively common virus that belongs to the same family as the herpes virus. Most people who get infected experience no symptoms. However, for those who do, the symptoms are similar to those of the common cold, including a mild fever and feeling run down.

CMV can be passed through saliva and urine. Once a person becomes infected, the virus remains alive but usually dormant within that person's body for life, but they are generally immune to recurrent infections. Therefore, for the vast majority of people, CMV infection is not a serious problem.

The infection doesn't seem to affect a woman's fertility, but problems can arise if a woman passes it on to her unborn baby. This can lead to hearing loss, vision impairment and varying degrees of mental retardation later on in the child's life.[14] In men, CMV can affect a man's fertility by reducing his sperm count.[15]

OTHER DISEASES AND INFECTIONS

Of course, there are many diseases that can affect fertility, though not all of them are sexually transmitted.

Rubella (German Measles)

Rubella is generally contracted during childhood, when it is only a mild disease; however, if contracted while pregnant, it can have devastating implications for the health of your unborn baby, including causing deafness, blindness and heart disease, and, in some cases, it can cause miscarriage. This is why young women are now routinely vaccinated against it.

If you are trying to get pregnant, do ensure you have had your rubella immunisation. If you're not sure, your doctor can easily check to see if you are immune.

Toxoplasmosis

Toxoplasmosis is a rare but serious blood infection caused by the parasite *Toxoplasma gondii*. The parasite can be found in cat faeces and may be passed to humans through contact with cat litter, by eating raw or partially cooked meat or eating contaminated fruit or vegetables. If you have had cats for some time, you may have already been exposed to toxoplasma and developed immunity to toxoplasmosis.

Although toxoplasmosis may not affect your fertility, if you contract it while pregnant – and particularly during the first three months of pregnancy – it can be very harmful for your unborn baby. Effects on the baby can include stillbirth, premature birth, low birth weight, fever, jaundice, abnormalities of the retina, mental retardation, abnormal head size, convulsions and brain calcification. It can also increase the chances of miscarriage.[16]

To avoid infection, make sure your partner empties the cat-litter tray and washes his hands thoroughly afterwards, or better still he should wear disposable gloves. It is also advisable to avoid raw or undercooked meat, wash your hands frequently (particularly if handling raw meat), wear gloves while gardening and be sure to wash all fruit and vegetables before eating them.

Chapter 9

Eating for Fertility

In this chapter we'll be looking at the importance of maintaining a healthy, balanced diet. We'll look at which foods are particularly beneficial to your fertility and which ones are best avoided – in reality there is no such thing as a good food or a bad food, but healthy and unhealthy diets certainly exist. This chapter also provides a clear and straightforward guide to the all-important vitamin and mineral supplements, as backed up by recent medical research. Much has been written about the kind of supplements women should take when they're trying to get pregnant – and a lot of this is either contradictory or just plain confusing! Ensuring that your body has the right nutrients really needn't become time-consuming or expensive.

Diet is the single biggest controllable factor in getting yourself fit for fertility. Enjoying a sensible and healthy diet will help to keep your hormone levels balanced and will provide your body with all the nutrients it needs. Not only will this make you feel and look better, it will also increase your chances of conceiving and of having a healthy baby. It's always a good idea to introduce changes to your diet before trying to conceive as, for example, sperm can take up to three months to mature, so it makes sense to start your healthy lifestyle sooner rather than later. Adopting a healthy diet isn't about giving up all the things you enjoy; it's really about taking responsibility for your own health and wellbeing – which can only be a positive thing!

As a nation, we now have much more exposure to information on what is and isn't good for us. We're bombarded with television programmes and magazine articles telling us what we mustn't eat and what the latest 'miracle' food is. In fact, there's so much information it's hard to figure out exactly what we should be doing.

Remember, keep things simple. Changing your diet doesn't have to be complicated, and following a healthy-eating plan doesn't have to mean deprivation, hunger and endless tofu stir-fries. By making small changes to your diet, you increase your chances of maintaining a regular menstrual cycle, producing good eggs and enjoying a healthy pregnancy. Similarly, your partner will make strong and healthy sperm.

KEEP HYDRATED

I personally think that a significant number of people are routinely dehydrated in their daily life. It is a terrifying fact that if you are 2% dehydrated, which is very little fluid, then your performance is down by up to 10%. If we looked at this in the athletic world, this means that a 100m runner would be running at about 11 seconds compared to his usual time of 10 seconds. This would mean the difference between being in the Olympic semi-finals and not even qualifying.

If you equate this to one's daily life, this can have an equally huge impact, and so I really encourage people to be well hydrated. This means drinking about eight glasses (or two litres) of fluid a day. I encourage couples to look at their urine colour. If it is a light straw colour, you are drinking enough, but if it is a dark, concentrated colour, this indicates that you are dehydrated.

Eating food isn't just about replenishing our energy stores so that we can get through the day, nor is it just about socialising or enjoying new flavours. What we eat affects our bodies at a *cellular* level and has an enormous impact on the functioning of our body systems – from our circulatory system and nervous system to our digestion and reproductive organs. It can also affect our frame of mind. That is why it's so important to take a bit of time to make adjustments – and they need not be big adjustments: you may already have a very good diet.

There are countless faddy diets around, many of which are not particularly balanced. I'm not going to suggest you diet in the conventional sense or try to restrict your eating – on the contrary, I'm going to be encouraging you to eat lots of food rich in nutrients and essential food groups, all of which will contribute to your fertility health. Of all the diets that are cramming the shelves of bookshops, the ones that are most frequently endorsed by the medical profession are the low-fat, high-fibre diet and the low GI (glycaemic index) diet. The advice you'll find over these next few pages will largely reflect this. Good basic advice is to eat fresh organic food, rich in protein. Please do not forget to stay well hydrated.

THE FOUR MAIN FOOD GROUPS

Although we may talk about certain nutrients being important for fertility, we eat food and not nutrients. It's important therefore that we translate key nutrients into food sources. One way this can be done is by grouping together similar foods. Wen looking at fertility we can use the following four groups: carbohydrates, fats, proteins and fibre. All of them are crucial and play different roles in preparing the body for fertility.

Carbohydrates

Scientifically speaking, carbohydrates are organic compounds made of carbon, hydrogen and oxygen. When eaten, carbohydrates are turned into glucose – the body's basic fuel source. As energy providers, carbohydrates are vital for fertility since they help to maintain healthy hormone levels and balance sugar levels.

Carbohydrates can be divided into two categories: simple carbohydrates and complex carbohydrates.

Simple carbohydrates, also known as fast-releasing or refined carbohydrates, are the main reason why carbs in general have been given such a bad rap recently. These carbs tend to produce a fast increase in insulin and blood sugar followed by a sudden slump, while not providing the body much in the way of nutrients. Food sources include sugar, white breads and other snack foods made from refined white flour, added glucose and glucose syrup and processed foods. In order to maintain a healthy blood sugar level, the amount of simple carbohydrates in your diet should be kept to a minimum. Some fruit, fruit juices and dried fruit also come under this category and do have their place in a balanced diet, but not in excess, and I would always recommend that fruit juice is taken diluted with water.

Complex carbohydrates, also known as slow-releasing or unrefined carbohydrates, are made up of more complicated sugars and starches as well as different types of fibre. They cause a more moderate insulin and glucose response and, provided you don't have too much of them, can help protect from high insulin levels and energy swings and can regulate bowel movements.

Food sources include wholegrain breads and cereals, brown basmati rice, some vegetables, beans and pulses and certain fruits, like apples and berries. These are the best carbohydrates since they can help to maintain energy levels and provide you with some of the fibre your body needs. Carbohydrates should make up around one-third of your daily food intake, or roughly five portions a day, where a portion is one slice of wholemeal bread, two egg-sized potatoes, two tablespoons of cooked rice, pasta or noodles or three tablespoons of breakfast cereal.[1]

What Is GI?

Just to complicate matters, carbohydrates – and the other food groups – are also categorised by their glycaemic index, or GI. This is something of a buzz word, but it is actually the result of many years' research within the scientific world and has long been recommended by doctors and nutritionists.

GI is a measure of how much a particular food will raise your blood glucose level – and how quickly. The index is a long list of all the different carbohydrate foods, which have been given a numerical rating. This number tells you whether that particular food will cause a sharp rise in blood sugar and insulin levels or whether it will be broken down and enter your bloodstream at a steadier pace. The numbers given to each food range from zero to 100. The lower the glycaemic rating of a carb, the more preferable your body's glucose and insulin response will be. Eating foods with a high glycaemic value means your body is likely to experience a sudden and sharp rise in blood glucose, which can lead to mood swings, hormone imbalances, sugar cravings, obesity and, potentially, diabetes.[2]

What is often surprising to people following a GI-type diet is that foods with a high rating include some vegetables, like carrots and potatoes, as well as most grain-based products like bread and rice. And, on the flip side, certain foods such as fruit juice and some fruits actually have a lower GI rating.

GI sounds complicated at first, but in fact it does make very good sense. Keep your blood sugar and insulin levels balanced and you'll avoid those energy swings that can so often lead to sugar cravings and extreme tiredness. Your hormone levels are more likely to maintain a healthy balance; you're less likely to suffer from high blood pressure; and you won't be putting a strain on your vital organs. GI can also be of benefit to sufferers of PMS (premenstrual syndrome); this all bodes well for your fertility health as well as that of the developing embryo when you do become pregnant.

To find out what the GI ratings are for different foods, have a look at the various GI websites on the internet – many include a comprehensive index – or there are a number of GI-based books available. Your GP may also be able to provide you with a general list of common foods and their GI rating.

Remember, the lower the glycaemic value of a carbohydrate, the better your body's glucose and insulin response will be to that food.

Fats

Fats have been given a bad press in recent years, and although it's true that some fats are not very good for you, there are some that are vital to your health and fertility. Fat is a nutrient that, in the right form and the right quantity, can balance hormone levels and support the circulatory system. In some cases, the right type of fats are even thought to reduce the risk of heart attack.

Fats can be broadly separated into two categories: saturated and unsaturated.

Saturated fats are found in meat, eggs, dairy products and some oils. These fats are best kept to a *minimum*, as they can lead to heart disease, obesity, high cholesterol and an increased risk of some cancers and heart attacks. The more saturated a fat, the harder it is for the body digest, and this can lead to weight gain. Saturated fats also inhibit the body's absorption of essential fatty acids.

Unsaturated fats are quite different. They are found in nuts, seeds, grains, fish and olive oil. Certain unsaturated fats, those called omega-3, omega-6 and omega-9 oils (collectively known as essential fatty acids), are essential for the body's production of prostaglandins, which work to regulate our hormones – hence their importance for good fertility fitness. For a more detailed look at the vital role of essential fatty acids in fertility fitness, see page 123.

Good sources of essential fatty acids include oily fish,

pumpkin seeds, sunflower seeds, linseed and flaxseed. If your current diet doesn't include much in the way of omega-6 and omega-3 oils, then it's a good idea to start now. You could either take a supplement or better still have a portion of mackerel or sardines once or twice a week and include a handful of nuts and seeds in your morning cereal or in salads.

The government recommends that fat should provide no more than 35% of your daily food energy, with saturated fat providing around 11% and unsaturated fats around 21%.[3]

Oily Fish

Oily fish, such as sardines, herring, mackerel, trout and salmon, are all rich sources of omega-3 fatty acids, as well as being a good source of vitamins A and D.

You can check which fish are oily and which aren't in the list below:[4]

Oily Fish
anchovies
bloater
cacha
carp
eel
herring
hilsa
Jack fish
katla
kipper
mackerel
pilchards
salmon
sardines
sprats
swordfish

trout
tuna (fresh)
whitebait

Non-oily Fish
ayr
catfish
cod
coley
dogfish/rock salmon
dover sole
flounder
flying fish
haddock
hake
halibut
hoki
John Dory
kalabasu
lemon sole
ling
marlin
monkfish
parrot fish
plaice
pollack
pomfret
red fish
red and grey mullet
red snapper
rohu
sea bass
sea bream
shark
skate

tilapia
tuna (tinned)
turbot
whiting

As you can see from the list, fresh tuna is an oily fish and is high in omega-3 fatty acids, but when it is tinned, these fatty acids are reduced to levels similar to white fish. So, although tinned tuna is a healthy choice for most people, providing protein, B vitamins and iron, it doesn't count as oily fish.

How Much Oily Fish Should You Eat?

Most people should be eating more oily fish because omega-3 fatty acids are very good for our health. However, oily fish can contain low levels of pollutants that can build up in the body. For this reason, there are recommendations for the maximum number of portions of oily fish we should be eating each week (a portion is about 140g, cooked). Girls and women who wish to have a baby or who are pregnant or breastfeeding are advised to eat a maximum of two portions of oily fish per week. Other women (who do not plan to have children), men and boys can safely eat four portions.

Protein

Protein is an essential nutrient made up of more than 20 biological compounds called amino acids. Our bodies are only able to make 12 of these; the rest must come from the food we eat. These are the essential amino acids. Protein is necessary for the repair and renewal of the body's cells, for producing hormones, for growing muscle and tissue and for making antibodies to help fight infections, so healthy eggs and sperm require protein.[5]

Good sources of protein include white meat or lean beef and

lamb, oily and white fish, lentils, the grain quinoa, rice, some vegetables (such as peas and beans), cheese, nuts and seeds, and eggs. Proteins from animal foods contain all of the essential amino acids and are called 'high biological value' or 'high-quality' proteins. With the exception of soya beans, which are classed as a high-quality protein, proteins from plant sources do not contain all of the essential amino acids and are called 'low biological value' or 'low-quality' proteins. However, if the proteins from different plant sources are eaten together (or at least over a day), the deficiency in one plant protein is made up for by an excess in another. So even if you are a vegetarian or a vegan, there is no reason why your intake of protein cannot be as good as that of a meat-eater. One thing to watch out for, though, if you are a vegetarian, is an over-reliance on dairy products, particularly cheese. Whilst there is nothing wrong with cheese, too much can lead to a diet that is very high in saturated fat and may lack iron. I usually advise people to include more beans, nuts and seeds in their diet. Beans on toast, a lentil soup or hummous and pitta are all good alternatives.

Fermented dairy products such as live yoghurts not only provide protein but also probiotic 'good' bacteria, which supports the growth of good bacteria in the gut and boosts the immune system, so they're a particularly good choice. In total, and whatever the source, protein should make up around 15% of our food energy.

Recently, there has been a lot of coverage in the media about high-protein, low-carbohydrate diets. Protein increases the levels of ammonium, a metabolic by-product. High levels of ammonium have been thought to reduce a woman's fertility and possibly increase the risk of miscarriage, though this is still being researched.[6] As ever, my advice would be to exercise moderation when it comes to any sort of diet. It's more important that both you and your partner are getting adequate amounts of essential amino acids, along with nutrients from the other food groups.

A WORD ON LIVER AND LIVER PATE

These foods can contain a lot of vitamin A. An excessively high intake of vitamin A can harm an unborn baby. This means women should avoid eating liver and avoid taking supplements containing vitamin A or fish liver oils, (which contain high levels of vitamin A). However, liver is rich in fertility-boosting nutrients and so men can still enjoy eating it!

Fibre

Fresh fruit and vegetables are one of the best sources of fibre as well as being packed with essential nutrients such as vitamin C (in oranges and kiwis) or antioxidant phytochemicals (in canned tomatoes and red onions). Think about buying organic where possible. There is no agreed evidence that organic food is definitely better than conventional produce but many couples are particularly concerned about the impact of pesticide use. Unlike conventional farming, organic methods of farming do not use pesticides, DDT and other chemicals. Some of these chemicals contain xenoestrogens, which behave like low-dose synthetic oestrogens in the body. Not only do these chemicals put the liver under great pressure, they also upset the balance of male and female hormones, and the resulting increase in oestrogen affects fertility. It must be said that it is perfectly possible to produce normal food with minimal residues, and in fact they are not detected in about 70 per cent of produce sampled by the Pesticides Residue Committee. (Food Standards Agency 2003.) Ultimately, buying organic is a personal choice, but given that many people report that it simply tastes better than conventional food, and that therefore they are likely to eat more of it, I would support the decision. It also enables you to feel that you are doing everything possible to increase your chances of conception, which can only be a good thing.

Specialist companies are emerging who will ship a wide range of organic vegetables and fruit direct to your door. Often called box schemes, these vary from company to company but all are based around purchasing a box of supplier-selected vegetables. Your box will be delivered to your door with a range of seasonal vegetables and fruit (minus any you have told them you don't like). Box schemes are a particularly good way of supporting local producers and an excellent way of eating in tune with the seasons.

As well as fruit and vegetables, if you can, try to buy organic meat, eggs and other produce. If you can't get to a good supply of organic produce, make sure you wash all fruit and vegetables before use to remove as much pesticide as possible. It is very important to incorporate lots of fruit and vegetables into your daily diet. A minimum of five portions is the recommended daily amount.

Portion Control

Here are some examples of what is actually meant by one portion:[7]

Fruits
1 orange or apple
1 small banana
½ large grapefruit
1 150ml glass of 100% fruit or vegetable juice (you can only count juice as one portion a day, however much you drink)
1 large handful of blueberries
1 tablespoon of dried fruit or 3 dried apricots
10 grapes or strawberries
2 kiwi fruit
1 slice of melon (2-inch slice)

Vegetables
4 heaped tablespoons of runner beans
8 cauliflower florets

3 heaped tablespoons of chickpeas
1 large parsnip
3 heaped tablespoons of canned sweetcorn
3 heaped tablespoons of peas
½ pepper
1 cereal bowl of mixed salad
2 heaped tablespoons of cooked spinach
1 tomato or 3 cherry tomatoes
8 Brussels sprouts
2 spears of broccoli

FERTILITY FITNESS 'GOOD' AND 'BAD' FOODS

Provided you are enjoying a balanced diet, which includes plenty of nutrient-rich fruit and vegetables, you should try not to get overly hung up on food. Faddy diets are really just that – fads that are dreamed up by so-called experts who may actually have little knowledge of nutrition. Of course, it's important to take control of your diet – and you'll feel better and more positive for it, but don't let it become an obsession. Overly strict dieting that results in severe weight loss can, as we've seen, disrupt ovulation in women or reduce sperm formation in men.

Couples coming to my practice often ask what particular foods they should be having in order to boost their fertility. Unfortunately, there is no 'miracle' food that will suddenly guarantee getting pregnant. However, there are foods that I would positively recommend, and there are some that are best avoided or taken only in moderation. Overall, nutrition has a subtle but powerful effect on all of the body's systems, including the reproductive system.

Top Ten 'Good' Foods

These are the 'super foods'. Try to incorporate more of them into your and your partner's diet. It can be very helpful to keep a food diary to chart your progress – try to increase your intake week by week with the aim of eventually eating these foods three or four times a week – more is even better!

1. **Brazil nuts** are rich in the important antioxidant selenium, important in protecting sperm and eggs from free radical damage. A low intake of selenium has been linked with heart disease and cancers as well as male infertility and pre-eclampsia in women.

2. **Broccoli** (along with other green leafy vegetables, such as kale and spinach) is a wonderful provider of folic acid. Folic acid reduces the risk of neural-tube damage (brain and spinal cord) in the developing embryo; women who have been on the contraceptive pill can be deficient in folate. Broccoli will also provide you with vitamin B5 (pantothenic acid), which is important for foetal development.

3. **Sardines**, mackerel, herring and tuna, are full of the essential mineral selenium and essential fatty acids, which act as hormone regulators.

4. **Pumpkin seeds**, along with sunflower seeds, grains and pulses, provide a wonderful source of zinc, the all-important mineral so necessary for maintaining a healthy menstrual cycle and for the production of the hormone progesterone. Zinc is also vital for your partner, as it balances the levels of testosterone and increases sperm count (see page 158).

5. **Pure orange juice**, one small glass will provide 100% of the recommended daily intake of vitamin C , a powerful anti-oxidant nutrient that maintains quality of sperm and eggs as well as your general wellbeing. It is also a great source of potassium and will count towards your daily fluid intake. Make it your routine by adding a glass at breakfast. If you don't like orange juice have a kiwi instead for just as much vitamin C.

6. **Mangoes** are also rich in vitamin C, which as we've seen is essential for producing a healthy baby. Mangoes also have

an alkaline pH so work to correct acidity, while the anti-oxidants help to prevent the damaging action of free radicals (see page 119).

7. **Dates** were traditionally believed to be a powerful aphrodisiac and have long been associated with fertility. There's more than legend to this, however: dates contain a good source of carbohydrate energy along with protein and fibre; they contain several essential minerals and vitamins including above average amounts of iron and are a particularly good source of potassium.[8]

8. **Oats** are an excellent source of protein and do not contain the fat that you find in traditional sources, like meat. Oats release energy slowly, so you won't get a sudden dip in blood sugar levels after eating them, and provide the body with manganese. A deficiency in this mineral may lead to defective ovulation and will inhibit the synthesis of sex hormones.[9] Oats make horses frisky and have long been considered a male sexual energiser, hence our phrase 'sowing his wild oats'. Some herbalists suggest that oats boost male human fertility as well. So why not both help yourself to a fertility-enhancing bowl of porridge each morning?[10]

9. **Eggs**, in particular the yolks, have a broad range of nutritional benefits, particularly with regard to fertility fitness. They provide amino acids, necessary for egg and sperm production, vitamin A, vitamin B1, vitamin B2, vitamin B5, vitamin B6, iron, manganese *and* zinc. Not bad for an egg![11]

10. **Wheatgerm** is a good source of vitamin E (sometimes known as the 'fertility vitamin'), which carries oxygen to the sex organs, as well as zinc, the B vitamins and selenium.[13] Wheatgerm can be added to breakfast cereals or used in baking.

'Super Foods' Food Diary

	Breakfast	Lunch	Dinner	Snacks
Monday				
Tuesday				
Wednesday				
Thursday				
Friday				
Saturday				
Sunday				

Top Ten Foods to Forget

Don't become obsessed, but do try to limit your intake of the following foods, wherever possible:

1. **Salt** is something we are all aware we should not consume too much of, and research does show that too much salt can affect your fertility fitness. Tests carried out on mice that were fed a diet high in salt were found to have impaired ovulation, plus increased blood pressure and a reduction in fertility.[14] Despite improved awareness and government campaigns about eating less than 6g a day, many of us are still consuming too much salt, as so much of our salt intake is found hidden in foods we would not normally expect, such as breakfast cereals and bread. Avoid eating processed foods (see below), check food labels to increase your intake of foods that contain only a little

salt (less than 0.25g per 100g of product) and try not to add salt to your food, or replace it with herb salt.

2. **Monosodium glutamate** doesn't sound like something any of us would willingly eat, but it is used to flavour countless everyday foods, such as Chinese food and processed foods, including some ice creams and salad dressings. Not only has the consumption of monosodium glutamate (MSG) been linked to sight problems[15] and obesity,[16] it has also been shown to reduce pregnancy success. Male rats fed MSG before mating were found to have a less than 50% success rate in conceiving, whereas those not fed MSG had over a 92% success rate.[17] Try to get into the habit of reading the labels on food you buy – or, better still, avoid processed food altogether and stick to organic and fresh produce.

3. **Aspartame**, like MSG, is a hidden 'ingredient' likely to be found in anything labelled 'diet' or 'sugar free'. When the temperature of aspartame exceeds 30°C the wood alcohol in it converts to formaldehyde (a poison used to preserve body parts) and then to formic acid, which is even more toxic. Much research has been done on the effect aspartame has on our health. It has been shown to be linked with depression, weight gain, dizziness, palpitations, memory loss, joint pain and much more.[18] And if that isn't enough to put you off altogether, it is also linked with infertility and miscarriage.[19] Remember to check the labels on processed foods and drink, and try to avoid all diet drinks, mints and chewing gums.

4. **Quinine** is the key ingredient in tonic water and is also used in some antimalarial medication. Some researchers have suggested it may cause birth defects if taken while pregnant.[20]

5. **Refined carbohydrates** are best kept to a minimum when trying to conceive. As explained earlier, diets high in added sugar can put stress on the immune system and can lead to unwanted weight increase and hormone fluctuations, known to affect your fertility fitness. Like salt, sugar is found in many processed foods, so read the label first! Replace white

bread, pasta and rice with wholegrains, and try to cut out foods like cakes and biscuits.

6. **Caffeine**, should be reduced in your diet. Many scientists have concluded that women trying for a baby should consume no more than 300mg of caffeine a day, (1 mug of instant coffee will provide 100mg of caffeine). High levels of caffeine can result in babies having a low birth weight, or even cause miscarriage.

7. **Processed foods**, particularly snack foods, can contain high levels of added salt and sugar. Try to limit the salty, sugary snacks and go for fruit, nuts and seeds instead.

8. **Fried foods**, and too much saturated fat in general, will lead to health problems, weight gain, the incorrect metabolism of omega fats and fatigue. Fried foods, such as crisps and chips, are found to contain acrylamide, a chemical that appears to form as a result of a reaction between specific amino acids and sugars found in foods heated to high temperatures. Research into the effects of acrylamide showed that, among other side effects, rats exposed to the chemical had a decreased rate of fertility.[21]

9. **Unpasteurised foods** (those made from raw milk) may become contaminated with listeria. There has been widespread coverage of the dangers of pregnant women contracting listeriosis, as it can cause miscarriage and premature birth.[22] Brucella is another kind of bacteria passed via raw milk and can lead to human brucellosis. In animals, brucellosis can cause miscarriage and infertility.[23] Avoid eating soft cheeses and unpasteurised foods both while you're trying to get pregnant and during pregnancy.

10. **Acrylamide,** produced by certain starchy foods that have been heated to a high temperature, such as crisps, chips and crispbreads. Acrylamide causes cancer in animals and decreases fertility in rats, so it may also be a danger to human health. Research is currently being conducted but until more is known, the best advice is to avoid crisps and chips or limit your intake.

HORMONE-BALANCING DIET: THE RULES

In summary, here are my key rules for balancing your hormones and getting you fit for fertility. Do bear in mind, though, that probably the single most important thing to do is eat a balanced diet that you actually enjoy.

1. Eat five portions of fruit and vegetables every day, and make sure you include a good variety of colours.
2. Eat wholegrains, such as granary bread, brown rice, oats, muesli, millet, quinoa and rye. Avoid white refined carbohydrates.
3. Buy organic foods where possible.
4. Eat foods containing phytoestrogens, such as beans, lentils, chickpeas and soya products.
5. Eat oily fish three times a week, as well as plenty of nuts and seeds.
6. Drink *at least* two litres of fluid a day (water, diluted fruit juices).
7. Reduce your intake of saturated fats (cakes, biscuits, pies, pastries, fatty meat, full fat dairy products).
8. Avoid additives, preservatives and chemicals such as artificial sweeteners.
9. Reduce your caffeine intake.
10. Reduce your alcohol intake.
11. Try to avoid sugar (glucose) drinks and foods with added sugars such as sweets, cakes and sugary breakfast cereal.

Meal ideas

Breakfast

- Porridge with skimmed or semi-skimmed milk or water and raisins
- Muesli with no added salt, with fresh fruit or nuts added, with low-fat yoghurt
- Wholegrain toast with chopped banana

- Breakfast smoothie made with skimmed milk, low-fat yoghurt, fruit and wheatgerm

Lunch

- Omega-3 enriched eggs, scrambled on toast
- Chicken and avocado salad with added pumpkin seeds
- Jacket potato with tinned salmon and reduced-fat cream cheese and cucumber
- Baked beans on wholemeal toast
- Lentil soup with wholemeal bread roll
- Turkey and cranberry salad in wholemeal pitta

Evening meal

- Lean beef and broccoli stir fry
- Chickpea curry and brown rice
- Salmon or trout with pesto topping, potatoes and green vegetables
- Spanish omelette with ratatouille vegetables
- Home-made chilli con carne made with lean mince and served with brown rice
- Chicken or vegetable fajitas with avocado and salad

Snacks

- Fresh fruit (carefully washed)
- A handful of dried fruit such as apricots
- Tinned fruit in natural juice with low-fat yoghurt or fromage frais
- A handful of mixed nuts and raisins
- A small bowl of breakfast cereal with skimmed or semi-skimmed milk
- A couple of slices of maltloaf with a thin spreading of butter
- Low-fat natural yoghurt or fromage frais with chopped Brazil nuts
- Raw vegetable sticks peeled or carefully washed, such as carrot, pepper, cucumber etc, with a tomato salsa dip

YOUR GUIDE TO VITAMINS, MINERALS AND NUTRITIONAL SUPPLEMENTS

Eating a healthy, balanced diet with plenty of fruit and vegetables is essential for making sure your body is getting the nutrients it needs. There is no substitute for a healthy diet as many of the compounds found in plant foods – the phytochemicals – are simply not available in supplement form. A balanced diet, and the nutrients provided, will help you look and feel better, have more energy, improve your ability to cope with stress, improve your mood, help you to fight off infections and achieve the right weight. Eating a good diet will also enhance your fertility – and that of your partner. As we've seen, the food and drink we consume – our everyday diet – play a vital role in balancing the body's hormones, ensuring that the delicate mechanisms of the reproductive system are in good working order and preparing the body for conception and a healthy pregnancy.

All women, regardless of their diet, are advised to take a daily folic acid supplement (0.4mg) while trying to conceive and during the first 12 weeks of pregnancy. This is to reduce the risk of neural-tube defects such as spina bifida in the unborn baby. Many good multivitamin and mineral preparations that contain the correct amount of folic acid are now available.

A great deal of scientific knowledge now exists about the use of nutritional supplements and their beneficial effects on both male and female fertility, particularly where known problems exist. Supplements can have a number of roles, including improving your and your partner's overall health and rebalancing hormones; they can provide additional antioxidant nutrients to counteract damage and provide the necessary 'raw ingredients' to help the production and functioning of eggs and sperm.

Many couples want to do 'everything they possibly can' when trying for a baby and so take one-a-day supplements as an 'insurance policy' while improving their diet. These are available via a good chemist on the advice of a pharmacist, from your doctor, qualified nutritionist or dietician. They typically contain most of the nutrients needed for fertility and general health and there are now recognised pre-conception and pregnancy formulations which also include the correct dose of folic acid. Others may consider the need for individual high-dose supplements to act as 'nutritional medicine'. Consultation with a nutritionist or dietician specialising in fertility and fertility treatments is strongly advised.

Taking an excess of vitamins and minerals can be more harmful than not consuming enough, particularly when using mega-dose single supplements as opposed to the multi-formulas. For example, vitamin A in the form of retinol can cause harm to an unborn baby; a prolonged high intake of zinc can have a negative impact on the immune system; and there is a risk of selenium toxicity when taking supplements. I will often consider running blood tests on couples to assess vitamin and mineral levels.

Another important point to realise about supplements is that they are unregulated. Unlike medicines, which have undergone years of scientific trials to show effectiveness and must meet stringent levels of purity, nutritional supplements do not have to demonstrate effectiveness. Cases of supplements that don't contain what the label states have been found, and contamination with other substances is not unknown. It really is a case of 'buyer beware'.

A respectable brand of supplements will be produced to pharmaceutical-quality standards of GMP (Good Manufacturing Practice), which offers a greater level of confidence in a product.

RDAs AND RNIs

In Europe, RDA stands for Recommended Daily Amount. The RDA is an estimate of the amount of vitamins and minerals sufficient to meet or more than meet the needs of *groups* of adults. RDA values are part of European Union food law (EU RDA) and reflect the variation in opinion across Europe. There is only one figure for each nutrient, derived

---

from figures for adults, rather than a range of figures that vary with age, sex and physiological status as exists for UK Reference Nutrient Intakes, or RNIs. RNIs were developed by the Committee on the Medical Aspects of Food Policy (COMA) for the Department of Health. The RNI is the amount of an individual nutrient that is enough to ensure that the health needs of nearly all the group (97.5%) are being met. By definition, many within the group will need less. Both RDAs and RNIs are valid, but RDAs tend to be used for food-labelling purposes (the whole of Europe needs to use these by 2010), whereas RNIs will be used for guidance on nutritional intake by health professionals.

Randomly taking individual vitamins and minerals is not advised as there can be interactions between nutrients as well as with food. If you are not able to consult a nutritionist or dietician to look at your overall diet and lifestyle, then it is far safer to use a one-a-day multinutrient formulation, which should have levels of vitamins and minerals close to 100% of the EU RDA or RNI.

Vitamin A

There are three active forms of vitamin A:

- retinol
- retinal
- retinoic acid

In food, most vitamin A is found in the form of retinol. All three types can be formed from the plant pigment carotenes (usually red or yellow plants, such as carrots). The most common carotene is beta carotene.

Vitamin A is essential for eyesight, for the development of many organs and processes during the early stages of embryo development, and for fertility, growth and optimum neurological and immune function throughout life. Like other vitamins, vitamin A has important antioxidant properties.

Vitamin A is needed in the production of male and female sex hormones. Without vitamin A, ovarian hormone production will be reduced and the prostate gland in men stop producing secretions. Results from studies on birds provide strong evidence that vitamin A requirement begins during the first two to three weeks of human pregnancy, so it is important to get adequate vitamin A nutrition during the early stages of pregnancy.

Recently, concerns have been raised over the use of vitamin A by women trying to get pregnant and during pregnancy. This is largely because in the past women were encouraged to eat liver. Vitamin A is stored in the liver (in animals and in humans) and so it follows that liver and products made from liver (e.g. pâté) contain the highest source of vitamin A in the form of retinol; in fact, just 3g of calves' liver (about the size of an acorn) will provide 100% of the RDA for vitamin A. Retinol has been linked to foetal abnormalities when consumed in large amounts.[24] Fortunately, it appears that beta carotene – the pigment in plants that is converted into vitamin A – does not cause such defects.[25] The corpus luteum (the structure in the ovary that produces progesterone and helps to maintain pregnancy in the first three months) is rich in beta carotene, so plays a key role in the regulation of the reproductive-cycle hormones.[26]

To avoid an excessive intake of vitamin A, it is advisable for women to avoid retinol-containing supplements, fish-liver oil, liver and liver products. Many multivitamins and supplements aimed at women use beta carotene as a safe and effective way of supplementing the diet when needed.

Food sources: carrots, green leafy vegetables (e.g. broccoli, watercress and spinach), orange-yellow vegetables and fruit (e.g. carrots, sweet potatoes, cantaloupe melon and mangoes), whole (full-fat) milk, butter, margarine and spreads, cheese, eggs, oily fish, liver and liver pâté (women should avoid if planning a pregnancy or pregnant).

EU RDA: 0.8mg. There is no RDA for beta carotene.[27]

UK RNI for males aged 19–50 years: 0.7mg.

UK RNI for females aged 19–50 years: 0.6mg.

Vitamin B1 (Thiamin)

Thiamin converts carbohydrates, fats and alcohol into energy for metabolism. It promotes healthy nerves and, alongside other nutrients such as pantothenic acid (vitamin B5), can help the digestion of food. It is also needed for ovulation and implantation.

Food sources: lean pork, potatoes, nuts, wholegrain cereals, B1-fortified breakfast cereals and seeds.

EU RDA: 1.4mg.

UK RNI for males and females aged 19–50 years: 0.4mg/ 1,000kcal.

Vitamin B2 (Riboflavin)

Deficiencies in B2 have been linked to sterility, miscarriage and low birth weight.[28] B2 helps fight infections, aids red blood cell formation, helps the body to process protein and is used by the liver to clear old hormones, including oestrogen and progesterone. If these are not excreted, the body thinks there is enough and less production occurs, resulting in hormone deficiencies.

Food sources: milk, cheese, yoghurt, fish, beef, eggs, wholegrain bread and cereals, avocadoes and mushrooms.

EU RDA: 1.6mg.

UK RNI for males aged 19–50 years: 1.3mg.

UK RNI for females aged 19–50 years: 1.1mg.

Niacin (Formerly Vitamin B3)

Niacin is needed to release energy from carbohydrate-rich foods, is involved in blood sugar control and keeps the skin, nervous and digestive systems healthy. Some of the body's needs are met from tryptophan – an amino acid found in many proteins contained in rich foods – which the body can convert to the active form of the vitamin. When provided as a supplement rather than naturally through the diet, niacin is in the form of nicotinamide, which has no side effects and so is safe for couples trying to conceive. Another form of the vitamin is nicotinic acid, which is sometimes used in high doses to treat raised blood cholesterol level and should only be taken under medical supervision.

Food sources: chicken and turkey, lean beef, fish, nuts, pulses, potatoes, fortified breakfast cereals, eggs, milk and cheese (low in niacin but high in trytophan, which can be converted into niacin).

EU RDA: 18mg.

UK RNI for males and females aged 19–50 years: 6.6mg/1,000kcal.

Pantothenic Acid (Formerly Vitamin B5)

Pantothenic acid is important for foetal development so is essential before and at conception. It is also used to manufacture stress hormones, and when stress hormones are overproduced, for example during long periods of anxiety or emotional upset, the body's need for pantothenic acid increases. The name 'pantothenic' is derived from the Greek and means 'widespread', as it is present in all food of animal or vegetable origin, though some food sources are particularly good.

Food sources: lean meat, poultry, dried fruit (e.g. prunes and apricots), nuts, yoghurt and legumes (e.g. peas, chickpeas and lentils).

EU RDA: 6mg.

UK RNI for males and females aged 19–50 years: 3–7mg.

Vitamin B6 (Pyridoxine)

Along with zinc, B6 is essential for the production and balance of female sex hormones. Research has shown that women who had previously had difficulty in conceiving saw a marked increase in their fertility after being given B6. Periods were regulated, and the incidence of pregnancy rose.[29] Vitamin B6 also helps the body use magnesium and linoleic acid and fight infections.

Food sources: lean meat, poultry, fish, eggs, wholemeal bread, wholegrains, brown rice, nuts, bananas, yeast extract and soya beans.

EU RDA: 2mg.

UK RNI for males and females aged 19–50 years: 15mcg/g of protein.

Vitamin B9 (Folic Acid or Folate)

Folic acid, also called folacin or folate is a B vitamin that was first identified in the 1940s and found to be vital for every cell division in the body, for the formation of DNA (the body's genetic blueprint) and RNA (so that cells duplicate normally), and for protein synthesis. Folic acid is essential for making red blood cells. It has been given a lot of attention recently as studies now show that folic acid helps to prevent babies developing neural-tube defects.[30] As well as eating folate-rich foods, women should start taking 400mcg of folic acid from three months before trying to conceive until at least week 12 of their pregnancy. Pre-conception folic acid is especially relevant for those who have previously taken the contraceptive pill, which can deplete the levels of folic acid in the body.

Your partner can also benefit from taking folic acid before you start trying to conceive. After showing that a folate-restricted diet made sperm counts plunge 90% in rats, researchers at the University of California in Berkeley showed that folic acid deficiency has a similar effect in men.

While there are good food sources of folate, it is thought that around 10% of Americans and Europeans fail to eat enough in their daily diet. In addition, some experts believe that only about half of the natural folate in foods is absorbed by the body, whereas when foods are fortified with folic acid or folic acid supplements are given, the absorption is far greater.

Folic acid works with other B vitamins, especially B12 and B6 and so these should be supplemented together.

Food sources: green leafy vegetables (e.g. Brussels sprouts and broccoli), orange juice, liver (for men only), pulses (e.g. lentils, aduki beans, soya beans and borlotti beans), nuts, yeast extract, wheat germ, wholemeal bread and fortified breakfast cereal.

EU RDA: 0.2mg.

UK RNI for males and females aged 19–50 years: 0.2mg. (For women, when you're trying to get pregnant, you should take a daily 0.4mg folic acid supplement from the time you stop using contraception – ideally three months before trying to conceive – until you are 12 weeks pregnant.)

Vitamin B12 (Cobalamin)

B12 is essential for the synthesis of DNA and RNA, which make up the blueprint for the genetic code of the entire body. It also aids the absorption of iron and helps to process fats, carbohydrates and proteins.

Research shows that B12 is also needed to maintain fertility in men. In one study, a group of infertile men were given vitamin B12 supplements for 2–13 months. Approximately 60% of those taking the supplement experienced improved sperm counts.[31]

Any diet containing some animal protein should provide adequate amounts of B12, so if you follow a vegetarian diet but you consume milk and eggs, you will still obtain the required amount. A vegan diet, however, should include soya milk and breakfast cereal that has been fortified with the vitamin to ensure needs are met.

Food sources: lean meat, poultry, fish, eggs, B12-fortified soya milk and breakfast cereals.

EU RDA: 1μg (microgram).

UK RNI for males and females aged 19–50 years: 1.5μg.

Vitamin C (Ascorbic Acid)

Vitamin C is active throughout the body. It is good for the immune system, aids healing, strengthens blood vessels and cell walls and is crucial in the formation of collagen (a protein found in skin, bones, cartilage and gums) – all important factors when you are trying to look after your health and a developing embryo.

Vitamin C is a powerful antioxidant and helps to protect the body from free radicals. It may also help protect sperm and its DNA from damage and improve sperm motility and quality. Semen contains a protein vitamin E complex called non-specific sperm agglutinin (NSSA). NSSA exists in two forms, an oxidised form, which can't bind to sperm, and an unoxidised form, which binds to sperm to act as a 'non-stick' coating. Together, this prevents sperm clumping together and increases sperm motility. If 20% or more of sperm are clumped, subfertility occurs. Vitamin C has an antioxidant effect on NSSA and keeps it in its reduced form so it can bind to sperm and prevent them sticking together.

Studies show that men who are subfertile because of sperm clumping can be helped by vitamin C. Men taking supplements of 500mg of vitamin C twice a day had a reduction in sperm clumping from 37% to 14% after just one week. After four weeks, sperm clumping can be reduced to as little as 11%. Research shows that the overall quality of sperm, including numbers of normal sperm present, motility and lifespan, is also improved by taking vitamin C.[32]

Although most of the research has focused on vitamin C and sperm improvements, a few studies have looked at the role of antioxidants in female fertility problems. Scientists in one study gave half of the women with a luteal-phase defect a daily dose of 750mg of vitamin C and half of the women a placebo (a 'dummy' supplement). They reported that the pregnancy rate was significantly higher in the women who took the vitamin C – 25% versus 11%. The authors also reported that serum progesterone levels were significant higher in the treatment group, which may help support a pregnancy.

Studies have also shown that women taking the ovulation-inducing drug clomifene are more likely to start ovulating if they take this medication in conjunction with vitamin C.[33]

Food sources: oranges and orange juice, kiwi fruit, tomatoes, strawberries, green leafy vegetables (e.g. watercress, broccoli and spinach), blackcurrants, red peppers and potatoes.

EU RDA: 60mg (but if you are taking large amounts – up to 1,000mg per day – then doses of 200mg are best taken with meals. Women should avoid taking more than this as it may dry cervical mucus. It may also cause stomach upsets in sensitive individuals.)

UK RNI for males and females aged 19–50 years: 40mg.

Vitamin D

Nicknamed the 'sunshine vitamin', vitamin D is a hormone that is produced within the body when the skin is exposed to sunlight. Vitamin D is also found in a few foods. It is essential for strong, healthy bones and teeth as it is needed to absorb calcium and phosphorus. Many nutritionists are concerned that levels of vitamin D in our bodies are too low due to an inadequate dietary intake, but more importantly, due to a lack of sun on our skin. In northern latitudes, the sun's rays are too weak to stimulate vitamin D production in the winter, so gentle exposure to the sun over the summer months becomes important. People at most risk and for whom dietary supplements become important are those who spend a long time indoors, babies, the elderly and women who wear clothes that almost completely cover their bodies.

Food sources: oily fish (e.g. sardines – one small can provides double the EU RDA, eggs, fortified margarine and spreads (UK food law demands this) and fortified breakfast cereals.

EU RDA: 5µg.

UK RNI for males and females aged 19–50 years: not set (although the RNI during pregnancy and breastfeeding is 10µg).

Vitamin E (Tocopherol)

This is also a powerful antioxidant and plays a very important role in male and female fertility. Research shows that taking vitamin E can result in a significant increase in fertility – in both men and women.[34] What's more, there is evidence to suggest that taking antioxidants like vitamins C and E can significantly reduce age-related ovulation decline; clearly, such findings could have an enormous impact on older women's fertility.[35] Studies also indicate that taking vitamin E before and during IVF treatment increases the success rates for those couples in which the man has a good sperm count but low fertilisation rates.[36] Taking vitamin E can also help to prevent abnormal clotting, so should be taken by those who have had a miscarriage.

Food sources: vegetable oils, wheat germ, wholegrains, nuts (e.g. almonds), seeds (e.g. sunflower seeds), eggs and broccoli.

EU RDA: 10mg.

UK RNI for males aged 19–50 years: none set as it depends on the individual's polyunsaturated fat (PUFA) intake, but likely to be at least 7mg.

UK RNI for females aged 19–50 years: as above, but likely to be at least 5mg.

Iron

We need iron for the formation of red blood cells, to transport oxygen to our organs and muscles, for healthy blood and bones and to resist stress. A lack of iron can cause breathlessness and tiredness, as the body is literally being starved of oxygen. If you think you are deficient in iron, it's well worth asking your GP to check for you.

A good deal of research has suggested that iron deficiency can affect a woman's fertility. Studies show that women who have experienced fertility problems have gone on to become pregnant after being given iron supplements.[37] It is also thought to guard against miscarriage.

Iron can be found in animal and plant foods. About 25% of the iron in meat, called haem iron, is absorbed by the body, whereas people may absorb less than 10% from plant sources (non-haem iron), such as vegetables, dried fruit, nuts and breakfast cereals. The good news is that more of the iron from plant sources is absorbed if they are eaten with food and drink that is rich in vitamin C (e.g. orange juice, green peas, potatoes and red peppers). It is only the absorption of iron from plant foods that can be affected by dietary factors; absorption of iron from animal sources is not affected. Along with vitamin C, other factors can influence non-haem iron absorption:

Which Dietary Factors Affect the Absorption of Iron From Plants?

Food	Active Substances	Effect
Fruit and vegetables	Vitamin C	+
Meat, chicken and fish	Cysteine-containing peptides (protein)	+
Wine and beer	Alcohol	+
Wheat bran	Phytates	-
Tea	Polyphenols	-

If you need to take an iron supplement, you should take it with orange juice rather than with tea as polyphenols (natural chemicals) in tea inhibit its absorption. If you do drink tea, make sure you leave at least an hour between taking an iron supplement and enjoying your cuppa.

Food sources: red meat, game, oily fish (e.g. sardines), poultry, eggs, dried apricots, muesli, iron-fortified breakfast cereals, green leafy vegetables, nuts, figs, wholemeal bread, lentils and beans.

EU RDA: 14mg.

UK RNI for males aged 19–50 years: 8.7mg.

UK RNI for females aged 19–50 years: 14.8mg.

Magnesium

Magnesium has many roles within the body, including energy production, nerve function, muscle relaxation and the formation of healthy bones and teeth. A study of infertile women and women with a history of miscarriage suggests that low levels of magnesium may impair reproductive function and contribute to miscarriage. Oxidation, a process that is damaging to cell membranes, can lead to a loss of magnesium. The same study suggests that the antioxidant selenium protects the cell membrane, thereby maintaining appropriate levels of magnesium. The authors of the study suggest taking both magnesium and selenium supplements.[38]

Food sources: wholegrain cereals, wheat germ, pulses, nuts, sesame seeds, dried figs and green leafy vegetables.

EU RDA: 300mg.

UK RNI for males aged 19–50 years: 300mg.

UK RNI for females aged 19–50 years: 270mg.

Manganese

This seems to be a largely underrated trace element in terms of its effect on fertility. It's actually terribly important. Studies show that a deficiency in this trace element can lead to defective ovulation. It also appears that the lack of manganese may inhibit the synthesis of cholesterol, so limiting the synthesis of sex hormones – leading to infertility.[39] Research also suggests that women with low manganese levels are more likely to have babies with a malformation.[40]

Manganese is also needed for healthy skin, to regulate blood sugar levels and for cell protection.

Food sources: wholegrain bread, nuts, seeds, brown rice, wheat germ, pineapple, pulses (e.g. lentils, chickpeas and kidney beans) and tea.

EU RDA: none set, but the US has suggested 2.5–7mg.

UK RNI for males and females aged 19–50 years: none set, but likely to be at least 1.4mg.

Selenium

This mineral is also an antioxidant and helps to protect your body against free radicals. Selenium helps the pancreas to function properly and build healthy tissues. Research studies show that selenium is very important for male and female fertility. Its antioxidant qualities prevent chromosome breakage, known to be a cause of miscarriage and birth defects. Evidence shows that some women who have suffered from recurrent miscarriage have a deficiency in selenium.[41]

Selenium is also vital for the healthy formation, quantity and protection of sperm. Research has shown that without adequate selenium sperm have reduced motility and density, while in some cases the tails kink and break off completely. Men given selenium supplements were found to have increased sperm motility and increased chances of conception.[42]

There is genuine concern amongst many nutritionists and health professionals in the UK over the fall in selenium intakes over the last few decades. This is largely because of a decrease in imported flour from North America in favour of selenium-poor flour from European countries. Recent dietary surveys indicate that the average intake of selenium may be as low as 30–40µg per day, well below the RNI of 75µg for adult men and 60µg for women. There are no obvious signs of selenium deficiency, and as one of the most important supplements for fertility, it is a good idea for both you and your partner to include a multi-vitamin and mineral formula that includes at least 100% of your needs up to a maximum safe level of 0.2mg per day.

Food sources: brazil nuts, eggs, meat, fish (e.g. tuna), poultry, sunflower seeds, wholegrains and brown rice.

EU RDA: 55µg.

UK RNI for males aged 19–50 years: 75µg.

UK RNI for females aged 19–50 years: 60µg.

WHAT ARE FREE RADICALS AND ANTIOXIDANTS?

Free Radicals

In order for us to live, the body has to continuously react with oxygen as part of the energy-producing processes within cells. As a result of this, highly reactive molecules, called free radicals, are produced. Free radicals can interact with other molecules within the cell, which can cause damage to proteins, membranes and genes. This damage has been implicated in the cause of certain diseases. such as cancer, and has an impact on the body's aging process.

Antioxidants

It's the job of antioxidants to neutralise free radicals. Our body produces its own 'antioxidant army' to defend itself from free-radical attack. The metabolic processes that produce antioxidants are controlled and influenced by an individual's genetic make-up and environmental factors (such as diet, smoking and pollution) to which our body is exposed.

Unfortunately, changes in our lifestyle, which include more environmental pollution and poorer diet, mean that we are exposed to more free radicals than ever before.

Our own internal production of antioxidants is insufficient to neutralise all of the free radicals, but there is an abundant supply of antioxidants in a wide variety of foods. By increasing our dietary intake of antioxidants, we can help our body to defend itself. Examples of dietary antioxidants include vitamin C, vitamin E, beta carotene and selenium.

High Doses of Antioxidants

While being very important nutrients, there are some concerns about the use of high-level supplementation of antioxidant nutrients such as vitamin C. We simply do not know the exact amount to give and for how long, nor do we fully understand the interactions vitamin C has when combined with other antioxidants such as vitamin E, beta carotene and selenium. Antioxidants at high concentrations (far in excess of the RDAs) can act as pro-oxidants (i.e. promote damage), and recent studies on animals have shown that although antioxidants can counteract the female aging effect on egg quality and number, they may cause unwanted side effects on the overall fertility fitness of a woman. Similar concerns have been raised in men's health as there is a delicate balance of damage and repair that exists in healthy semen and sperm formation.

However, when weighing up the overall balance of supplementation versus no supplementation, if a known fertility problem exists where inflammation or damage is likely (e.g. varicocele in men or endometriosis in women), then a daily amount of 500–1,000mg of vitamin C, up to 400iu of vitamin E and up to a maximum of 0.2mg of selenium seems a good idea. For men with low testosterone and low sperm production, a multivitamin and mineral supplement containing 20mg of zinc is widely recommended.

DID YOU KNOW?

A serving of just two brazil nuts can contain up to 2ooµg of selenium. They are an excellent source of this essential mineral.

Zinc

Zinc and its links with fertility receive a good deal of press, and rightly so. In women, a deficiency in zinc can upset the menstrual cycle and slow down the metabolism of protein, which is necessary for the production of good-quality eggs. If you have taken the contraceptive pill, you are more likely to be deficient in zinc. Zinc is also essential for cell division and so it is important that you have an adequate amount at the time of conceiving and during IVF treatment. Research has also shown that women with inadequate levels of zinc are more likely to experience pregnancy complications, abnormal deliveries and a variety of intrauterine malformations.[43]

In men, a deficiency in zinc has been shown to reduce sperm count, levels of testosterone and lead to poor sperm motility. In a controlled trial, men with low sperm counts and motility were given zinc supplements twice daily. After three months, there was significant improvement in sperm count, sperm motility and the fertilising capacity of the sperm.[44]

Taking vitamins B6 and C may aid the absorption of zinc, and, as with iron, it is best to avoid taking the supplement at the same time as drinking tea or coffee.

Food sources: oats, oysters, nuts, wholemeal bread, sunflower seeds, rye, wheat germ, ginger, mushrooms, sweetcorn, carrots, tomatoes, almonds, peas and eggs.

EU RDA: 15mg.

UK RNI for males aged 19–50 years: 9.5mg.

UK RNI for females aged 19–50 years: 7mg.

Amino Acids

Amino acids are the building blocks of protein. Certain amino acids have been identified as having particular roles to play in fertility.

L-Carnitine (LC) and Acetyl-L-Carnitine (ALC)

The name 'carnitine' is derived from the fact that this amino acid was first isolated from meat (carnus) in 1905. L-carnitine (LC) and acetyl-L-carnitine (ALC) play a key role in energy metabolism and the maturation of sperm. LC is a 'transporter vehicle' in that it carries fats into the cell where they can be broken down into energy, which the sperm can use for growth and good motility. Besides moving fatty acids into the cell to produce energy, LC is also responsible for removing excess (and toxic) waste products from sperm metabolism. In addition, ALC works as an antioxidant by helping to repair sperm membranes if damaged by free radicals. Finally, under certain conditions, sperm need another form of energy from ALC. Sperm must be both motile and flexible in order to reach and fertilise an egg. The flexibility of a sperm's cell wall is determined by the amount and quality of polyunsaturated fatty acids that make up the sperm's outer layer, or membrane. Mature sperm are made up of more polyunsaturated fatty acids, and this process needs ALC.

A variety of studies support the conclusion that LC and/or ALC at total daily amounts of at least 3g per day over a period of at least three months can significantly improve both sperm concentration and sperm count among men with low sperm motility and/or low sperm count, and they have been shown to improve sperm concentration, motility and morphology in men with mild to moderate varicoceles.

Food sources: meat, poultry, fish and milk.

EU RDA: there is no RDA for LC or ALC as the body can usually make enough for its needs. However, due to its possible role in improving poor sperm health, supplemental amounts of LC and ALC are usually 500–2,000mg a day.

L-Arginine

This is an amino acid found in many foods, and the head of healthy sperm contains a large concentration of this nutrient, which is essential for sperm production. Men with abnormal sperm quality often have deficiencies of L-arginine in their semen. Supplementing with L-arginine can help to increase both the sperm count and quality.

Animal experiments have shown that L-arginine can create greater metabolic activity as well as increased energy supply in sperm cells. A recent treatment trial of L-arginine for a group of 15 infertile men with low or absent sperm counts resulted in a 20% rate of pregnancy initiation. L-arginine has been shown to increase sperm motility as well as sperm count.

Anyone who suffers herpes attacks (either cold sores or genital herpes) should not supplement with L-arginine because it stimulates the virus.

Food sources: turkey, chicken, meat, wholemeal bread, peanuts and other nuts and seeds.

EU RDA: there is no RDA for L-arginine as the body can usually make enough for its needs. However, due to its possible role in improving poor sperm health, supplemental amounts of L-arginine usually contain 500–1,500mg a day.

Essential Fatty Acids

I touched on the importance of essential fatty acids (EFAs) earlier in this chapter, but I would like to go into more detail here as they play such a vital role. EFAs must be obtained through the diet because the human body cannot make them. The essential fats are the polyunsaturated fats found in many plant foods, such as sunflower seeds, olives, evening primrose and linseed. EFAs are also found in fish. As we've seen, there are different groups of polyunsaturated fats: omega-3 from fish oils, linseeds and linseed oil (flaxseed oil), rapeseed oil and walnut oil; omega-6 from evening primrose, corn oil and sunflower oil; and omega-9 from olive oil.

ALA, EPAs AND DHAs

While all of the EFAs are important for health, it is the omega-3s that have attracted the most interest of late. There are two types of omega-3 fatty acids: docosahexaenoic acid (DHA) and eicosapentaenoic acid (EPA). You can make these fatty acids in your body from a parent essential fatty acid – alphalinolenic acid (ALA), which is found mainly in green leafy vegetables, nuts, seeds and their oils.

EPA is needed to make health-protecting 'eicosanoid' hormones that keep cell metabolism on an even keel. DHA is required for healthy sperm, brain development and function, vision and has heart-protective and anti-inflammatory functions as well.

Essential fats have a significant effect on all systems of the body, in particular the reproductive system. EFAs are needed to produce prostaglandins, which have hormone-like functions. Prostaglandins affect the function of virtually every system in the body: these molecules are used in the regulation of inflammation, pain, blood pressure, fluid balance, blood clotting and affect hormone production and function. In order to maintain a proper balance of prostaglandins, it is critical to have the proper amount of each fatty acid. PMS has been linked to an incorrect prostaglandin production. Tests show that women taking EFAs have experienced a significant change in symptoms of PMS, including dramatic relief from headaches, depression, irritability, bloating and menstrual pain.[45] Omega-3 oils are important for women who are pregnant or breastfeeding because they help a baby's nervous system to develop.

A study conducted with more than 8,000 pregnant women in Denmark showed that eating fish regularly reduced the incidence of low birth weight and premature delivery substantially. Women who ate about 12g of fish a day (i.e. about two 50g portions a week) were three times less likely to deliver low birth weight babies than women who ate no fish at all. The mothers who ate no fish were twice as likely to give birth prematurely than those who had their two portions of fish a week. This significant reduction in low birth weight and premature births was attributed to the increased intake in omega-3 fatty acids associated with eating fish.[46]

Equally, men could also be supplementing their diet with essential fatty acids. As with women, the correct balance of prostaglandins is crucial for fertility fitness. Proper levels of prostaglandins are needed for the good quality and motility of sperm. Research studies have shown that some men with abnormal sperm or sperm with poor fertility have less than adequate levels of prostaglandins in their semen.[47]

In addition to its role in prostaglandin levels, DHA is highly concentrated in the testicles, where sperm form. It is needed to regulate enzymes in the process of making sperm. Sperm itself has high concentrations of DHA, too. Here, DHA seems to be needed to help give the sperm energy and increase its mobility. In fact, infertile men have been found to have low DHA levels.

Food sources: linseeds and linseed oil (flaxseed oil), oily fish (e.g fresh tuna, mackerel, sardines and salmon), omega-3-enriched eggs, nuts, green leafy vegetables and pumpkin seeds.
EU RDA: 300mg.

PRACTICAL STEPS

Try to eat one or two portions of oily fish each week or take a good-quality fish oil supplement – this will provide 4.5g omega-3 fatty acids (DHA and EPA). Also include some omega-3-enriched eggs in your diet – one egg will contain approximately 0.7g of omega-3 fatty acids (DHA and EPA).

Make sure you also include a good source of ALA in your diet (e.g. one teaspoon of flaxseed oil a day, taken either on its own or mixed into dressings, etc.). Flax oil is also available in vegetable capsules. Alternatively, you could include four to five teaspoons of ground flaxseeds or rapeseed oil in your diet. It is important that the flaxseeds are ground or at least crushed; if left whole, much of the fat will not be used by the body. Replace fats high in omega-6 oils, such as sunflower oil or corn oil, with fats higher in monounsaturated fats, such as olive oil or rapeseed oil. This is because high levels of omega-6 fatty acids interfere with the process in which the body converts ALA into the even more beneficial EPA and DHA. Olive and rapeseed oil do not disrupt the formation of EPA and DHA.

The very small amount of fat in green leafy vegetables is ALA – broccoli has 0.13g/100g, and cabbage 0.11g/100g, so simply eating your greens is making a positive addition to your intake.

Other Supplements of Interest

Coenzyme Q10 (CoQ10)

CoQ10 is present at very high levels in human seminal fluid and shows a direct correlation with seminal parameters (sperm count and motility). In sperm cells, CoQ10 is concentrated in the mitochondrial mid-piece, where it is involved in energy production. It also functions as an antioxidant, preventing the fatty acids in the sperm's outer membrane layer from being attacked by free radicals. When sperm samples from 22 asthenospermic men (low sperm motility) were incubated in a test tube with 50 microM CoQ10, marked increases in motility were seen. 60mg of CoQ10 was given to 17 infertile patients for an average of 103 days, and although there were no significant changes in standard sperm parameters, there was a substantial improvement in the fertilisation rate.

Pycnogenol®

Pycnogenol® is a water extract from the bark of the French maritime pine. It contains a high concentration of active bioflavonoids (phytochemicals), which are also found in fresh fruits and vegetables, and is one of the most potent natural anti-oxidants against free radicals. There is also research showing it to have anti-inflammatory properties. 19 subfertile men were given 200mg Pycnogenol® daily orally for 90 days. Pycnogenol® therapy resulted in improved sperm morphology. The scientists suggested that the increase in more healthy, normal sperm may allow couples diagnosed with teratozoospermia (less than 15% normal morphology) to forgo in vitro fertilisation and either experience improved natural fertility or undergo less invasive and less expensive fertility-promoting procedures, such as intrauterine insemination.

A Word About Taking Supplements

High doses of supplements can have dramatic effects on the body's chemistry and so, even though supplements are freely available from shops and via the internet, you should be well informed before taking them. Do get advice before you begin to take supplements as some can interfere with prescribed medication or counteract the effects of other nutritional supplements or diets. There is also an issue with the lack of regulation for supplements. A dietician or nutritionist with an interest or speciality in fertility and/or men and women's health should be in the best position to offer guidance. Most doctors or pharmacists practising in fertility clinics should also be able to advise you.

As always, don't let taking supplements become an obsession. Looking after your health and making sure you're getting a good balance of nutrients is something positive that you can do for yourself, but don't let it rule your life or break the bank.

Chapter 10

Stress Reduction

As a nation, we are all working much longer hours than ever before. We battle our way to work, spend hours at computer screens in airless offices dealing with numerous problems at once; we eat on the run, drink coffee to keep us going and return home to a glass or two of wine, exhausted.

The stresses of modern-day life might not be life-threatening, but they can seem relentless, and over time stress can take its toll on our bodies. You may find it hard to sleep, lack energy, become irritable, suffer from digestive disorders and notice a decrease in sex drive. The body is highly sensitive and will respond to stressful situations and periods of consistent stress in a number of ways. This may include interfering with the normal workings of the reproductive system – in both men and women.

This is not to say you should give up your job or somehow attribute your fertility difficulties to not 'coping' with life's stresses. What this shows is that in *some cases* a particularly stressful lifestyle that continues over a prolonged period of time may affect your fertility fitness. The important thing here is to be aware of where the stress lies in your life and to take steps to minimise it. This may mean talking to your boss at work about your current workload and seeing whether there may be a way to share it with a colleague, or perhaps asking if you could work from home one or two days a week. Or it may be that you can help yourself by taking some gentle exercise, treating yourself to a massage or talking worries over with someone. By recognising where the stressful areas of your life are and taking small steps to alleviate them, you'll start to feel more positive and in control, and this will have a good effect on your health.

> 'The trouble about always trying to preserve the health of the body is that it is so difficult to do without destroying the health of the mind.'
>
> *G.K Chesterton*

If you are trying for a baby and have perhaps been trying for some time or are receiving treatment for infertility, this itself can become a major source of stress for both you and your partner. This is completely understandable and is a common experience for many couples. Each month can seem a rollercoaster ride of emotions, from hope and expectation to anxiety and disappointment. You may feel as though your whole life revolves around your monthly cycle, wondering if this might be the month that you conceive or obsessing about what you should have done differently the month before. On top of this, you may find that your sex life has started to lack spontaneity and become an unromantic, military operation, and this can put your relationship under further stress. Nor will questions from well-meaning family and friends help much! It's no wonder that stress is so often the common experience of couples trying to conceive.

We'll be looking at the stress that often comes with assisted conception treatment in more detail in Part 4. For now, let's look at ways to combat stress.

STRESS AND FERTILITY

Stress can take its toll on the reproductive system, and, in turn, having problems conceiving can add to existing stress, creating something of a vicious circle. The American Society for Reproductive Medicine found that cases of extreme stress can affect fertility in men and women.

When we experience stress, our adrenal glands release the steroid hormone cortisol. If this is happening over a prolonged period of time, the excessive amount of cortisol in the body can upset the balance of other hormones. In women, the hormone prolactin may be overproduced and interfere with normal ovulation, causing menstruation to become irregular.[1] In men, research has shown that stress can lead to a drop in sperm count and a rise in the number of sperm with abnormalities.[2]

If you lead a particularly stressful lifestyle – and reports suggest that more and more of us do – then take stock now! It's important that you don't let stress become just another aspect of your life.

CASE STUDY

Mr and Mrs G were both 42 years old and were very busy businesspeople. They ran a local car salesroom and petrol station together. Mrs G did all the accounts for the company, and her husband sold the cars and worked in the petrol station, and as a sideline he did some car mechanics. They were both working extremely long hours and were highly stressed individuals who did a limited amount of exercise and worked seven days a week. Occasionally, they would take weekends off, but in the last four years they had only spent five days away from the business.

At the age of 42, Mrs G's parents died and she was left a reasonable inheritance. The couple decided to have a complete break from the business in order to regroup. They sold their business, started enjoying life more and began to look at a villa in Portugal to buy. Prior to this, although they had been trying to get pregnant, they did not have time to go to infertility clinics and had not had any investigations. Mrs G's periods had been regular. Neither of them had had children in the past. They had been trying to conceive for seven years.

Mrs G had started feeling tired and bloated and had not had a period for seven months, so she visited her GP, who felt her abdomen and, suspecting that there was an ovarian cyst, referred them on.

I duly saw them and performed a transabdominal scan and was both surprised and delighted to be able to tell Mrs G that she was 24 weeks pregnant! A healthy baby girl was duly delivered 14 weeks later. At no stage prior to this had they even thought there may be a pregnancy.

To me, it shows what a significant impact their stressful life had had on their infertility. The stress could not only have affected Mrs G's chance of conceiving but also Mr G's semen analysis and their frequency of intercourse.

THE MARES AT STUD STORY

Many years ago, I worked in a stud in the Midlands where there was a big barn with approximately 20 mares in. The pregnancy rate was very good, but we did notice fluctuations in it. The rate was highest at times when the barn was fairly full. When we put thought to this, we realised that the echo within the barn was different when the barn was full compared to when it wasn't so full. The echo upset the mares and reduced their fertility. We decided to put other horses in the barn when necessary to make sure the environment was always the same for the mares. This maintained the pregnancy rate.

This shows to me that, in animals, stress can have a negative effect on pregnancy. Stress can have a similar impact on humans.

COMBATING STRESS

Identifying the cause or causes of stress in your life is the first step in starting to overcome it. It may help if you and your partner take turns to list the factors that each of you feel is contributing to your stress levels. Or it might help to write them down in a journal.

Often stress becomes heightened through our own imaginings of what the worst outcome might be. It can become a vicious circle in which stress leads to obsessive worrying and unrealistic fears, which in turn lead to further stress. By identifying the real issues that are causing you to feel stressed, you become better equipped at dealing with them.

Often couples say to me that they haven't got the time to do stress-relieving techniques. I emphasise that they have had time to make an appointment to see me today – so why not schedule this once a week? I encourage patients to put into their diary 'appointment with Mr Dooley' on a weekly basis, which basically means time for themselves.

Ten Ways to Minimise Work Stress

1. Pay attention to lighting: make sure you're not having to strain your eyes or that you are not squinting in the glare of a light.
2. Don't stay seated for too long – this is bad for your circulation. Make sure you get up and walk about every hour or so. Rather than send an email to a colleague, go to see them in person.
3. Make sure you have a good chair that is at the right height for your desk.
4. If you work with a VDU, ensure that you have regular breaks.
5. Limit your caffeine and sugar intake, and drink plenty of water.

6. Develop assertiveness skills to help you deal with difficult colleagues – say no.
7. Learn to delegate.
8. Put a plant by your desk to help moisten the air.
9. Do plenty of exercise.
10. Get out into the fresh air.

If you are feeling anxious about being unable to conceive, take time to talk through your worries with your partner or a close friend. 'Control the controllables' (see page 173) by taking the right steps to improve your fertility fitness, and if you are still feeling concerned, make an appointment to see your GP so that you can get some professional advice on how best to proceed. Often stress is due to a lack of information and a fear of the unknown. By educating yourself and learning about what steps to take to improve your chances of conception, you will start to feel empowered and in control, which will create a wonderful sense of optimism and confidence – both of which are extremely powerful stress-busters.

Relaxation

Research has demonstrated the power of relaxation in increasing one's immune response. Relaxation can create a state of wellbeing and improve your ability to cope, which is an added plus in battling infertility. Alice Domar, PhD, is Director of Women's Health Services at Harvard Medical School's world-renowned behavioural medicine division. Her research on the effects of stress on female wellbeing shows that the practice of self-nurture can treat a host of women's health problems, including infertility.[3]

Breathe

The way you breathe reflects the amount of stress you are under. When you are feeling relaxed, your breathing will be calm and regular (10–14 breaths per minute) and you will feel your diaphragm moving in and out. When you are feeling anxious or tense, your breathing speeds up (to about 15–20 breaths per minute) and becomes more shallow and irregular. Your diaphragm no longer moves in and out, but rather your ribcage jolts up and down, and you may find your shoulders become tense and high.

Very few of us breathe properly – we get into the habit of only taking half a lungful of air rather than a deep, nurturing breath. Take some time each day to practise deep-breathing techniques: you'll soon notice the benefits.

If you can, lie comfortably on the floor with one hand resting on your upper chest and the other on your stomach. Close your eyes and breathe gently in and out for a minute or so, feeling the way your stomach rises and falls with each breath. The hand on your upper chest should barely move. Now turn your attention to your outward breath, breathing out through your nose for a count of five. Pause, then breath in for a count of five and repeat. Do this for a few minutes each day, until you start to recognise how slow, gentle breathing should feel.

Think Positively

'The one thing I am sure of, regardless of what a patient is suffering from, is the reaction to their situation and their state of mind is of critical importance, and to ignore them in the face of high technology and medical practice is to court disaster.'

Sir David Weatheral, FRS, University of Oxford

Positive thoughts lead to positive results. Enjoy the beauty of life. Look at a flower for five minutes each day and wonder at its creation.

We can often make stress worse by concentrating too much on the negative and allowing negative thoughts to overwhelm us.

The idea of positive thinking is to challenge the negative thoughts that play over and over in your head. So, for example, if you start with a negative thought such as 'I'll never have a baby' turn it around into something that is positive like 'I'm doing everything I can to try to get pregnant.' This may sound simple, but it's effective.

Avoid using words that exaggerate circumstances and find ways of turning negative thoughts like 'I can't cope with change' to positive thoughts like 'I can cope with change; changes are challenges, and challenges are opportunities to learn.'

'A man is not old until regrets start taking the place of dreams.'

Anonymous

Have a Loudhailer

I always remember talking to Adrian Moorehouse, the Olympic gold medal swimmer, about negative and positive thoughts. He gave a lovely story about his visualisation of having two people, a man and a woman, talking in his brain.

The bad man was large, ugly and kept on giving negative thoughts. These included 'You can't do it', 'You're not good enough' and 'Really, you haven't trained adequately'.

The small, pretty lady had a very, very soft voice and was saying things like 'Adrian, yes, you can do it', 'You are the world's best' and 'Believe in yourself'.

Adrian was always concerned that the large, ugly voice over-powered the soft, little voice, but eventually he learnt to use positive visualisation to control the two voices in his brain. With time, he was able to overcome the negative voice by giving the lady with the little voice a loudhailer!

Keep a list of positive affirmations in your bag or by your desk at work, and whenever you think negative, irrational thoughts, replace them with positive affirmations. The more you do this, the more quickly your old negative belief system will start to become positive and optimistic.

Protect Yourself

It's important that you learn to look after yourself. This means eating well, getting enough good sleep, spending time with your partner and loved ones and taking time to be on your own – even if it's only for a few minutes each day.

Trying for a baby can bring up all sorts of difficult emotions – particularly if you've been trying for some time without success. One of the hardest things to cope with is seeing other people with their babies. This is perfectly understandable and not something you should feel guilty about. There's no rule to say you must spend lots of time with your new niece or your pregnant best friend. It's quite all right to protect yourself from scenarios that may feel too painful or difficult.

Take time to relax, whether by simply giving yourself an hour to read or meditate or through practising yoga or some form of light exercise. Remember, stress can affect your libido, so it's good idea that you *both* do what you can to counter this.

Massage

Massage is an excellent way of relieving stress and one of the oldest healing techniques. Giving and receiving a massage is a wonderfully relaxing and pleasurable experience. You don't have to visit a professional masseuse or learn a specific technique to feel the benefits either. It is something you can get your partner to do with you – perhaps taking it in turns. In times of stress, this can be a great way of bringing you closer together.

Lie face down on a firm surface; make sure the room you are in is warm and quiet. Get your partner to warm some massage oil (try adding a few drops of lavender to your base oil) by rubbing the oil in his hands before starting. Then he should begin with long, simple strokes that follow your body's contours. As a rule, you should always stroke towards the heart, concentrating on the areas most prone to tension: the shoulders, neck, lower back and head. Your partner can then vary the pressure and length of stroke he uses, making sure to keep one hand in contact with your body at all times. Once your partner has finished massaging your back, turn over, and, again working towards the heart, he can massage the front of the body, taking care not to apply too much pressure. Once the massage is finished, take some deep breaths and focus your thoughts on how relaxed you are feeling.

Aromatherapy

The art of using essential oils in holistic healing was well known to the ancients, including the Egyptians, Persians, Greeks, Romans and Hebrews. Today, most people come into contact with aromatherapy as a beauty treatment, where pleasant smells are used to pamper. However, practitioners of clinical aromatherapy would argue that there is more to it than nice aromas. Knowledge of the therapeutic and chemical properties is used to help the body and the body's systems to self-heal by restoring equilibrium. Aromatherapy has been used successfully to treat wounds, infections, respiratory disorders, muscular and joint disorders, stress, anxiety and many other conditions.

Ask your GP to recommend a practitioner. A consultation will include a detailed medical history, then, in agreement with your GP, the therapist will decide on an individual prescription and make up a cream or oil with this in mind.

Sleep Well

Stress and anxiety are the most common causes of lack of sleep, which in turn become a main reason for stress. A good night's sleep is essential for our mental and physical wellbeing. This is why when we go without sleep for too long, we become depressed, irritable, unfocused and more susceptible to illness. Lack of sleep can also lead to a decreased sex drive, which, when you're trying for a baby, is not the best scenario! Don't let sleepless nights become a habit. Remember HALT: do not get Hungry, Angry, Lonely or Tired. Try the following techniques to ensure a good night's sleep.

Ten Tips for a Good Night's Sleep

1. Avoid eating too late at night, or drinking tea, coffee, alcohol and any other stimulants.
2. Have a warm bath before bedtime. Add some soothing aromatic oils, like lavender or rose.
3. Make your bedroom a haven – not a chaotic mess.
4. Drink a herbal tea, such as valerian or chamomile.
5. Listen to a piece of calming music.
6. Try not to panic if sleep doesn't come. Instead, focus on tensing and relaxing each of the muscles in your body.
7. Avoid going to bed on an argument. If something is bothering you, try to talk it over with your partner – but do this outside of the bedroom.
8. If you haven't fallen asleep after an hour or so, get up and make yourself a warm drink, before going back to bed.
9. Try to get into the habit of going to bed and getting up at the same time each day.
10. Have sex.

Hypnosis/hypnotherapy

Clinical hypnosis is the use of a state of deep physical relaxation and hypnotherapeutic suggestions within the framework of a specific protocol. The protocol must have a specific objective. This objective is discussed before the hypnosis takes place. When done properly, the clinical hypnosis can optimise the individual's ability to influence a number of the events that can affect fertility.

It is easy to learn and can be used as often as required; its efficacy will increase with time and repetition, and it has no known side effects.

Clinical Hypnosis and Stress Management

Stress is part of any type of change. How an individual deals with stress can directly affect their internal environment – it can create hostile cervical mucus, for example. Part of the clinical hypnosis procedure involves relaxation, which is of physical benefit, and suggestions can be made to enable the individual to deal with stress more effectively. An example would be suggestions to 'be able to deal with any situation, no matter what, in a calm way'.

Clinical Hypnosis as a Distraction

Clinical hypnosis can be used as a means of distracting the individual from something that has become a focus of attention. For example, part of wanting to become pregnant causes the woman to start to see babies 'everywhere', and this can create its own stress. Another example in which clinical hypnosis can be helpful as a means of distraction is during medical procedures, some of which can be less than pleasant. The patient can be taught self-hypnosis as a way of creating a mental space during the procedure.

Clinical Hypnosis for Visualisations and to Deal With the Past

One of the most interesting ways in which hypnosis can be used is to create visualisations of internal states, strong and healthy – a fertile environment. It can also be used to create a space for dealing with emotional histories that may be affecting the patient's capacity to conceive, for example unresolved grief in connection with a miscarriage or guilt about an abortion.

Research

There have been many research projects into how clinical hypnosis can be integrated into medical practice, the most recent of which was at Soroka University in Israel, where it was found that hypnosis doubled the success rate of IVF.

Counselling – Talk About It

If you have tried various ways of dealing with stress, but find that none of them seem to be working, it might be a good idea to talk to someone about it. This could be your partner, best friend or mother, or it could be a professional counsellor, who is trained to listen and respond to people suffering from stress, in complete confidence. There are many types of counselling but they can be divided into what I term three basic types: support counselling, which offers you and your partner emotional support; implication counselling, which allows you to explore the implications of a particular course of treatment such as egg donation or surrogacy and therapeutic counselling, which allows you to explore *why* you are not conceiving and may in itself function as a treatment.

EXPRESS YOURSELF

A study presented at a British Psychological Society conference in Leeds found that men who were able to talk about their feelings, rather than bottle up difficult emotions, were more likely to be fertile. Although the fertile men reported stress-causing incidents day to day over a two-week period, they were far more likely to talk about them than those men who had problems with fertility. The report's author, psychologist Keith Hurst, said that bottling up stressful events was far more likely to lead to higher stress level overall.[4]

By talking through your worries – whether they're related to work, your relationship or about trying for a child – you are more likely to find ways of coping and of putting situations that seem overwhelming back into a healthier perspective. By verbalising your concerns, solutions are allowed to emerge. Counselling can help to nurture more positive ways of responding to situations and encourage a clearer and more rational outlook.

All centres licensed under the Human Fertilisation and Embryology Authority (HFEA) must offer counselling.

Ten Things Counselling Offers You

1. Complete confidentiality
2. An appropriately trained practitioner
3. To be able to talk at ease in a friendly and safe environment
4. To be non-judgemental
5. To allow you to reach your own conclusions
6. To allow you to express your feelings
7. Available from your clinic
8. Help for both you and your partner
9. To be informed of any costs beforehand
10. To be available before, during and after treatment

Chapter 11

Taking a Team Approach

We have seen how trying to conceive can often become a great cause of stress. This in turn can impact on your relationship with your partner – and your relationships with friends and family. This is quite understandable, and those who know you well will no doubt see this.

Your close relationships can be a wonderful source of comfort and reassurance, so remember to make use of that. Spending time with people you care about – and who care about you – is a good way of taking some of the focus away from your day-to-day concerns, particularly those surrounding your fertility.

YOU AND YOUR RELATIONSHIPS

You and Your Partner

Trying for a baby can put pressure on most couples; after all, you are both planning to embark on a life-changing adventure. If there are difficulties in conceiving, then naturally there may be an added feeling of pressure, particularly if you are receiving fertility treatment.

Sometimes when I see couples who are experiencing difficulty conceiving, the spouse or partner with an infertility factor expresses their fear that the other partner will leave and find someone who is able to have children. Or, in some instances, once treatment has begun, one spouse may feel that the other is less motivated to succeed. In the majority of cases, such fears prove to be unfounded, but the feelings that surface are nonetheless very real. Avoid attributing blame or feeling guilty – these aren't helpful emotions. Keep communicating and letting each other know how you're doing, what you're feeling and offering each other as much support and reassurance as you can.

The demand to have intercourse at the 'proper times' can provoke frustration. Avoid planned sex, particularly when one partner has a business trip, is working late or just isn't in the mood for sex. Couples who go through cycles of sex on demand often find that lovemaking loses its spontaneity and playfulness. Sex becomes a chore to be performed only at certain times of the month. Sometimes the pressure to perform is so great that a man has trouble with his erection or is unable to ejaculate.

Women may have trouble getting aroused, causing vaginal dryness or muscle tension, which can make intercourse painful. And it isn't uncommon for couples to have distracting thoughts during sex, about whether this time will be *the* time, which further reduces the pleasure that partners feel from lovemaking.

Try to find a balance. Don't become so obsessed that babymaking is the only focus in your lives. Make time for other things that you can do together. Plan trips away or days out together to help bring some renewed energy back into your relationship. It's interesting to see how often it's only once couples decide to stop 'trying' so hard, or go away on a relaxing break, that they end up falling pregnant. Vary your sex life. By all means have sex around the time of ovulation, but enjoy having sex at other times, too. Give yourselves a break, and remember to keep talking and keep taking care of the relationship.

You and Your Children

If you or your partner already have children – together or from a previous relationship – remember that they too need and require your love and attention. Children can often feel forgotten or inadequate when their parents are going through fertility treatment. So make a real effort to let them know just how important and special they are to you.

You and Your Family

Sometimes one or both sides of the family can put pressure on a couple to have children. This may be meant very innocently, but nevertheless it can be hard to handle, especially if you've been trying to conceive for a while without success. It may be that you'd like to confide in your parents about your hopes and concerns but your partner might feel he doesn't want this kind of information shared outside of your relationship. There is no right or wrong answer, but by deciding how to handle this, as a team, you will protect your relationship. Try not to let the hopes of others come between you.

Other Relationships

For many couples, trying to conceive becomes the main focus of their lives. Other relationships may be neglected, friends with children avoided or family members left out. Do remember how important good relationships are. Whether or not you have children, you are always going to need good friends and a good support system, so take time to cultivate and nurture relationships.

You don't have to tell people that you're trying to get pregnant – though you may decide you'd like to – but try not to become so obsessed about conceiving that you neglect your friendships. By maintaining good relationships outside of your own partnership, you are doing wonders for your emotional and mental wellbeing.

AFRAID TO TELL

I always remember working in one fertility unit in Southern Ireland where there was a culture that young married couples were to have children. I saw a lady in the fertility clinic and did her investigations, and the blood tests were rather unusual. On close questioning, I found out that she was actually on the oral contraceptive pill! I asked her why she was on the pill when she was trying to get pregnant. She indicated to me that she and her husband had decided not to have children, but there was such pressure from her family to have children that it was easier to say to their parents, 'We are attending the fertility clinic,' rather than tell them the truth.

Be honest with yourself about exactly what you want.

GETTING A PLAN

At an early stage, it is very important to get a plan for your fertility. I think the plan should encompass a journey of about 18 months. This plan could include: keep trying naturally, further investigations, lifestyle management, etc. If you don't have a plan, then you could end up waiting for long periods, wondering where to go next. It is a bit like if one considers a journey in a car: when you come to a set of traffic lights, you don't want to be fumbling around, looking at the map and wondering where to go. You will have already planned the journey and will know whether to go straight on, turn left or right. Indeed, there may be information that you have gained on the journey to that traffic light that may change your plan slightly, but at least you know where you are going at that point.

Chapter 12

Male Fertility Fitness

Despite the fact that around 35% of a couple's fertility problems generally lie with the man, it is often the case that the woman is the first to raise the issue of whether there could be a general fertility problem. While I have many couples coming through my door each day, I also see many women without their partners. I only occasionally see men on their own.

Even if the main factor affecting fertility lies with the woman, there's really no reason why your partner shouldn't be involved right from the start – after all, he's hoping to become a parent, too, and he's certainly got an important role to play! Do try to get your partner involved in *all* aspects of the journey you're on, not just the conception bit. By taking responsibility for his health and by being as supportive and encouraging as he can be, your partner will be contributing to your joint fertility fitness and upping the odds of a healthy and successful conception.

Often men find it hard to contemplate the idea that they may have some kind of fertility problem. This can challenge the way they think about themselves and their masculinity. Even in these relatively equal times, men still have strong notions about what their role in a relationship entails. Issues surrounding fertility can undermine this and leave men feeling frustrated and confused.

Until quite recently, men were largely sidelined in fertility clinics – which were very much geared towards making the woman feel comfortable and secure. Thankfully, this is changing. Men shouldn't have to feel as though they must put on a brave face or simply avoid confronting their fears altogether. It is important that your partner can talk openly about his concerns so that you can both move forward together as a team.

There is much that your partner can do to ensure he is in peak fertility fitness, which needn't involve making big changes. In some cases, he may need to take the time to see his GP to discuss having some preliminary tests, which will quickly ascertain if an underlying problem may be preventing conception. Once this has been established, your partner can then take steps to correct this, or he may need to receive some treatment.

Some of the following points have already been covered in the earlier chapters, but I think it is worthwhile having a dedicated section for men, as they are so often overlooked in fertility treatment, and it is important that they know exactly how to improve their own fertility fitness.

FACTORS AFFECTING SPERM QUALITY

Temperature

The optimal temperature of the testes for sperm production is slightly lower than body temperature, which is why the testes hang away from the body in the scrotum. Men with low sperm counts are frequently advised to minimise lifestyle factors that may overheat the testes, such as wearing tight (e.g. 'bikini-style') underwear or frequently using spas and hot baths.

Alcohol

As we saw in Chapter 6, alcohol is toxic to sperm and drinking too much can reduce sperm quality and fertility. Alcohol is known to produce a rise in oestrogen levels, which can interfere with sperm development and affect the balance of hormones. Alcohol is also a major cause of impotence.

Smoking

Research has shown that men who smoke cigarettes have a lower sperm count and motility and increased abnormalities in sperm shape and function.[1] Added to this is the damage that second-hand smoke can do to the female partner, increasing the risk of miscarriage.

A study by Queen's University, Belfast, found that men who smoke cannabis are damaging their fertility. The active ingredient found in cannabis – THC (tetrahydrocannibol) – appears to impair sperm's ability to reach the egg and its ability to digest the egg's protective coat with enzymes that aid its penetration.[2] As more and more people now smoke marijuana, this may well be a significant factor in male infertility.

Stress

It is important for men to stop and recognise the effect that stress can have on their physical health, emotional wellbeing, personal relationships and even their sex life. Whether the stress is caused by work, an active lifestyle or concerns about trying for a baby, men should take time to relax each day to allow the body to unwind and recharge. See Chapter 10 for ideas on how to combat stress.

Your Environment

Research suggests that extensive exposure to certain chemicals may impact on a man's fertility. Exposure to heavy metals, particularly lead, pesticides and anaesthetic gases has been associated with potential impairments to sperm quality. The below table shows chemicals that may affect male fertility.[3]

POTENTIAL TOXIN	ORIGIN	EFFECT
Alkylphenols	Industrial and domestic detergents	Hormonal disrupter
Bisphenol A	Lacquers to coat foods, dental treatments	Hormonal disrupter
Dioxins	Paper production, transformer disposal	Hormonal disrupter
Organochlorine pesticides (Lindane, DDT, etc.)	Lindane used on cereals, soft fruits, cabbage	Hormonal disrupter
Phthalates	Plastics industry	Hormonal disrupter, testicular toxin
Phytoestrogens (found in certain types of plant products)	Some soya products	Hormonal disrupter
Vinclozolin	Fungicide used on foods	Hormonal disrupter

A study showed that men who regularly use laptops may be lowering their fertility. It was found that the combination of the legs-together posture required to balance a laptop and the heat generated by the machine increased the temperature of the testes by up to 2.8C. This temperature rise was thought to be enough to impact sperm quality.[4]

General Medical Problems

Fever

Influenza, pneumonia or even a severe cold can cause a high fever, which will adversely affect sperm production and quality. These changes usually last only a few weeks.

Diabetes

In the longer term, diabetes can produce problems with erection and ejaculation through damage to the function of the automatic nervous system.

High Blood Pressure

High blood pressure can cause problems with erection, either directly or as a side effect of medication (e.g. amlodipine).

Coronary Artery Disease

Coronary artery disease can cause problems with erection. This could be due to generalised hardening of the arteries, in the penis as well as the heart, or to medication used in the treatment of heart problems.

Neurological Disorders

Multiple sclerosis, stroke and spinal-cord injury and disease can all cause problems with erection and ejaculation.

Kidney Disease

Chronic renal failure, which results in a build-up of waste products in the body, can adversely affect sperm quality and fertility. It can also cause erectile problems.

Cancer

Cancers that affect the genital tract or endocrine (hormone-producing) systems may directly reduce fertility. Otherwise, medication and radiation used to treat cancer may severely reduce sperm production or even stop it altogether.

Mumps

When mumps develops after puberty, it damages the testicles in 25% of men afflicted with the disease. However, it is extremely rare for this to lead to sterility. (Interferon, an antiviral drug, may help to prevent infertility in adult males with active mumps, but the drug is highly toxic and caution is essential.)

Hernia

Recently, hernia repairs were linked with male subfertility. A study in Israel found that men who had had a previous hernia repair had a one in eight chance of a small, shrunken (atrophic) testis, compared with an incidence of less than one per hundred in men who had not had a hernia repair. When semen was analysed, the quality was significantly poorer in men who had had a hernia repair. It's thought that testicular function is either affected by reduced blood supply (e.g. damage or scarring during the operation) or from some as yet unidentified immunological reaction.[5]

If you are concerned that your sperm may be affected by an operation, then I would advise you to talk to your surgeon to consider the possibility of freezing sperm.

Chlamydia

Researchers have found that chlamydia not only affects the fertility of women; it can also affect the fertility of men. According to scientists at Unrea University in Sweden, a couple's fertility can drop by 30% if the man has chlamydia. This is why it is important that you both get yourselves screened for infections. Although chlamydia does not have easily recognisable symptoms, once diagnosed it can be quickly treated with antibiotics.[6]

THE SPERM MYTHS

Myth: Men with high sex drives have very fertile sperm.
Fact: There is no correlation between male fertility and virility. Men with high sex drives may have no sperm at all.

Myth: Masturbation is bad for male fertility. Many boys are bought up believing that if they masturbate a lot their sperm supplies will 'run out' early.
Fact: The testicles produce and store sperm from puberty through most of adult life. Masturbation does not pose any risk to sperm quality or quantity.

Myth: A man can judge his fertility by the amount of semen he ejaculates.
Fact: Just because you produce a lot of semen does not necessarily mean that you are very fertile. Most semen is made up of seminal fluid, only a small part is actual sperm. Contrary to popular belief, your actual sperm count is not the most important indication of fertility; it is the amount of motile (moving) sperm that matters in terms of fertility, so tests that simply check sperm counts are not that helpful.

Myth: Looking like an Adonis will give me better sperm.
Fact: A six-pack and bulging muscles may be a stereo-typical image of a red-blooded fertile male, but in fact excessive exercise, especially muscle-building exercise, could lower your sperm count indirectly by lowering the amount of testosterone in your body. Any form of steroids taken for building muscle can cause testicular shrinkage, resulting in infertility.

Myth: A small penis makes less sperm.
Fact: The size of penis has no effect on the quality or quantity of sperm that is produced. A man with a small penis could easily produce more sperm in both quantity and quality than

a man with a large penis. It could even be argued that sperm that comes from a small penis doesn't have so far to travel and so is likely to be livelier as it enters the cervix.

Myth: As long as I don't drink or smoke for a few weeks before trying to conceive, my sperm will be healthy.
Fact: The entire production of sperm formation to maturation takes about 72 days. So a binge-drinking session at Christmas will mean your sperm is still adversely affected in early spring. After quitting smoking, it takes approximately three months for sperm to be restored to its normal state. Even a long stint in a sauna can damage sperm for up to two months afterwards.

Myth: Having a beer belly will not affect my sperm count.
Fact: Being overweight can cause male fertility problems. Too much excess weight can cause hormonal disturbances, which can decrease sperm count and functionality.

Myth: A man's sperm count will be the same each time it is examined.
Fact: A man's sperm count will vary. Sperm number and motility can be affected by time between ejaculations, illness and medication.

IMPROVING SPERM QUALITY: THE SIMPLE MEASURES

As we've seen, it takes around three months for sperm to develop and fully mature. That's why it's a good idea for your partner to start implementing positive changes to his diet and lifestyle *before* you plan to try for a baby.

Here are some relatively simple suggestions that will do much to improve your partner's fertility fitness:

Ten Ways to Improve Your Sperm Quality

1. Stop smoking.
2. Cut down on alcohol.
3. Make sure you're getting enough of the good foods listed on page 97.
4. Avoid having too many of the bad foods listed on page 100.
5. Take the supplements recommended below.
6. Avoid too much stress and use stress-relieving techniques.
7. Drink plenty of water, as this is necessary for the production of semen.
8. Avoid environmental toxins.
9. Have regular enjoyable sex.
10. Get active – but don't overdo it.

The World Health Organization guidelines define a healthy sperm sample as the following:
Volume: at least 2ml
Number of sperm/ml (i.e. sperm count): at least 20 million/ml
Percentage of sperm that are moving (motility): at least 50% (i.e. more than half – they will also examine the quality of that movement)
Percentage of abnormal sperm: less than 85%

Supplements for Healthy Sperm

As we saw in Chapter 9, taking certain supplements has been proved to be a great way of boosting fertility fitness – for both men and women. This, of course, shouldn't be *instead* of a healthy balanced diet (that's just as important), but by taking a good multivitamin or a combination of vitamins and minerals, your partner is guarding against deficiencies.

Men may be resistant to the idea of taking supplements, but it is important that they are reminded of their crucial role as provider of healthy, motile sperm. What's more, he really need only take the supplements for a few months. And he'll more than likely enjoy the benefits that this brings to his health and well-being in general. So, to recap, here are the key supplements for healthy sperm production and fertility fitness (see Chapter 9 for recommended doses):

Zinc

Zinc plays an important role in testicular development, production of sperm and sperm motility. Supplementing the diet with zinc has been shown to improve sperm counts in both fertile and subfertile men.

Selenium

Fertile men have been found to have significantly more selenium in their sperm than infertile men.[7] This mineral is essential for making the tail of the sperm strong and motile.

Vitamin C

Vitamin C protects sperm from free radical damage (see page 113). It also helps to reduce sperm agglutination (a condition where sperm clump together). It's also been found to improve motility and reduce the number of abnormal sperm.

Vitamin E

In trials, vitamin E given daily to both partners of infertile couples led to a significant increase in fertility.[8] Like vitamin C, vitamin E is a strong antioxidant and helps to fight free radicals, which could otherwise harm sperm's DNA.

Manganese

A deficiency in this mineral may affect the production of male sex hormones.

L-arginine

L-arginine is an amino acid and is essential for sperm production. Preliminary research shows that several months of supplementation increases sperm count, quality and fertility.[9]

L-carnitine

This is also an amino acid and is essential for the normal functioning of sperm cells. In trials, supplementing with 3–4g per day for four months helped to normalise sperm motility in men with low sperm quality.[10]

Vitamin B12

In a study, a group of infertile men were given oral vitamin B12 supplements for 2–13 months. Approximately 60% of those taking the supplement experienced improved sperm counts.[11]

Folic acid

This can be an essential nutrient for men with low sperm counts and higher doses of up to 5mg a day should be considered.

SIZE DOESN'T MATTER . . .

Human sperm measure just 0.06mm in length, whereas the humble fruit fly boasts a sperm length of 58mm!

Chapter 13

Using Complementary and Alternative Techniques to Boost Fertility

'Though I believe passionately in scientific medicine, I also believe that some aspects of the complementary approach have a lot to offer. I think they could be put to scientific tests, and should be, but whether this will happen is far from certain.'

Sir David Weatheral, FRS, University of Oxford

AN INTEGRATED APPROACH

I am a firm believer in looking at a person as a whole – not just as a set of symptoms. This is one of the reasons why I have built up the Poundbury Clinic and have helped to develop the clinic at Westover House, which takes an *integrated* approach to health-care. By bringing together complementary and alternative medicine (CAM) and modern Western medicine, patients can receive the kind of care that treats them as a whole person. This means taking into consideration the many different facets that make us who we are. Physical symptoms are important, but so are the emotions, professional demands, relationships, beliefs, strengths and weaknesses that can so often lie beneath symptoms and that make up our own unique characteristics.

'To create success, everyone's noses must be pointing in the same direction.'

Sir John Harvey Jones

THE JIGSAW STORY

I always remember treating a couple who had obviously been to see a huge array of different practitioners in both orthodox and complementary medicine. During the consultation, I asked whether they had seen an acupuncturist. They had. Then I asked if they had seen a reflexologist. Again, they'd seen one already. Then I asked in turn whether they had seen a medical infertility expert, a medical herbalist, a hypnotherapist and a traditional Chinese medicine doctor. The answer to all of these was 'yes'.

What concerned me was that none of the practitioners were talking to each other. If communication does not occur, then I am not sure how individual practitioners can get the best for the patient. When I was working at the Olympics, we all worked together; the teams had good communication and therefore all worked for the good of the patient. I use the example of building a house: if someone was trying to build a house and the electrician did not tell the plumber where the sockets were going to go, and if the bricklayer did not tell the carpenter where the windows were going to go, then the house would be a chaotic mess!

The management of infertility is like a jigsaw. Even if all the parts are in the right place and the right way up, you'll only be able to see the whole picture properly when they are slotted together. The care of individuals is a team approach, and only when you are all working together, with a common aim, will we be able to see what is best for that individual.

In order to get individual practitioners to communicate, we have developed the integrated cooperation card below. This can also be downloaded from my website, www.thepoundburyclinic.co.uk.

The Poundbury Clinic

INTEGRATED HEALTHCARE CARD

Golden Rules

Remember to update this card after each visit to your practitioner

Please document any over-the-counter products you are taking

Please document any side-effects you may experience

Remember to document any change in your condition on a regular basis

Please add in any new complaints that you have

If you have any concerns always seek help from your practitioner

Useful Contacts

THE POUNDBURY CLINIC
Middlemarsh Street, Poundbury,
Dorchester, DT1 3FD
Tel: 01305 262626
www.thepoundburyclinic.co.uk

**PRINCE OF WALES'S FOUNDATION
FOR INTEGRATED HEATH**
12 Chillingworth Road,
London, N7 8QL
Tel: 020 7619 6140
www.fihealth.org.uk

WOMEN'S HEALTH CONCERN
PO Box 2126, Marlow,
Bucks, SL7 2RY
Tel: 01628 488065
www.womens-health-concern.org

ACUPUNCTURE
www.acupuncture.org.uk

HOMEOPATHY
www.trusthomeopathy.org
www.the-hma.org

HERBAL MEDICINE
www.nimh.org.uk

OSTEOPATHY
www.osteopathy.org.uk

REFLEXOLOGY
www.reflexology-uk.co.uk

Ask your practitioner for any useful written information and contact numbers

© Michael Dooley & Sarah Stacey

Practitioners' Details

Name/Address/Telephone/Email

Name/Address/Telephone/Email

Name/Address/Telephone/Email

Name/Address/Telephone/Email

Name/Address/Telephone/Email

Name/Address/Telephone/Email

Please contact The Poundbury Clinic
if you have any comments on
this Healthcare Card

'Never doubt that a small group of thoughtful people, committed people can change the world. Indeed it is the only thing that ever has.'

Margaret Mead

Complementary treatments are holistic. This means they look at all areas of a person's life – not just the physical manifestations. Like Western medicine, CAM does not guarantee success, but by allowing the two to work together, a great deal can be achieved.

I will be looking at the different ways in which CAM can be used alongside conventional fertility treatment later on in Part 4. But, as I will show in this chapter, CAM can also be very helpful in boosting fertility fitness and in helping to give you and your partner the best chance of conceiving naturally.

An estimated 5.75 million people in the UK are now going to see a complementary practitioner for some kind of treatment.[1] Unfortunately, not all therapies are available on the NHS yet. Around half of the GP practices in the UK can now provide access to CAM in some form.[2] So when considering trying CAM, you will need to take into account your budget and where you might have to travel to.

Not all complementary therapies will work for you, but if you are able to, do try to incorporate one or perhaps two of the therapies outlined below into your Fit for Fertility Programme and see how it works for you.

Trust and Communication

It is very important that you keep everyone informed. Your GP should always be your first port of call, and it's important that you let him or her know first about any symptoms you are experiencing and any medication you may be taking which he or she hasn't prescribed. It is also vital to tell your complementary practitioner of any medical conditions you have and any medication you are taking. Once you start complementary treatments, be sure to tell your GP. Different treatments can sometimes have an effect on each other, which could make them work less well or even pose a danger for you.

When you first see a complementary practitioner, they should take a detailed medical history from you. This should include finding out what other treatments you are taking – conventional and complementary – and what previous medical conditions and procedures you have had.

An integrated approach to your fertility health is more than likely going to be the best approach and will help treat you as an individual rather than simply as a patient. However, it's important to keep everyone in your 'team' in the loop and aware of the various treatments you are receiving and that means good communication between all parties involved, whether it's your GP, fertility consultant, herbalist, acupuncturist or homeopath.

Finding a Practitioner

If you are going to choose a practitioner privately, rather than through your GP, make sure your chosen practitioner is registered with a professional association or regulatory body (see Useful Contacts and Websites).

TYPES OF COMPLEMENTARY AND ALTERNATIVE MEDICINE

Herbal Medicine

Herbal medicine, sometimes referred to as herbalism or botanical medicine, is probably the oldest form of healthcare known to mankind and has been used by all cultures throughout history. A herb is a plant or part of a plant valued for its medicinal, aromatic or savoury qualities. Herbs produce and contain a variety of chemical substances that act upon the body. Herbalism is the use of herbs for their therapeutic or medicinal value.

161

Much of the medicinal use of plants seems to have been developed through observations of wild animals, and by trial and error. Until well into the twentieth century, much of the pharmacopoeia of scientific medicine was derived from the herbal lore of native peoples. And, today, many of the medications commonly prescribed are of herbal origin, something like one in seven of all conventional doctors' prescriptions are derived from plants.[3]

Once a herbalist has taken your medical history, he or she will give you the appropriate herbal preparations for you to use at home. It is essential that you discuss treatment with a medical herbalist and do not self-prescribe. Herbal remedies come in various forms, but the easiest and most effective way of taking herbs is in tincture form, diluted in water.

Throughout time, fertility and reproduction have always occupied key positions within cultures. No doubt this is why there are so many herbal remedies specifically made to treat and enhance fertility.

Chaste Tree (*Vitex agnus castus*)

The common name of this pretty herb is chaste tree, harking back to the Crusaders' belief that it would dampen their wives' libidos while they were off crusading. Whether it actually achieved this effect is doubtful, as it is now recognised as boosting female fertility and easing menstrual symptoms.

Agnus castus has the effect of stimulating and normalising pituitary gland function, especially progesterone function. It works to balance out the levels of hormones, whether there is a deficiency or an excess. This makes it a particularly helpful herb for women who suffer from irregular periods, luteal-phase defects or ovulatory problems and for women who have recently stopped taking the pill. The herb not only increases progesterone levels but also inhibits prolactin, high levels of which have been connected to infertility.

Agnus castus is also extremely helpful in treating menopausal problems and PMS. A trial published in 2000 showed 42% of the 1,634 women involved reported that they no longer suffered from PMS after taking *Agnus castus*. Overall, 93% of the women on the trial reported that their PMS symptoms either disappeared or decreased. Interestingly, 23 of the women on the trial fell pregnant while taking *Agnus castus*, 19 of whom had previously had fertility problems.[4]

Dong Quai (*Angelica sinensis*)

Dong Quai is an ancient Asian herb widely recognised for its beneficial uses for fertility. Although it doesn't contain any known phytoestrogens, Dong Quai does seem to act like an oestrogen 'modulator' that activates or suppresses oestrogen receptors within the pituitary gland to even out the production of hormones. Dong quai is also believed to increase metabolism within the uterus and ovaries and has been attributed with helping to build a receptive uterine lining. The herb can also be used to treat other gynaecological disorders including vaginal dryness, menstrual cramps and symptoms of PMS and menopause. It has also been promoted to help circulation and regulate menstrual cycles, particularly after a woman has been on the pill.[5]

False Unicorn Root (*Chamaelirium luteum*)

This herb, which came to us via the North American Indians, is thought to be one of the best tonics and strengtheners of the reproductive system in herbal medicine. It works by balancing out the levels of female sex hormones – whether they are in excess or deficit. False unicorn root is particularly useful for treating delayed or absent menstruation. It is also thought to help prevent threatened miscarriage. Though primarily used for the female system, it can be equally beneficial for men in balancing hormone levels.[6]

Saw Palmetto (*Serenoa serrulata*)

This North American herb is generally prescribed as a tonic for men for use in the treatment of prostate problems. It is thought to work by reducing levels of a very active form of testosterone considered to be the primary cause of enlargement of the prostate.[7] It is also used to treat low libido, potency problems and for the balancing of hormone levels. Saw palmetto may also be used by women as a reproductive tonic and to increase milk production. It can also be used in polycystic ovarian syndrome.

Liquorice (*Glycyrrhiza glabra*)

Native to the Mediterranean region and parts of Asia and cultivated worldwide, liquorice appears to modulate oestrogen, much in the same way as dong quai. A Japanese study showed positive results in its treatment of irregular periods due to elevated androgen levels, as seen in women suffering from polycystic ovarian syndrome.[8]

Winter Cherry (*Ashwagandha*)

This is one of the most respected herbs in Ayurvedic medicine. It is most often used as a rejuvenating herb after illness or during times of stress, but it is also thought to boost the reproductive systems of both sexes. In a study, 101 normal healthy male volunteers aged 50 to 59 took 3g of powdered *Ashwagandha* daily for three months. All showed significantly increased red blood cell counts, and 71% of the volunteers reported improved sexual performance.[9]

Damiana (*Turnera aphrodisiaca*)

This South American herb has been used as an aphrodisiac since ancient times by the native people of Mexico. Traditionally, the herb is Mexico's version of Viagra and consumed only by men, although Mexican women have used it for stomach ailments, menstrual problems and hormonal imbalances.

It is thought that the herb's alkaloid content could have a testosterone-type action that affects sexual appetite and function. It is found to be helpful in treating premature ejaculation, impotence, vaginal dryness and absence of periods.[10]

Traditional Chinese Medicine

The philosophy and practice of traditional Chinese medicine (TCM) has been evolving over thousands of years, beginning long before the evolution of Western medicine. It developed continuously in China, Japan and other Asian countries and is still a primary treatment in many countries.

The theory behind TCM is that the body is a dynamic energy system. The aim of Chinese traditional medicine is to maintain and/or restore harmony in the body and the balance of the two types of energy ('Yin' and 'Yang'). Traditionally, Yang is associated with heat, dryness, brightness, upward or outward movement, forceful action, lightness and speed. Yin represents the corresponding qualities of cold, moisture, dimness, downward or inward movement, quietness, heaviness and slowness.

In TCM, acupuncture is considered to be Yang because it works from the outside in, while Chinese herbalism is thought to be Yin because it works from the inside outwards. The two practices are often used together and so making a 'whole'.

Diagnosis forms a key part of TCM and usually consists of a four-step process:

1. **Visual examination.** The doctor notes the patient's expression, complexion and general physique, as well as making a detailed examination of the tongue for colour, shape and coating (if any).

2. **Listening/smelling.** The doctor listens to the patient's breathing and looks for any unusual body sounds or odours.
3. **Verbal questioning.** This phrase is similar to history taking in a Western medical examination.
4. **Palpation.** The doctor feels the patient's organs through the abdomen, the 'Qi' points along the meridians and the pulse (see below). Traditional Chinese medicine distinguishes three different pulse points on each wrist and as many as 30 different pulse qualities at each point. Pulse diagnosis takes years to master in the Chinese system and is regarded by patients as an important measure of a doctor's skill.

Acupuncture

A branch of traditional Chinese medicine, acupuncture involves placing very fine needles into the skin at different points (called acupoints) in order to stimulate the flow of Qi (pronounced 'chee'), the body's energy. The acupuncturist works to balance this flow of energy along a network of pathways called meridians. Electroacupuncture and the burning of Moxa over acupuncture points, for thse with a needle phobia, may also be performed.

Over the centuries, acupuncture has been used, successfully, in the treatment of fertility problems in both men and women. There is now an impressive body of evidence to support this success.

A large-scale trial conducted at New York's Weill Medical College of Cornell University concluded that acupuncture treatment has the following fertility-boosting benefits:

- increased blood flow to the uterus and therefore uterine wall thickness, improving the chances of a fertilised egg implanting
- increased endorphin production, which, in turn, has been shown to affect the release of a gonadotropin-releasing hormone (GnRH) involved in regulating reproduction
- lower stress hormones that interfere with ovulation

- normalised fertility hormones that regulate ovulation
- improved ovulation cycles in women with polycystic ovarian syndrome (PCOS), a condition that makes conception difficult
- improved pregnancy rates in women undergoing IVF[11]

Chinese Herbal Medicine

Another branch of traditional Chinese medicine, this is the use of herbs and plants to treat illness and restore health by correcting imbalances within the patient's body. Chinese herbal medicine includes preventative treatment and was – and in many cases still is – a customary, everyday part of people's lives.

Once diagnosed, you will usually be given a number of herbs to be taken in combination. These might come in pill form or be prepared as a tea.

Chinese herbs have a long history of use in aiding fertility. Records indicating herbal treatment of infertility and miscarriage date back to AD 200, including mention of formulas that are still used for those purposes today.

No one herb is singled out as particularly good for fertility; it is the combination of herbs that is effective. There are some exotically named materials that are frequently found in fertility formulas, such as deer antler and sea horse, but the prominent materials are derived from roots, barks, leaves, flowers and fruits. Formulas for men and for women tend to be different, but there is considerable overlap in the ingredients used.

Treatment is ideally given for a period of three to six months prior to attempting conception. When pregnancy is attempted or confirmed, the treatment is usually stopped.

It is important to have one's liver function tested prior to and during treatment, to ensure that no damage is done to your liver, although it should be noted that this is rare.

Homeopathy

Homeopathy comes from the Greek words '*homoios*' – meaning 'same' – and '*pathos*' – meaning 'suffering'. The idea being that like will cure like. Homeopathy is a system of medicine based on three principles:

1. **Like cures like** – so, for example, if the symptoms of your cold are similar to poisoning by mercury, then mercury would be your homeopathic remedy.
2. **Minimal dose** – the remedy is taken in an extremely dilute form.
3. **A single remedy** – no matter how many symptoms are experienced only one remedy is taken, which is aimed at all of the symptoms.

Homeopathy works in harmony with the immune system, unlike some conventional medicines, which suppress the immune system.

Homeopathic remedies have long been used to treat symptoms of PMS. Pulsatilla is particularly beneficial for women who experience bloating and cramps, and sepia is used to treat constipation, lethargy, irritability and weepiness. Because homeopathic medicines can be effective in re-establishing health in women's reproductive organs, it follows that they can be helpful in re-establishing fertility. Since remedies are prescribed specifically for the patient concerned, there is not one particular remedy that can be singled out as *the* fertility remedy. However, there are a number frequently prescribed that can help to regulate periods, correct vaginal dryness or treat loss of libido.

Reflexology

Cultures throughout the world, including India and China, have used foot (and hand) treatments as a way of treating the whole body for thousands of years.

Reflexology is based on the principle that certain points on the feet and hands, called reflex points, correspond to different parts of the body. By applying pressure to these specific points, a practitioner can help to release tensions and aid the body's natural healing processes.

Reflexology teaches that the body is divided into different vertical zones, with each running from the head down to the feet. All body parts within each zone are thought to be linked via the nervous system and mirrored in the soles of the feet. So, the heels correspond to the left and right pelvic areas, and the ankles to the reproductive organs.

Research carried out at Derriford Hospital in Plymouth showed that reflexology has proved to be successful in treating PMS, heavy periods, irregular periods, low sex drive, unexplained fertility, hostile cervical mucus, polycystic ovaries and recurrent miscarriage. Patients reported feeling more positive, relaxed and having more regular cycles, and a good percentage went on to conceive successfully.[12]

Reflexology is not a magic cure-all, and of course cannot guarantee a pregnancy, cannot unblock fallopian tubes, treat chlamydia or cure endometriosis. However, by encouraging the body to work more efficiently, it can create a healthier environment for pregnancy to occur.

Aromatherapy

Aromatherapy is a form of treatment using scents. It is a holistic method of caring for the body using botanical oils, such as rose, lemon, lavender and peppermint. It's one of the fastest-growing fields in alternative medicine and is now widely used in clinics and hospitals. In Japan, engineers are incorporating aroma systems into new buildings. In one such application, the scent of lavender and rosemary is pumped into the reception area to calm down the waiting customers, while the perfumes from lemon and eucalyptus are used in the bank-teller counters to keep the staff alert!

Usually, however, the essential oils are added to the bath, massaged into the skin or inhaled directly. Aromatherapy is used for the relief of pain, care for the skin, to alleviate tension and fatigue and to invigorate the entire body. Essential oils can affect the mood, reduce anxiety and promote relaxation. When inhaled, they work on the brain and nervous system through stimulation of the olfactory nerves.

Work carried out by Dr Gary Schwartz, Professor of Psychology and Psychiatry at Yale University, found that the aromas of some essential oils affect the nervous system and reduce blood pressure. The scent of spice apple was found to reduce blood pressure by an average of three to five points in healthy volunteers. Infertility problems and the pressure to conceive can create enormous emotional stresses, and aromatherapy is an excellent therapy to help counter such stress and induce relaxation.[13]

The essential oils of clary sage, sage, fennel, bergamot, ylang ylang and yarrow have traditionally been used to help the body produce oestrogen, testosterone and progesterone and so may prove to play a vital role in balancing hormone levels in both men and women.

REVISE YOUR GOALS

Keep making and assessing your goals and mini goals and give yourselves a timeframe. So, for example, you may choose to postpone taking ovulation-inducing medication for three months in favour of a course of acupuncture. Remember to follow the Fit for Fertility Programme. Once the three months is up, you can then consider again what options are available to you. Perhaps your periods will have regulated, in which case you will probably want to keep trying without medical intervention. Or, if you're still not ovulating, you may then feel it is the time to embark on a course of Western medical treatment, perhaps in conjunction with CAM. We'll look at more conventional options in Parts 3 and 4.

Chapter 14

Positive Steps to Boost Fertility

Many women who come to see me say how frustrating it is to have spent so much of their lives doing all that they can *not* to get pregnant (and sometimes panicking that they might be), only to discover that, when they decide the time is right to get pregnant, it doesn't happen right away.

As we've seen, compared with other animals, reproduction in humans is not always reliable. There are many different processes that all need to be working together to enable conception to happen, and that can be why you don't necessarily become pregnant as soon as you stop using contraception. The human body is an extraordinary and complex machine, and that means your body needs time to adjust to changes in the different factors that influence us daily.

I do think the inherent difficulty of conceiving is a fact that is worth repeating: humans, on average, have around a 25% chance of conceiving each month.[1] If you break that down, based on having intercourse twice a week, the chances of conceiving each time you have sex are only about 1–3%! This figure does, of course, depend on your age, as the percentage likelihood of you getting pregnant each time you have unprotected sex decreases as you get older.

One of the main concerns that I have is that couples do not have intercourse enough. A recent survey from Manchester demonstrated that after three years of marriage, couples decrease intercourse from three to four times a week to three to four times a month. In order to maximise your chance of conception, you should be having intercourse two to three times a week. This is not meant to depress you, but rather to illustrate just how normal it is to take time to fall pregnant. Don't put pressure on yourself or feel as though there must be something terribly wrong just because you don't become pregnant right away. Give yourself time – and try to enjoy the process of reaching your goal.

THE FROG IN MILK

This is the story of a frog in a bowl of milk. Normally, frogs would not be able to survive in milk, but this particular frog had the ability to remain positive and so kept on swimming and swimming and swimming. Eventually, by swimming and swimming and swimming, he turned the milk into a thick cream and was thus able to climb out of the milk. The moral of the story? Stay positive!

You have decided to start a family, and, for now, that is likely to be your ultimate goal. Having a strong desire to succeed at anything – be it winning a race, landing the job you've always dreamt of or having a baby – is a fundamental part of achieving that success.

World-class athletes all share a focused and determined desire to win, and much of their training programme will concentrate on building up not just muscle and stamina but a positive belief that they can and will achieve their goal. Focus on achieving your goal.

Studies show that being optimistic, believing in yourself and holding on to the expectation that things *will* work out well is an attitude that will halve our risk of dying from either accident or disease.[2]

HOW TO STAY POSITIVE

Of course, it's not easy to simply decide to be positive, and if you've been trying to conceive without success for some time, then you may be feeling pretty negative. I have worked with Dr Stephen J. Bull, who is a leading consultant in sports psychology and who has worked with British Olympic teams over many years. He strongly advocates the importance of 'controlling the controllables' as an important first stage in taking charge and boosting positivity.[3]

Controlling the Controllables

What can you control?
- your diet
- your smoking habits
- your stress levels
- your alcohol intake
- the number of times you have sex, etc.

What can't you control?
- the fact that you have blocked tubes
- the fact that your partner has had a vasectomy
- the fact that you have had an ectopic pregnancy
- your age, etc.

It is no good worrying about things that you cannot control, the 'uncontrollables'. All you can do is to try to control the 'controllables'.

> 'Worry is like a rocking chair – you can do it all day and get nowhere.'
>
> *Anonymous*

SNIOPS

Staying positive involves keeping a positive environment. That is why it is important to avoid SNIOPS. This stands for:

S – Surrounded by the
N –Negative
I – Influence of
O –Other
P – People

This means avoid wasting emotional, mental and physical energy on those factors about which you have no control and instead focus on the things you *can* do something about. It may be that you can't afford to visit an acupuncturist, but you can make sure you eliminate alcohol and processed foods from your diet. Or, you can make an appointment with your GP to screen for infections, even if you can't get there for another two weeks.

Goal Setting

The next important element that Dr Bull cites in staying positive is goal setting. You know what your ultimate goal is, but by creating smaller, time-based goals, your long-term goal will seem less daunting. What's more, by reaching the mini goals that are taking you towards your ultimate goal, each small success will provide you with an important confidence boost that will keep you on your positive path.

It's a good idea to write down these goals and next to them give yourself a timeframe. So you might have a list something like this:

Long-term goal:
  Have a healthy baby!   By 2008

Intermediate goals:

Regulate periods	By end of 2006
Reduce weight by x kg	By end of 2006

Short-term goals:

Cut out alcohol	Start now
Increase intake of green leafy vegetables	Start now
Take supplements daily	Start this week
Have sex at least twice a week	Start this week
Practise yoga once a week	Start next week

Don't choose goals that are going to be impossible to achieve, as that will only deter you. Think SMART: Specific, Measurable, Achievable, Realistic, Time-based. And try to review your goals regularly so that you can assess how you've achieved your original targets and how you can adapt and create new goals accordingly. Acknowledge how well you've done by implementing these changes; it's not always easy, particularly when you lead a full and busy life, and it can be difficult explaining to friends and family why you're not drinking or perhaps socialising as much.

Having a route set out before you is a powerful way of maintaining focus and positivity. Later on, I'll be showing how this can also be applied to fertility treatment and the different paths that inevitably arise from this.

Positive Visualisation

I remember once going to a seminar with the Olympic swimmer Adrian Moorehouse who used to help the British equestrian team. He informed me that he could sit in bed with a stopwatch and swim his race. He would know exactly when he should turn and the time he should be on. This is an ideal use of positive visualisation. It is also like writing down your goals and writing down your journey. If you ask me to use a bow and arrow in order to hit the bull's eye and you did not allow me to see the target, I would more than likely miss it. That is why writing down your goals, seeing your goals, makes it easier to obtain them.

Visualisation is a technique that uses the power of the imagination to help increase self-confidence and reduce stress. By focusing on what it is you really want and visualising a positive outcome, you move towards manifesting these desires. You can use tapes that guide you through a visualisation or simply try it yourself.

A good time to practise visualisation techniques is just before you go to sleep at night. This allows your subconscious mind to reflect on what it has learnt and will improve the chance of a successful result.

Visualisation exercises should always involve images and imaginings that are relevant to your particular situation. So if, for example, you are experiencing irregular periods, you might choose to visualise your ovary releasing a healthy, strong egg each month, and see it move along the fallopian tube to meet the sperm.

It's also very powerful to try to create a fully formed visualisation of your ideal outcome. That could go along the lines of the following:

1. Choose a pertinent positive affirmation, such as 'I am a healthy and fertile woman with a healthy reproductive system that is in its optimum condition for conception.'
2. Each night, as you go to bed, imagine the healthy egg being released and travelling along the fallopian tube to meet the strong and healthy sperm swimming like an Olympic finalist towards it!
3. Feel your confidence grow as you picture the sperm penetrating the surface of the egg.
4. Now imagine your fertilised egg gracefully gliding along the fallopian tube towards the uterus, where it successfully and safely implants into the soft wall of the uterus.
5. Now repeat your positive affirmation slowly and carefully to yourself.

6. Keep repeating this to yourself as you concentrate on the wonderful and positive feeling of having successfully conceived.
7. Repeat this procedure every night for a week, staying awake throughout the entire process. The following week, repeat the process but let yourself fall asleep when you're ready. The visualisation and affirmation should soon become part of your everyday thinking patterns.[4]

GO FOR IT!

The question I often ask people is, if you had three frogs on a lily and one decided to jump off, how many would be left? The answer is simple: three. This is because the frog has only *decided* to jump off and has not actually done it. The decision is easy, but doing it is difficult.

PART 3

SEEKING PROFESSIONAL MEDICAL HELP

As we've seen in Parts 1 and 2, the human body is highly sensitive and complex, and the systems that work to keep us alive and well, that keep our cells repairing and replicating and that allow us to reproduce can all be affected by seemingly small factors. Diet, the number of hours we work and a deficiency in nutrients – all of these factors contribute to the overall wellbeing of our bodies. What's more, these factors can have a huge impact on our fertility. Over the course of Part 2, you have seen how changes to your diet and lifestyle play a fundamental role in improving your fertility fitness. By taking control of these areas of your life, you are almost immediately increasing your chances of conceiving – and sooner, rather than later.

If, however, once you have made the suggested changes, you find that you are still trying to conceive without success, then it might be time to seek medical help. This doesn't mean you should start thinking the worst or letting yourself become consumed with worry, nor does it mean that there is something wrong with you or your partner. One of the most reassuring things about going to see your GP is that they can often, very quickly, eliminate various possible causes of infertility. This sort of peace of mind can sometimes be enough for some couples, who then simply decide to just carry on trying for the time being.

In this section I'll be outlining the various different tests that you and your partner can have. These tests are there to help establish what might be affecting you and your partner's fertility and, if necessary, how this can then be treated. It's always worth getting as much information as you can. Not only will this enable you to make appropriate choices, but it will help you and your partner clarify what your next few steps are going to be. By setting out your plan and having goals along the way, you'll have a greater sense of control over the situation, an idea of what you need to do and what you have achieved so far. This is important if you are to avoid wasting time and energy on worrying unduly.

Chapter 15

Finding Help

WHEN SHOULD I SEEK MEDICAL HELP?

You will probably hear different theories regarding when to get medical advice on fertility, but my motto remains 'If in doubt, give a shout.' If you're concerned, then worrying without doing anything is simply going to prove counterproductive.

As we have seen already, the standard definition of infertility is the inability to conceive within one year of regular intercourse without the use of contraceptives. Up to 90% of couples with normal fertility will be pregnant at the end of one year and up to 95% will be pregnant by the end of two years, but couples over the age of 35 or those with a history of health problems may need to get help more quickly.[1]

Follow your gut instinct. If you're worried, then ask. At best, you'll discover that there is absolutely nothing wrong, and, with this peace of mind, you may go on to conceive. At worst, you'll find that you're going to need treatment. At least in the case of the latter, by finding out early on, you may be able to get yourself on to an IVF waiting list and save yourself a good deal of time. Taking control now saves time and worry. (See also the Fit for Fertility Checklist on page 55.)

WHO DO I SEE, AND WHERE DO I GO?

Once you and your partner have decided to seek medical help, your first stop is likely to be your GP. Before you go, it's a good idea to work out exactly why you're going for help. This might sound obvious, but my experience shows that different couples have different agendas. Some couples want to know why they're not getting pregnant; others simply want to get pregnant and are less concerned about the whys and wherefores. Some will be happy to be reassured and sent away for six months or so, while others may feel they need concrete answers and a clear plan of action.

Why Are You Here?

This is a question I often ask my couples. Four potential answers are:

1. We are here to find out why we are not getting pregnant.
2. We are here to find out why we are not getting pregnant, and we would also like a pregnancy.
3. We would like a pregnancy, and we would also like to find out why we are not getting pregnant.
4. We don't mind why we are not getting pregnant; we just want a pregnancy.

Preparing for the Appointment

Your GP may give you both a history sheet to fill out. This is used to establish an overall picture of your health including your past medical history, your past surgical history, your drug history and your history with regard to your infertility.

Make some time beforehand to note down anything that you think your GP should know about. For example, any over-the-counter medication or supplements you regularly take, the length and regularity of your menstrual cycle, health concerns that you might not have raised with them previously and any kind of family health history that could be significant. Don't worry about noting seemingly trivial things – the more information your GP has, the better. If you haven't been given a history sheet, then it is a good idea to look at the one I have included at the end of this book (see page 343) and fill it out and take it with when you go. It's likely that your GP will be asking you and your partner many, if not all, of the questions listed in the history sheet.

As we've already seen, it's just as important for you to jot down what you want from your appointment and any particular questions you would like answering. Your GP or gynaecologist may not be able to answer them straightaway, but it's still worth doing.

It Takes Two to Make a Baby

Often it is the woman who will go to see her doctor if she has concerns about why she's not getting pregnant. If you can, do try to go together. Fertility is not a 'woman's issue'; it is something that affects you both. It can feel awkward discussing quite intimate details with your doctor, but remember that doctors are quite used to this. Keep focused on what is you want – a baby! – and work as a team. Your doctor will want to take a history from both of you, and by going together, you will save time waiting for a further appointment and be able to discuss your options as a couple.

It's worth your partner making an appointment with someone he feels relatively comfortable talking to. Some men prefer to see male doctors, while others find it easier to discuss health and personal issues with a female doctor. Some, of course, are quite comfortable talking with either! You may choose to go to the consultation together and have your histories taken at the same time, or in some cases it may be more appropriate to see your doctor at separate times.

In order to conceive, the basics are quite simple, as I explained in Chapter 1 – you need an egg, a sperm and the two have to get together in a healthy body. The basis of diagnosis is using history, examination and investigations to assess these areas.

Remember, do not be afraid to ask for medical help, and make sure you get what you need from your GP. It may be that he or she will have to refer you elsewhere in order to get answers to your questions, but at least this will start the ball rolling.

Throughout my childhood, my father's belief was that he never wanted me to come back to him and say, 'Why did you not tell me?' I have the same belief for my patients. I want all my patients to know all the negative options and then choose the most appropriate plan for them. This is the core to my DR AID approach, which I explained in the Introduction.

CASE STUDY – WHEN SHOULD WE ASK?

Kate was 23 when she first came to see me, and her partner, Peter, was 28. They had been trying to get pregnant without success for a year. They had no family history of any fertility problems and no past surgical history or known medical problems. When I saw them, they were both very worried. Kate had regular periods and experienced no pain with intercourse. Peter was also healthy and had suffered no past injuries to his testicles. They were desperate to get pregnant and concerned that something might be wrong.

Because of their good health and because they were both young, I was wary of rushing into carrying out elaborate investigations. When considering the possible tests and investigations, your GP or consultant should always weigh up the benefits versus the risks. If the benefits of any operational procedure are greater than the risks, then that is reasonable. If, however, the risks are greater than the benefits, it's sensible to resist going ahead straightaway. Also, I often ask myself, 'Will such a test affect how I manage the problem?' If not, why do it?

So, in this case, I took a thorough history, examined Kate, arranged for Peter to have a semen analysis and for Kate to have her progesterone levels checked to ensure she was ovulating. On receiving the results and establishing that everything appeared to be normal, I spoke to them both about their diet and lifestyle and put them on the Fit for Fertility Programme. I then arranged to see them again in six months. Happily, they rang not long after to cancel their appointment, as Kate had become pregnant. They are now the proud parents of a healthy baby boy.

Another couple, Sophie and Richard, came to see me when they were both aged 40. They had only been trying for six months but, like our previous couple, were worried. Because of their ages, I was much more rigorous in my management of their case. I arranged for Sophie to have a laparoscopy, for Richard to have a semen analysis and for both of them to have hormone blood tests.

The laparoscopy revealed normal tubes, but we did diagnose polycystic ovarian syndrome (see page 242). As Sophie was slightly overweight, I put her on a diet programme and asked that she come back in three months. On her return, Sophie had lost the excess weight but was still not pregnant, so I prescribed clomifene, which is used to trigger ovulation. We arranged for her to return in two months. When the appointment came around, a very delighted Sophie announced that she was four weeks pregnant. She and Richard have since given birth to a beautiful baby girl and are now expecting their second child.

Depending on your GP's surgery, your age, the length of time you have been trying to conceive and your GP's own specialist interest, you may be referred straightaway to a general gynaecology clinic. However, most GPs will be able to deal with the range of initial tests such as history taking, examination and routine investigation (which we will look at in Chapter 17). Some treatment may also be initiated by your GP, but again this does very much depend on his or her diagnosis and own expertise.

Ten Instances When You Should Be Referred Without Delay to a Specialist

1. You request it.
2. Either of you is older than 35.
3. You have long or short cycles (less than 21 days or greater than 35 days).
4. You have had a diagnosis of pelvic inflammatory disease.
5. You have had an ectopic pregnancy in the past.
6. You have had a diagnosis of endometriosis in the past.
7. You have been trying to conceive for more than three years.
8. You have a family history of premature ovarian failure.
9. You have had three or more miscarriages.
10. Your partner's sperm tests are abnormal.

What Might Happen at My Initial Appointment?

Your doctor will want to assess your overall health. This will involve asking questions on the following subjects:

- your diet
- your weight and body mass index (BMI)
- your smoking and drinking habits
- any prescribed medications you are taking
- a review of your family history
- details of any kind of recreational drug use – particularly marijuana (for men)
- any history of genitourinary infections or STDs
- whether you have been screened against rubella
- your occupation and working hours
- any previous testicular injury
- any previous pregnancy
- any operations
- your general stress levels

- the regularity and nature of your menstrual cycle
- any past operations and surgery (including hernia operations)
- whether your partner has had mumps
- details of any radiation treatment or chemotherapy
- whether your partner has pain in the testicles

Depending on your individual circumstances, your GP may also suggest a standard gynaecological examination. This may include a cervical smear, if you haven't had one within the last three years. Swabs for infection and chlamydia will also be taken. A routine examination of your partner may also be advised.

If your GP is satisfied that you both appear to be fit and healthy with no obvious signs of potential problems, he or she may recommend a pre-conception diet – much like the one in Part 2. He or she may also suggest taking folic acid and zinc for you and your partner respectively, and is then likely to reassure you both that, with time, you *will* conceive.

Making a Plan

It always amazes me that if you go on holiday lots of time is spent planning – the journey and a comprehensive itinerary is written out. Think of your treatment plan in the same way.

At the end of your appointment, try to work out some sort of plan with your partner and GP. Communication is vital, and although we may all worry about taking up our doctor's time, it is absolutely your right to expect a plan of action.

I will often dictate a letter in front of the couple. This will summarise what was discussed in the consultation and what the next steps will be. Even if your doctor provides you with a very simplified version of the letter below, it's well worth having some kind of plan in writing.

Carol and Frank J.
23 New Way Road
Other Place
Anywhere

4 August 2004

Dear Carol and Frank,

It was nice meeting you today, and I hope you found the consultation helpful. As we discussed, the important things we found were as follows:

- Carol is aged 26 and works as an insurance broker, and Frank is aged 32 and works as an airline pilot.
- You have been together for five years and have been trying to get pregnant for the last 18 months.
- Neither of you has had children in the past.
- You are both fit and lead a reasonably healthy lifestyle, except Frank, you smoke 15 cigarettes a day.
- Carol, you are finding the delay in getting pregnant stressful, and you are anxious about this stress.
- Neither of you has any significant past medical or surgical history.
- Carol, your periods are regular.
- Due to Frank's job, he is away a lot, and intercourse only occurs once to twice a month.
- Examination of both of you was normal.

Following the discussion, we've agreed the following plan:

1. Frank, as we discussed, smoking can reduce fertility and can cause a high percentage of abnormal sperm to be produced. You are going to reduce and eventually stop smoking, and you will look into joining the NHS Stop Smoking Programme.
2. Carol, we discussed your stress, and it appears to be centred around your wish for pregnancy. We discussed,

*in general, stress-relieving techniques. You are now
going to have regular massage and hypnosis because you
find this beneficial.*

3. *I am concerned about the number of times you have
intercourse each month. You are going to try to increase
this. I would encourage you to have intercourse two to
three times per week across the week.*

*The above are lifestyle issues, and we have also arranged
the following investigations:*

1. *I have taken swabs from Carol to make sure that you
have not got an infection. Please could you call the
nurse, Susan, in order to obtain the results next week,
and, if necessary, we can arrange appropriate treatment.*

2. *Carol, as you are having regular periods with cycles
lasting 28–30 days, we will arrange for you to have a
blood progesterone test on day 21 of your next cycle.
Day 1 is counted as the first day you need to use
sanitary protection.*

3. *Frank, I have arranged for you to have a semen analysis.
Please remember to get the sample to the laboratory
within 30 minutes of production. Also, I would advise a
period of abstinence between two and five days – no
longer and no shorter.*

4. *In order to test Carol's tubes, I have arranged for you
to have a hysterosalpingogram (HSG). This will allow
me to assess the shape of your uterus and tubes and see
whether your tubes are open. This should be performed
within ten days of your menstrual period so that there is
no chance of pregnancy. However, we will not do it if
you are bleeding. Please also use contraceptive
precautions for that cycle. The procedure can be
uncomfortable, and please bring someone with you to
chaperone you home. It may be helpful to take a couple
of over-the-counter painkillers an hour before the*

procedure. Please do not forget to take the antibiotics I have given you to cover the procedure.

In summary, we have arranged the following:

Lifestyle Issues
1. *Frank, you are going to stop smoking.*
2. *Carol, you are going to address your stress and start regular massage.*
3. *You are going to have more regular intercourse.*

Investigations
1. *We have arranged a semen analysis.*
2. *I have done swabs on Carol.*
3. *We have arranged a 21-day progesterone test.*
4. *We have arranged a hysterosalpingogram.*

I have arranged to see you again in my clinic in three months' time, but obviously if you do conceive between now and then, please do not hesitate to contact me.

When we meet again, we can discuss the results and decide whether more investigations are required and what the next course of action is.

Between now and then do keep in touch, and if you have any concerns, please contact my clinic nurse on the number I have given you.

All best wishes

Yours sincerely

Mr Michael Dooley
Consultant Obstetrician and Gynaecologist

Cc GP

It's terribly important for your own sense of purpose and focus to feel as though you are moving on to the next stage. We saw in Chapter 14 how setting goals and reviewing your progress can be immensely beneficial – in terms of organisation, saving time and from a psychological perspective. It is equally important to apply the same strategy here. Even if the plan is to do nothing other than continue to have regular sex for the next six months, it is still a vital next step for you and your partner.

Chapter 16

Seeking Private Medical Help

NHS OR PRIVATE?

Unfortunately, it is not always easy to get fertility treatment on the NHS, and often there are long waiting lists to contend with. Waiting for appointments, scheduling tests, waiting for results and then follow-up consultations can take a lot of time. For many couples, understandably, this makes for a particularly stressful process. This is why I would always recommend that you seek medical help sooner rather than later. Get an appointment scheduled in your diary – even if it's months away. It may be that by the time your consultation comes round you have already fallen pregnant. The important thing is to get the ball rolling and to feel that you are doing something.

The extent of investigation and treatment that the NHS can provide still depends on certain criteria and can vary according to the health authority that is responsible for the area in which you live.

The National Institute of Clinical Excellence (NICE) has issued guidelines for clinics that include the following recommendations:

- Screen all women for chlamydia before they undergo procedures to check if their fallopian tubes are blocked.
- Offer women who do not have any history of problems with

their fallopian tubes an X-ray to see if their tubes are blocked, rather than an invasive procedure.

- Offer six cycles of intrauterine insemination (IUI) to couples with unexplained fertility problems, slightly abnormal sperm count or mild endometriosis.
- Offer three cycles of stimulated IVF to couples in which the woman is aged 23–39, who have an identified cause of their fertility problems or unexplained fertility of at least three years.[1]

However, because these guidelines are not always easy to implement, you will still find significant variations from one area of the country to the next. Waiting times to see a gynaecologist may vary from two weeks to up to three years.

Because of the long waiting lists, many couples choose to go privately. A study carried out showed that 75% of couples end up on long waiting lists and, if they had the money or health insurance, would choose to go privately. Do be aware though that your insurance policies may not cover investigations or treatment.

Infertility can be an expensive business if you do decide to go privately. It's important that you and your partner take time to consider the financial implications and ensure that you will not be putting yourself into debt or overstretching your budget.

WHAT CAN YOU EXPECT TO PAY IF YOU GO PRIVATE?

You must always get a full breakdown of the costs from your clinic before you embark on treatment.

The average cost of a single private IVF attempt without drugs is around £2,800. This is for actual treatment, of course. An initial consultation along with blood tests will be much lower. But you must take into account hidden costs – such as medication – later on down the line. You should also note that clinics won't refund your money if there is no pregnancy as a result of any treatment.

CHOOSING A PRIVATE CLINIC

As a paying customer, you have every right to pick and choose when it comes to finding the right clinic. You may find that larger, well-known clinics are too impersonal for you and look instead for a smaller, more informal unit. It's a good idea to visit a few to get a feel for them. You can also send for brochures or check out the different websites that most clinics now use. It's also worth speaking to friends.

Cost will obviously play an important role in your decision making, but you should also take into account travelling times and overall convenience. If you don't have a car and a particular clinic is miles from the nearest station, then more than likely that clinic isn't going to be the right place for you. Or if the unit is close to home but there is no parking available, then you need to weigh up how much time finding a parking space is going to add to your journey. These may seem rather trivial factors, but if you are going to have treatment, then you will be making a number of visits, so it's important that you do what you can to make life a little easier for yourself.

Ten Tips on Choosing a Clinic

1. Read up on a handful of clinics to get a feel for what seems best for you.
2. Read the leaflet titled 'Choosing a Clinic', published by the Infertility Network UK (see Useful Contacts and Websites).
3. Read *The HFEA Guide to Infertility and Directory of Clinics*, which contains league tables that show how successful the various clinics are (see Useful Contacts and Websites). Do make sure you read up on these. There is more information on this below.
4. When visiting clinics – or if you're speaking to them on the phone – ask as many questions as you can. It may help to write them out first.

5. Work out how long you think it will take to get there – from home and maybe also from work.
6. Look at the costs.
7. Ask about success rates.
8. Visit the clinic's website if they have one.
9. Have an initial consultation at the clinic; you must feel comfortable with the team treating you.
10. Try to visit the support group.

League Tables

The HFEA Guide to Infertility and Directory of Clinics is a comprehensive guide on the services, success rates and waiting times of all fertility clinics across the UK and was first published in 2005 by the Human Fertilisation and Embryology Authority, which regulates clinics. For the first time, patients now have a way of seeing how clinics compare. Although private clinics may produce their own tables, it's more reliable to look at those issued by the HFEA. The important figure to take into account when looking at league tables is what's known as the 'take-home baby rate' per treatment cycle. This rate does not take into account pregnancies that have resulted in miscarriage or ectopic pregnancies, but simply the number of successful pregnancies.

What's more, the clinics will now have to adhere to new HFEA guidelines on how this information is presented. By issuing specific guidelines, the HFEA hopes to provide clear, jargon-free information to patients. In the past, some clinics have enhanced their results, for example by treating only younger women. All couples will now be able to access the guide online or through their GP, look up the various rates of success and waiting times and then make a more informed decision about where they would like to be treated.

Useful Questions to Ask When Choosing a Clinic

When deciding on a clinic, it's well worth asking as many questions as you can. Remember, you are paying for their service, so you are absolutely entitled to ensure you are getting the best possible service for *you*. Couples' requirements and priorities differ; what may be very important to you might not even figure in another couple's decision-making process. Don't forget: this is about creating the right package to suit you. I have included useful questions to ask at the initial consultation, many of which are advised by the HFEA.

- What treatments and tests do you offer?
- What are the benefits of the treatment you've recommended, and why do you think it's the best option for me?
- Are there alternative treatments? If so, why do you think they are less suitable?
- How many patients at your clinic have had this treatment, and how many had a baby?
- Does my age affect the choice of fertility treatment?
- What medication will I have to take, and what are the side effects?
- Are there any alternatives to the medication you have mentioned?
- What lifestyle changes can I make that may boost my chance of having a successful pregnancy (e.g. diet, exercise, stopping smoking, etc.)?
- Can you break down all the costs involved in this treatment?
- Is there any way these costs can be reduced?
- Are there any hidden costs?
- What kind of counselling or advice do you provide, and what is the cost?
- Are there any patient groups or support groups I can join?
- Could you tell me more about the assessment process (welfare of the child) that is carried out before treatment can begin?

- What other options are available if this treatment does not work?
- What happens next? Do my partner and I need to do anything?
- Is there a waiting list?
- Will I see the same doctor each time?
- How often might I need to visit the clinic?
- What is the take-home baby rate?
- Do you offer complementary and alternative therapies in conjunction with conventional treatment?
- Do the consultants have specific expertise?
- Do you impose any restrictions on potential patients? (For example, some clinics prefer not to take women over a certain age.)
- Do you have a 24-hour, 7 days a week emergency number?

Once you have answers to these questions from a few clinics, you'll be in a position to make an informed decision about which is likely to suit you best. The more information you can get, the better – that way you'll also feel more in control.

Preparing for the Appointment

As before, follow the advice in Chapter 15 about writing down everything you think your doctor may need to know and any questions you may have for him or her. Make sure you have a detailed plan of action at the end of the appointment.

Chapter 17

Routine Investigations for Female Fertility –
General Tests and Ovulation Testing

Once you have seen your GP and a full history has been taken, your GP may suggest further investigations. (These procedures might not, however, be offered by your GP, in which case you will need to see a specialist either on the NHS or privately.) Further investigation may be recommended for a number of reasons. These include:

- Following your initial consultation, you have taken your doctor's fit for fertility advice but still have not conceived after a further six months.
- At your initial consultation, your GP feels your particular set of circumstances require attention sooner rather than later.
- You have requested further tests. As a rule, I am very careful not to dismiss couple's anxieties. When a couple are really concerned, I will often go ahead with further investigations in order to help minimise this stress, even if, from a medical point of view, I feel they should give it more time.
- You are concerned that you are not ovulating.

PHYSICAL EXAMINATION

A physical examination is very important, though I should stress this does not necessarily mean an internal examination.

Although I have continually emphasised the importance of going to appointments together, it's often a good idea to have your physical examination while your partner is out of the room. You may also use this opportunity to discuss previous pregnancies, illnesses or sexually transmitted diseases in private.

GENERAL APPEARANCE

Your doctor will want to make a note of your general appearance in order to gather any clues about possible hormonal problems. For example, polycystic ovarian syndrome (see page 242) is often accompanied with symptoms such as acne, increased body hair and excess weight.

Ten Important General Physical Findings

1. Abnormal hair growth
2. Overweight or underweight
3. Acne
4. Evidence of an abdominal operation
5. Milk coming from breast
6. Enlarged thyroid gland
7. Balding
8. Acanthosis nigricans (thickening and darkening of the neck)
9. Hoarse voice
10. Clinical evidence of chromosomal problems

PELVIC EXAMINATION

This is to check for any obvious signs of endometriosis (see page 249) and any tenderness or pain. Your doctor will also be checking for the shape and positioning of your pelvic organs. This examination doesn't require any kind of anaesthetic as it is quite straightforward, relatively non-invasive and should only take a few minutes.

This will check your vagina, cervix, uterus and ovaries. It is important at this time to you tell your doctor if you have any concerns or pain. If you are worried, talk about it at the beginning.

Ten Important Findings at Pelvis Examination

1. An abnormal vagina
2. An abnormal cervix
3. Fibroids
4. Endometriosis nodules
5. Tenderness
6. Swelling of one or both ovaries
7. Vaginal discharge
8. A fixed, immobile uterus
9. Bleeding from the cervix
10. Tight and painful entrance to the vagina

GENERAL HORMONE AND OVULATION TESTS

Ten Important Questions You Should Ask About Tests

1. Why am I being offered this test?
2. Is it safe? What are the risks?
3. Will it change the management of my case?
4. Are there any alternatives?
5. Will I be tested at a specific time in my cycle?
6. When will the results be back?
7. How will they be given to me?
8. Are there any costs involved?
9. Have I had this test before?
10. Are there any special instructions before I do the test?

Ten Baseline Tests That May Be Considered

1. Follicle-stimulating hormone
2. Luteinising hormone
3. Antimullerian hormone (not always available on the NHS)
4. Testosterone/androgens
5. Prolactin
6. Thyroid function
7. Full blood count
8. Rubella
9. Mid-luteal-phase progesterone
10. Swab for infection including chlamydia

Tests one to three are blood tests and are done at the beginning of your cycle (days 2, 3 or 4).

BLOOD TESTS

Simple blood tests will measure your hormone levels and establish whether there is any hormonal imbalance that could be affecting your fertility. It may be that, for a number of reasons, you are not ovulating or are only ovulating at irregular times. Your doctor will want to establish if this is the case and try to work out why. Looking at your hormone levels is the first and most straightforward way of finding this out. You'll remember from Part 1 that there are a number of female hormones that, through a rather complex balancing act, work together to maintain your fertility.

Your GP is likely to check the levels of the following hormones:

Full Blood Count

The full blood count assesses your levels of haemoglobin, (the substance that gives the red cells their colour and carries oxygen from the lungs to the cells). The test is primarily used to determine the presence of anaemia.

Follicle-stimulating Hormone (FSH)

As we saw in Part 1, FSH is produced by the pituitary gland and works to stimulate the growth of the ovarian follicles, which will eventually release an egg. A measurement of FSH is taken on days 2–4 of your cycle and is used to ascertain the quality and quantity of the eggs. A higher level of FSH indicates a reduced ovarian reserve, and if the FSH level is over 12iu/l (don't worry about the odd-looking measurements, the value is the important indicator), the ovaries are less likely to be ovulating regularly.

Luteinising Hormone (LH)

This hormone, like FSH, is controlled by the pituitary gland and has a number of jobs: it works to stimulate ovulation and causes the formation of the corpus luteum (this is the small cyst-like structure created after the egg is released), which then stimulates the release of progesterone.

LH is also tested for on days 2–4 of your cycle. High levels are associated with PCOS (see page 242), while very low levels can be associated with a condition in the brain called hypothalamic hypogonadism.

Androgens

Don't forget that all women do have a level of androgens 'the male hormones'; the main androgen is testosterone. An increased level of testosterone in a woman is one indicator of PCOS, although that doesn't necessarily mean you will have it. Elevated levels may also point to a general hormonal imbalance that could be affecting fertility.

Antimullerian Hormone

Testing for serum antimullerian hormone levels on day three of your cycle can give a useful indication of the health of your eggs. In a recent study there was a strong correlation between high concentrations of antimullerian hormone and healthy eggs and ultimately a higher clinical pregnancy rate. Other studies have confirmed that serum antimullerian hormone levels represent one of the best ways to assess the age related decline of reproductive function.

Prolactin

This hormone is secreted by the pituitary gland. Its main function is the control and production of milk after childbirth. However, it is also responsible for stimulating the production of progesterone. High levels of prolactin can be associated with a tumour of the pituitary gland and can upset ovulation. Mildly elevated levels of prolactin can indicate PCOS and higher levels will disturb ovulation.

Stress has also been known to cause an increase in prolactin levels, and your GP should take this into account when interpreting the results of the test.

Remember, doing blood tests are just a snapshot of a long and complex cycle. It is like taking one photo of an athlete doing a marathon. It helps us acknowledge that it may be repeated and reviewed. The purpose of all this is that we need to slowly create a picture of your and your partner's reproductive status. Don't forget that this also changes with time, so new information may be important.

Thyroid Function Tests

The thyroid-stimulating hormone (TSH) is also produced by the pituitary gland and works to control the thyroid function. This in turn is responsible for our body's metabolic processes and so ensures that all the different systems in our body are working properly. Thyroid disease is common in women[1] and irregularities in thyroid function, in particular an underactive thyroid, can, as we saw in Chapter 8, have a profound effect on fertility.

Rubella

It is important to check for rubella to make sure you are immune to this. Otherwise, if you do get pregnant and get a rubella infection, it can cause severe abnormalities in the baby.

Swabs

Your doctor may also want to take a cervical swab to test for chlamydia and other infections. This involves gently inserting a cotton swab into the opening of the cervix and taking a minute sample of the cervical mucus.

OVULATION TESTS

Ten Tests to Indicate Ovulation

Ovulation is difficult to confirm, but the following may help to indicate you are ovulating:

1. regular 28± five-day cycle
2. premenstrual symptoms
3. mid-cycle pain (known as 'mittelschmerz')
4. salivary ferning tests (see page 31)

5. temperature measurement
6. mid-cycle spotting (but do get your cervix checked)
7. mid-luteal-phase progesterone
8. LH hormone urine test
9. post-coital testing (cervical mucus changes)
10. diagnostic cycle/transvaginal ultrasound scan (TVS)

Mid-luteal-phase Progesterone

This test is carried out seven days after ovulation. It is often called the 21-day test because it's usually taken on day 21 of your cycle. This may not always be the best day for you. Your doctor will discuss the most suitable day with you depending upon the length of your cycle. Sometimes I do three tests across the cycle to try to get the correct date. This is used to test whether or not you are actually ovulating. You'll remember we saw in Part 1 how the hormone progesterone is produced when a follicle releases its egg. Checking that the right levels of progesterone are being produced at the right time helps establish that ovulation is taking place.

Because not all women have a 28-day cycle, the timing of the test can be adjusted. Make sure you let your doctor know if your cycle is longer or shorter than 28 days, and he or she will make the appropriate calculations. Results are relatively accurate; however, some doctors prefer to carry out the test over three consecutive months.

Because the 21-day test is looking for progesterone levels, your doctor will also be able to see if you have particularly low levels of the hormone. If there is not enough progesterone being produced, the lining of the uterus will not ready for implantation and so will be unable to maintain a pregnancy.

Low progesterone is also linked with PCOS along with more general menstrual-cycle irregularities. The test will therefore help to provide further clues as to what may be going on.

What If the Tests Show I'm *Not* Ovulating?

If the result of the 21-day test comes back showing low progesterone levels, then it is likely that you are not ovulating or the test was done on the wrong day. At this stage, your doctor may suggest one of number of options:

1. Repeat the 21-day test the following month on the same day and then do a further test or tests on days 19–23, i.e. two to three tests.
2. Refer you to a fertility consultant.
3. Prescribe you with the drug clomifene, although this should be done in conjunction with a fertility consultant.

Clomifene is the most frequently prescribed fertility drug for women. Although in most cases you will have been referred on for secondary care before you are recommended the drug, many GPs will also prescribe it themselves. We'll be looking at how clomifene works and its success rates in Part 4.

What If the Tests Show I *Am Ovulating?*

If the tests come back and indicate that your hormone levels are normal and that you are ovulating, your GP may suggest some further tests to help work out why you're not conceiving. (Sometimes – and I've seen this with my own patients – the very relief that women feel knowing that they are ovulating and that their hormones are happily working together can quickly result in a pregnancy.) It is snap-shut evidence, though you may ovulate one month and not another.

Luteinising Hormone Urine Test

If you are ovulating, your GP may recommend you try using a urinary LH home test in order to maximise your chances of conceiving (see also Chapter 1). Sometimes called an ovulation prediction test, this works by measuring the levels of LH in the urine in order to determine the time of ovulation. A sample of urine is applied to the test kit each day in order to measure the levels of LH.

As we've already learnt, LH is secreted by the pituitary gland and is the hormone that stimulates the ovary to prepare the follicle to release an egg. Once the follicle has matured, a sudden rise in LH levels (known as the 'LH surge') signals to the ovary to release the egg. (This is ovulation.) Ovulation typically occurs 10–12 hours after the peak of the LH surge. By determining exactly when you are going to ovulate, you can time intercourse accordingly.

Studies show that urine LH testing is a reliable means of predicting ovulation.[2]

Post-coital Testing

The idea of this rather unromantically named test is to see whether your cervical mucus is compatible with your partner's sperm. As you may remember from Part 1, the mucus needs to be of a particular, fairly fluid consistency in order to allow the sperm to swim through it. The post-coital test requires you to see your doctor, or attend your clinic, around the time of ovulation having had intercourse up to ten hours previously. Your doctor will then take a sample of the mucus and, using a microscope, look to see how your partner's sperm are behaving. The test is uncomfortable rather than painful, quite similar to having a cervical smear test, and takes about five minutes.

If the sperm are dead or moving only slightly and your partner has otherwise healthy sperm, this will indicate that something is happening to the sperm when it reaches the vagina that is causing them to die off. Your doctor may recommend certain medication or dietary changes to help get the mucus back to a good consistency.

This rather antiquated test is less commonly used these days, as it is now believed to have less clinical value than some of the other investigations now available. I very rarely do it, and the only time I do is to confirm that intercourse is actually taking place.

Diagnostic Cycle

In order to get a better overview of what's happening in your cycle each month, more fertility specialists and doctors are now using this process. A monitored cycle combines checking out your hormonal balances along with assessing your reproductive function via transvaginal scanning (TVS). The tests take place over one menstrual cycle, so theoretically it's also a faster way of establishing what might be going wrong. At Westover House we carefully link in with acupuncture, hypnosis and other complementary and alternative medicine diagnostic tests.

At the beginning of your cycle, around days 2–4, you'll be given a blood test so that your doctor can measure the levels of oestradial (the main type of oestrogen secreted by the ovaries) and LH, FSH and possibly antimullerian hormone to check out the quality and quantity of eggs. Then, around days 6–8 of your cycle, you'll have the first of three or four ultrasound scans.

The TVS will evaluate the genital tract. So, from the first scan, your doctor will be assessing the shape of your uterus, the thickness of the uterus lining, the shape of your ovaries and the size of the development in the ovaries. Subsequent scans will track the follicle growth and the thickness of the lining of your womb. After this, the development of the corpus luteum post-ovulation can also be seen. In combination with the scans, you will be asked to check your urine for the LH surge. Thus, you can detect both biochemical and physical signs of ovulation. Later, blood testing for progesterone will detect the efficiency of the luteal phase. I use the diagnostic cycle more and more in combination with CAM therapists.

TVS is a method of imaging the genital tract in women. The ultrasound machine sends out high-frequency sound waves, which bounce off body structures to create a picture. Something called an ultrasound transducer (a hand-held probe) is inserted directly into the vagina, allowing it to get close to the pelvic structures. The probe is then gently moved within the vaginal cavity in order to scan these structures.

Your bladder should be empty for this procedure. You may experience very mild discomfort from the pressure of the vaginal probe, but nothing more – it's really nothing to worry about. However, if you're anxious, why not get your partner or a close friend to come with you? If it does cause pain, then this can be significant.

If you want a transabdominal scan, which is when the scanner is placed on your abdomen and not in your vagina, you will need a full bladder. If you think this is going to be more comfortable for you, please ask.

How Is It Kept Clean?

The ultrasound scanner is cleaned on a regular basis and after each patient to make sure it is sterile, and a condom is used as well to give you absolute protection.

Ten Things a Transvaginal Ultrasound Scan Can Detect/Monitor

1. Shape, size and position of the uterus
2. Fibroids
3. Thickness of the lining of the uterus
4. Size, shape and position of the ovaries
5. Polycystic ovaries
6. Endometrial polyps
7. Incompetent cervix
8. Ovarian cysts

9. Monitor ovulation
10. Position and development of an early pregnancy, including an ectopic pregnancy

KEEP POSITIVE, AND REMEMBER YOUR GOALS

There may be some waiting involved in all this, which can in itself be stressful. While you're waiting to get your blood test results back from your doctor do try to keep up with your Fit for Fertility Programme. This is something you *can* control, and it's important not to neglect your overall health and wellbeing. Keep eating healthily and taking your supplements and taking time out to relax and unwind. And don't forget to keep the lines of communication with your partner open. Many couples can feel irritable during these waiting times, and it's important not to take this out on each other. It may be that you feel your partner is being *too* laid back and that you're doing all the worrying for the both of you. But remember that people all have different ways of coping with stressful situations, and this may just be his way.

Remember, visualise a pregnancy. Stick to your goals, revise them if necessary and think about how you can make new goals, too. Some couples put everything on hold until they receive the results of their blood tests. Rather than do that, use the time that you have to plan your next move and consider your various options.

Chapter 18

Further Investigations for Male Infertility

DIAGNOSING MALE INFERTILITY

Around 35% of infertility problems are attributed to the male partner. You wouldn't necessarily know this given the amount of focus that is placed on a woman in all matters related to fertility. So, for this reason and also as a matter of general support and solidarity, it's terribly important that your partner is involved in the diagnostic process right from the start.

Before you embark on further investigations, your partner should have a basic check-up with his GP – including a sperm test. Because most male fertility tests tend to be far less invasive than female fertility tests, it's often a good idea to proceed with these first – or at least at the same time.

Women who have suffered miscarriages often make the assumption that this is something to do with their fertility and reproductive system. In fact, miscarriage is often as a result of sperm abnormalities. This is why it is so important not to jump to conclusions, but to – in as far as you can – systematically rule out the different possible causes.

Because for so long fertility has been pigeon-holed as a 'woman's issue', men often find it hard to talk about and deal with the possibility that they may have fertility problems. It can challenge the way that they think about themselves and the role that they inhabit. Some men may feel they are less manly or that they are letting their partner down. This can lead to feelings of immense powerlessness and shame. What's more, women are generally more able to talk to one another about these kinds of emotional issues. Men sometimes find it more difficult, feeling that they must put on a brave face with their male friends – and with their partner. So, in some cases, getting your partner to make that first step of going to see their GP can be a very big move for them.

Try to keep talking to one another about your hopes and fears, and try not to get impatient if the other doesn't always see things your way. Remind yourselves that you are in this together and are both aiming for the same result.

THE INITIAL CONSULTATION

Read the advice in Chapter 15 for how to prepare for the initial consultation and what to expect. Whether you are seeing your GP together or going separately, you should both try to get a history sheet in advance so that you can have it filled out before you go.

Your partner should note down anything that springs to mind that could be of relevance, including old sports injuries and childhood infections. Don't worry about putting down information that may seem trivial to you – it's all useful for your GP and will give him or her a better picture to work from.

PHYSICAL EXAMINATION AND GENERAL APPEARANCE

After checking your partner's weight, body mass index (BMI) and blood pressure, the doctor will take a look at his general appearance. Noting the condition of the skin, body hair and glands. An abdominal examination will look for any abnormal masses and hernias along with scars from previous surgery that your partner may have forgotten to mention and that may have important implications for his fertility.

The genitals will also be examined, looking particularly at both testicles, checking for any swellings, tenderness or variation in size. The doctor will also check the testes for varicoceles (see page 259) and any other visible evidence of physiological problems, such as undescended testicles.

SEMEN ANALYSIS

Before you leave, your GP will ask your partner to provide a sperm sample within the following few days or weeks. At this point, he should make a follow-up appointment so that the results of the sperm test can be discussed.

Semen analysis is the primary screening test for male infertility, and the results can often provide a good deal of information that can be valuable in reaching conclusions.

The GP will provide your partner with a sterile container in which to ejaculate. He or she will also advise him to abstain from sex for two to four days before providing the sample. A fixed period of abstinence improves the standardisation of the test. He may also be required to give a urine sample, taken right after ejaculation. The sample should then be taken directly to the surgery for analysis. Some units have the facility for men to provide the sample on site. This is preferable as there will be no delay in transporting the sperm to the laboratory for full assessment.

Some men, for emotional, religious or other reasons may find it hard to simply produce a sample by masturbating while at the clinic. If this is the case, special non-latex, non-spermicidal condoms can be provided for use at home. Again, the sample will need to taken straight to the surgery – within the hour if possible – and be kept at body temperature. The surgery will advise him on the logistics of this.

What Does the Test Look For?

As soon as the lab has your partner's semen sample, they will measure it for the following factors:

- **Sperm count.** This is measured as the number of sperm/ml.
- **Motility.** This refers to the sperm's ability to swim and move quickly and is measured as a percentage.
- **Morphology.** This refers to the shape and maturity of the sperm cells to determine the quality and viscosity of semen. This is also measured as a percentage.
- **Clumping/agglutination.** Sperm that clump together are unhealthy and could be a sign of immunological infertility, in which your body is making antisperm antibodies (see page 222).
- **Volume of semen.** This measures the overall volume of ejaculate.
- **White blood cell count.** High levels of white blood cells in the semen may indicate infection.
- **Red blood cell count.** This may also indicate an infection.
- **PH.** Sperm is normally quite alkaline, so this will test for acidity.

Because it takes sperm around three months to fully develop and mature, any sample your partner provides at this point will, of course, be influenced by factors that happened three months previously. So, if he had an infection, took medication or was exposed to certain dietary and environmental factors, these may all affect the result of the test. Also, there are large swings in semen parameters – even in perfectly healthy, fertile sperm donors. For these reasons, some doctors prefer to take two samples over a few months.

Understanding the Results

Normally, your partner will have made a follow-up appointment at the time of the initial consultation. This need not be too long afterwards since the results of semen analysis can generally be made available very quickly, though this will vary from place to place. In my practice, I will phone or write to the patient as soon as the results become available.

The results that your partner gets back will probably look something like the data given below, which is based on the World Health Organisation's 1999 normal values:

SEMEN ANALYSIS	NORMAL VALUES
Macroscopic Examination	
volume (ml)	more than 2 mls
appearance	normal
liquefaction	complete
viscosity	normal
pH	7.2 – 8.0
debris	
agglutination	
Motility (% spermatozoa)	more than 50% (a + b); more than 25% (a)
(a) rapid progression	
(b) slow progression	
(c) non-progressive	
(d) immotile	
Vitality (% live)	more than 50%
Antisperm Antibodies (% bound)	more than 50% may not affect fertility
MAR test for IgA	more than 10%
MAR test for IgG	more than 10%
Concentration (x 10^6/ml)	
count/ml	more than 20 x 10^6/ml
total count in ejaculate	more than 40 x 10^6
Other Cells (x 10^6/ml)	
round cells	more than 5 x 10^6/ml
polymorphonuclear leucocytes	more than 1 x 10^6/μml
Morphology (%)	Multicentre studies in progress
normal	more than 15%
abnormal	
Head defects	
midpiece defects	
tail defects	
cytoplasmic droplets	
teratozoospermia index (TZI)	1.6 or less

Your GP should then go through the results with you both. I would always recommend that both partners attend; after all, this is affecting both of you, and often it can be hard for one person to take in all the information that is being given.

What Do the Terms Mean?

Oligozoospermia – reduced sperm count
Asthenozoospermia – reduced sperm motility
Teratozoospermia – reduced sperm morphology
Azoospermia – no sperm
Aspermia – no ejaculate
Normozoospermia – normal results

Sperm Count

What is considered to be a normal sperm count varies within the medical community. However, anything between 20 million sperm/ml of semen and 100 million/ml is generally considered to be normal. Do remember that any infections, cold or flu can affect this count, as can the frequency of ejaculation, and also keep in mind that men with sperm counts of well below 20 million have often been able to father children. Lifestyle factors – such as stress, alcohol intake and diet – will also affect sperm count. If the sperm count is lower than 5 million/ml, this may indicate a genetic defect such as carrying the gene for cystic fibrosis, and your partner will be referred for chromosome testing. If there is no sperm at all, then we may involve a urologist.

Sperm Motility

This refers to the sperm's ability to swim and move quickly. Just because the sperm are produced in high numbers and are shaped well doesn't mean they're all on the Olympic swimming team. Motility is one of the most important determining factors in the sperm's ability to fertilise the egg. At least 50% of sperm need to be motile in order to be considered 'normal'. They also need to be moving forward. When your partner finds out his motility percentage, this is the percentage of sperm that are moving. For example, 75% motility means that 75% of sperm are moving.

Motility is graded from a to d, according to the World Health Organization (WHO) *Laboratory Manual* criteria, as follows.

- Grade 'a' sperm are those that swim forward fast in a straight line.
- Grade 'b' sperm swim forward but either in a curved or crooked line or slowly.
- Grade 'c' sperm move their tails but do not move forward.
- Grade 'd' sperm do not move at all. Sperm of grade 'c' and 'd' are considered poor.

Immotility can be caused by a number of factors including infection, illnesses and frequency of ejaculation or substances such as alcohol, marijuana or tobacco. There may also be underlying medical reasons such as antisperm antibodies or defects in the sperm's tails.

Sperm Morphology

This refers to the shape of the sperm cells. Examples of poor morphology would include large numbers of sperm with two heads, no tails, two tails, no heads or deformed tails or heads. Numbers vary, from one school of thought to another, but around 15% and over of normal sperm is considered to represent normal fertility.

Again, infection and chemical substances can affect morphology. Age is also a factor. Studies show that after the age of 40 there is an increase in the number of immature sperm and in the number of abnormal sperm produced.[1] A very low percentage of normal sperm can also occasionally indicate genetic defects.

Agglutination

When sperm clump together, it is usually a sign of an immunological disorder causing the body to make antisperm antibodies. In some cases, vitamin C can help to reduce sperm agglutination.

Volume

Not to be confused with sperm count, which refers to the number of sperm in the seminal fluid, this is an overall measurement of the amount of seminal fluid produced in one ejaculate. A normal volume will vary from 2–5ml.

Contrary to some ways of thinking, a higher volume of seminal fluid does not indicate superior virility. A higher volume means a more diluted concentration of sperm. The volume can also affect their movement.

If the volume is low, it may be as a result of a past infection that could be blocking the ejaculatory ducts in the prostate, inhibiting the flow or production of seminal fluid. It may also suggest problems with the seminal vesicles or the glands. It could also indicate a condition called congenital bilateral absence of the vas deferens (CBAVD) (see page 260).

In addition to arranging for your partner to repeat the test (to allow for the inevitable fluctuations in semen quality that day-to-day lifestyle factors can cause), your doctor is likely to recommend you have a fructose test (see page 222).

White Blood Cell Count

High levels of white blood cells in the semen may indicate infection, ranging from a urinary infection to inflammation of the testes or prostate gland. Your partner's GP will also want to rule out other bacterial infections such as chlamydia.

Red Blood Cell Count

High levels of red blood cells in the semen aren't normal. Your partner will need to be evaluated for underlying infections.

pH

The pH of semen should be around 7.2–8.0; this is alkaline. Semen that is acidic and without sperm may indicate the absence of the vas deferens.

A Normal Result?

If your partner's test comes back normal, by which we mean it falls within the range described above, then this will probably come as a great relief to him – and to you. It is likely that he will not be referred for any further tests at this point. However, your GP may make certain dietary or lifestyle recommendations.

You and your partner may then want to decide on your next step. This may mean doing nothing further for the time being other keeping up with the Fit for Fertility Programme and continuing to have regular intercourse.

As ever, the important thing is to make a decision together, based on this latest piece of information, as to your next move.

The Next Step

Depending on specific results of your partner's semen analysis, his GP is likely to suggest one or all of the following:

- Reduce his intake of alcohol or stop drinking altogether.
- Stop smoking and, in particular, using marijuana and other recreational drugs.
- Follow a diet that includes the good foods listed in Chapter 9 and excludes the bad foods.
- Return in a month or two for another semen analysis; this helps to rule out old infections, binge drinking and other factors.
- Have further tests.
- Do nothing else

Before he decides whether or not to have further tests, you should both discuss the various options open to you and decide what feels to be the right way to proceed. If it looks as though there may be a wait before your partner can be seen for further tests, then you may decide it's worth getting on to the list now in order to save time later. Meanwhile, you can be continuing to follow the dietary and supplement advice given in Part 2, as this may well be all it takes to rectify semen abnormalities.

HORMONE TESTS AND FURTHER TESTS

Blood Tests

The first port of call, after semen analysis, is likely to be a simple blood test, to analyse your partner's hormones. This will measure the levels of the different sex hormones necessary for the production and development of healthy sperm. However, there is some debate as to the overall usefulness of this test in terms of understanding male infertility.

Testosterone

Because testosterone levels fluctuate during the day, with levels highest in the morning, the timing of the blood test is important. This is something your GP or consultant will discuss with your partner; however, this is more relevant in cases where the test results are borderline.

Low levels of testosterone (less than 10nmol/l) *may* indicate testicular failure; however, this will be assessed according to the levels of the other sex hormones. Low testosterone can also be due to a hypothalamic or pituitary dysfunction or a genetic defect. Because the production of testosterone is stimulated by the presence of other hormones, these will need to be assessed at the same time.

Follicle-stimulating Hormone (FSH)

FSH is essential for sperm development. High levels of this hormone can suggest primary testicular failure and, conse-quently, problems with sperm production. Your partner may be offered a testicular biopsy if this result returns. If the FSH level is low, again depending on the overall balance of the other hormones, your partner may be offered hormone-replacement medication to redress the balance.

Luteinising Hormone (LH)

LH stimulate the production of testosterone, which in turn helps produce healthy sperm. High levels of LH combined with low levels of testosterone may indicate testicular failure. A biopsy may be offered to confirm this and to ascertain whether it may be possible to retrieve sperm for intra-cytoplasmic sperm injection (ICSI) (see page 304).

The Next Step

Depending on the results of the blood test, your GP may suggest one or more of the following:

- If the hormone levels are normal, he or she may refer you for further tests (see below).
- If there is an imbalance, hormone treatment may be prescribed to correct this (see page 259).
- The results of the blood test may necessitate a testicular biopsy (see page 224).
- Do nothing else

FURTHER TESTS

Fructose Test: Checking for Obstructions

If there are no sperm present in the semen analysis, it could either mean none are being produced at all or that they are being produced but are unable to get through due to a blockage in the seminal vesicles. (The vesicles are the two sac-like structures that produce the part of semen that contains sperm.) Fructose is usually found in semen, so if when the semen is tested for fructose none is found, this usually means the seminal vesicles *are* blocked (assuming, that is, that the seminal vesicles are themselves present), preventing the fructose and sperm from getting through. However, if there is fructose found in the semen but no sperm, it could be that the testes are not producing sperm at all, and further investigations will be necessary.

Antisperm Antibodies Test

An antisperm antibody test detects whether a man's immune response is being triggered by his own sperm, causing the production of antibodies that then kill or disable the sperm.

It's as though his immune system is responding to the sperm in much the same way it would were it a bacteria or some other kind of foreign body.

Semen can sometimes trigger a similar response in women – it's a bit like developing an allergic reaction. Clearly, in both cases, this can impair chances of conception.

Sperm antibodies can be produced in response to an infection, after surgery on the reproductive tract or following testicular injury.

The test for antibodies is called the mixed agglutination reaction test (MAR). This is not always offered on the NHS, so you may have to ask specifically for it. If the sperm are found to be clumped together, then antibodies are likely to be present and medication may be prescribed. In the past that included steroids but this has been demonstrated to have limited benefits and increased risks so now ICSI is the more favoured treatment.

Sperm DNA Fragmentation Index

This is a relatively new kind of test, and, unlike routine semen analysis, it has little to do with the shape of the sperm or whether the sperm are moving. Rather, it works on the theory suggested by medical findings that damaged sperm DNA can affect conception and pregnancy outcome.

Studies have shown that sperm with high DNA fragmentation (damage) may fertilise an egg but embryo development stops before implantation or is more likely to result in miscarriage.[2]

These finding are particularly significant for couples who have previously been diagnosed with 'unexplained fertility', as men with otherwise normal semen analyses can have a high degree of DNA damage, and men with what was called very poor sperm quality can have very little DNA damage. It may also have important implications for couples who have had poor embryo quality after IVF implantation failure or recurrent pregnancy losses.

A sperm sample is all that is required for this test. The percentage of sperm with high DNA fragmentation is expressed as the DNA fragmentation index (DFI), with 30% and above indicating low to poor fertility.[3] Taking antioxidant supplements and avoiding environmental toxins (see page 148) can help limit further DNA damage in future sperm production.

In cases where diagnosis suggests the DNA damage may be a permanent condition, this will have important implications in terms of deciding what to do next. It may be that donor sperm is your next option.

Testicular Biopsy

If all other test results have come back normal or if your GP or consultant suspects your partner may have testicular failure, he may be referred for a testicular biopsy.

What Happens?

A testicular biopsy involves taking a small piece of tissue from the testis while the man is under either local or general anaesthetic. The tissue is carefully prepared and assessed under a microscope to determine the presence of sperm-producing cells and whether the sperm-production process is normal.

In a man with a zero sperm count, this test is done to determine if a blockage is present or if poor sperm production is the cause. In men with severe sperm production problems, this test can also determine whether small areas of sperm production are present in the testes, in which case sperm from the biopsy tissue may be used in infertility treatment. Even just a few normal sperm found in the biopsy tissue can be used in the assisted reproductive technique called intra-cytoplasmic sperm injection (ICSI) where a single sperm is injected into the egg by piercing the shell of the egg (see Chapter 24).

There are two types of testicular biopsy procedures:

A needle biopsy is a technique that can be performed under local anaesthetic that involves passing a small needle into the testis to obtain a sample of tissue about half the size of a match head.

An open biopsy involves removing a larger fragment of tissue about the size of a couple of grains of rice after cutting through the skin and the thick outer covering of the testis. This procedure is typically performed while the man is under general anaesthetic.

In either instance, it is important that your partner rests fully after the procedure and that either you or a close friend can be with him immediately afterwards.

Ultrasound Scanning

This is used to study the scrotum, testes and seminal vesicles in order to look for infection, inflammation, the congenital bilateral absence of the vas deferens (CBVAD), any obstruction and for the diagnosis of varicoceles (see page 259).

Chromosome Testing

This is only generally offered to men with very low sperm counts or no sperm at all. In some cases, low sperms levels or blockages resulting in no sperm in the semen can be caused by a chromosome abnormality. There are also a number of other genetic causes for male infertility and subfertility. A simple blood test will help to ascertain if there are genetic problems. Clearly, this can have significant implications for you and your partner – and also, in some cases, for your future offspring. It may be helpful for you both to see about having some genetic counselling to help work on any difficult feelings that this could bring up.

The test might be looking for the carriage of the cystic fibre gene, Young's syndrome (see page 261) and Klinefelter's syndrome (see page 261.)

MOVING FORWARD

These tests can all take time. There may be a waiting period before your partner gets seen by the appropriate doctor or specialist, and then there may be more waiting for results and follow-up appointments. This can be stressful for you both. Try to take time out together to do other things so that this doesn't become your sole focus. You are doing all you can right now, and it's important to remind yourselves of that from time to time.

Remember, it's about 'controlling the controllables' – doing what you can and not worrying too much about those things that you can't control. Keep eating healthily, taking time to relax, having regular sex and communicating with each other.

As tests results come back, make some time to discuss between yourselves and with your doctor what you feel the next move should be. For some couples, the prospect of more tests or starting treatment is too much – whether for emotional, physical, financial or other reasons – and they decide that although they would still love to have a baby, they would rather just see what happens over time. Whatever you decide, it needs to feel right for *you*. This isn't your doctor or your parents' choice, it's yours and your partner's.

If you decide to continue with treatment – be it conventional or alternative, or a mixture of both – remember that it is really important to draw up a plan of your short- and long-term goals so that you both feel involved and that you are heading in the right direction.

Chapter 19

Further Investigations for Female Fertility – the Fallopian Tubes

If the test results come back showing that your hormone levels seem normal, you are ovulating and your partner's sperm is OK, the next medical step will be to check for any blockages in your fallopian tubes. Your GP may refer you to the hospital straight-away or may suggest you give it another few months and then, if you haven't still conceived, refer you. This will depend on your age and other medical factors, such as whether you have had previous abdominal or pelvic surgery or you have a history of infections. And, of course, it will also depend on your own preference. Sometimes, even once you've been referred, there is a bit of a wait before the actual procedure, so you may decide to ask for a referral at this point in order to save time. You should discuss with your doctor what your best possible plan is – *at this stage*.

As we saw in Part 1, the released egg makes its journey from the ovary towards the uterus via the fallopian tube and this is where the sperm will meet the egg and fertilise it. The egg's journey from the ovary to the uterus takes around six days, though of course this journey is not completed if fertilisation doesn't take place. The fallopian tubes are about 8cm in length and only about the diameter of a pencil with a cavity the size of the pencil lead. The fallopian tubes are the only tubes in the body that naturally allow the passage of products both up and down. The sperm goes up the tube to meet the egg, which is coming down the tube. If fertilisation takes place, then the embryo travels down the tube to implant in the uterus.

THE CHANNEL TUNNEL STORY

People often ask me about the difference between an open tube and a functional tube. I liken the difference to the Channel Tunnel. The Channel Tunnel may be open (i.e. one can see through from one end to the other), but it may not be functional. One of the tracks in the middle of the tunnel may be damaged, so the tunnel could be open but the train would still not get through. To me, this is the difference between a functional tube and an open tube. This is an important analogy because although tubes may be open, the very fine lining within the tube may be damaged and therefore they may not be functional. A functional tube, by definition, is always open, but an open tube is not always functional.

TUBAL DAMAGE

Tubal damage is a common cause of infertility, accounting for 14–38% in the Western world.[1] Very often we refer to tubal problems associated with infertility as blocked tubes. In fact, not all women with tubal problems have blocked tubes. In some cases, they will have adhesions and scarring of the tubes, which restrict function and movement.

In cases where tubal blockage does occur, this could be partial or total and tends to most commonly affect the portion of the fallopian tube furthest away from the uterus. This blockage often leads to the accumulation of fluid and therefore a swelling of the tubes. This is known as hydrosalpinges. Consider the tube like a long, thin balloon with the end cut off. If you blow up the balloon, it remains flat and air goes through easily. If, however, the balloon is tied at the end (i.e. it is blocked), then as you blow it up, it will swell. In the fallopian tubes, this is a hydrosalpinges.

WHAT ARE THE CAUSES OF A BLOCKED TUBE?

Infections

The most common cause of tubal damage is an infection of the genital tract,[2] such as a sexually transmitted infection like chlamydia (see page 80) or an infection that may have come about after pelvic or abdominal surgery such as having the appendix removed.

Pelvic Inflammatory Disease (PID)

PID refers to any kind of inflammation of the pelvic organs. This inflammation, over time, leads to scarring around the fallopian tube, which is what makes it harder for the egg to make its journey. Usually PID is caused by chlamydia or some other kind of sexually transmitted infection. For more information on PID, see page 247.

Other Scarring

Endometriosis (see page 249) and previous abdominal or pelvic surgery may also result in scar tissue building up around the fallopian tubes.

Intrauterine Device (IUD) or the Coil

Studies show that the insertion of an IUD or the coil can sometimes introduce bacteria. This may lead to an infection and thus scarring of the tubes.[3]

WHAT TESTS CAN I HAVE TO DETERMINE THE BLOCKAGE?

The test or tests that your doctor will you refer you for are carried out to determine if there is a blockage of some kind and where exactly it is.

Please make sure that before you have any of these tests you have been screened for vaginal infections including chlamydia.

Hysterosalpingogram (HSG)

With names like this, it's really no wonder that the world of medicine can seem completely daunting to lots of people. However, don't be put off; this is not nearly as complicated as it sounds.

What Is It?

HSG is a series of X-ray pictures of the female reproductive tract. Dye that shows up on X-ray is passed into the uterus and tubes and spills into the abdominal cavity.

An HSG will show the shape of the inside of uterus and the fallopian tubes and whether or not there are any obstructions, adhesions, blockages or uterine cavity abnormalities such as fibroids or polyps. If the tubes are found to be blocked, the HSG will show exactly where the blockages are located. This can be useful if future surgery is planned.

Although the HSG is not a treatment, some reports suggest that gently forcing dye through the tubes may dislodge any material blocking them and so increase the chances of pregnancy.

What Happens?

To be sure you aren't already pregnant, the test is generally done on days 7–10 of your cycle when you are not menstruating.

Depending on the hospital or clinic you have been referred to and your medical history, you may be prescribed a course of antibiotics beforehand to clear any infection. It is essential to have swabs done to make sure that you have not had an infection, and it cannot be done during a period.

Before the HSG, you may be advised to take a normal painkiller or an anti-inflammatory like ibuprofen. This is really just a precaution as some women experience slight cramp-like pains – a bit like mild period pain – during or after the test. But don't worry, these will settle quickly.

You'll be provided with a gown to wear and will sit or lie up on the couch with your knees bent. The doctor will then place a speculum in the vagina so that the cervix is visible. Whilst X-ray pictures are being taken, a fine catheter will be passed into the cervix and dye injected into the uterus; the dye then passes through the tubes. The whole procedure should take no longer than ten minutes. Once the X-rays have been taken, you'll be able to go home.

As ever, do involve your partner. Although this test shouldn't be too uncomfortable, it is quite normal to feel nervous. Having your partner – or a close friend – there with you can help dissolve some of the anxiety.

For a couple of days after the HSG, you may notice a sticky vaginal discharge – this is just the dye leaking out and is perfectly harmless.

Understanding the Results

A radiologist and your gynaecologist will study the pictures and send a report to your doctor. The report may show that the dye flowed normally through the uterus and fallopian tubes and that the shape of the uterus is normal with no obvious signs of any kind of inflammation or disease.

At this point, your doctor may recommend that you have a laparoscopy and hysteroscopy (see page 233) in order to determine the abnormalities. Or he or she may feel that at this stage it may be better for you and your partner to simply carry on as before – having regular intercourse and taking good care of your health. This is something he or she will discuss with you, weighing up the pros and cons of further investigations.

If the report shows that the dye was not able to flow through the system as normal, then blockages will have been identified. Again, it is likely that your doctor will refer you for a laparoscopy to find out more.

Hysterosalpingo-contrast Sonography (HyCoSy)

An even more impossibly long tongue twister. Because of its convenience and safety, in recent years, this procedure has increasingly been used in preference to HSG and laparoscopy as a first-line investigation for infertility.

What Is It?

Unlike the HSG, which relies on X-rays, the HyCoSy uses ultrasound to assess the fallopian tubes. A solution is passed into the uterine cavity and, like the dye used in a HSG, observed as it flows along the tubes.

The advantages of the HyCoSy are that, unlike the HSG, there is no radiation risk involved. As well as tubal visualisation, other abnormalities such as fibroids that may not be apparent during a HSG can be seen, and it allows the examination of the other pelvic organs. Some units actually use 3D techniques to visualise the cervix in more detail. This is a research tool.

What Happens?

The test should take place on days 8–12 of your cycle. Although very similar in procedure, the HyCoSy takes slightly longer than a conventional HSG. As with the HSG, you might experience cramp-like pains during or after, so it's a good idea to take a painkiller beforehand.

Not all specialists are convinced by the efficacy and benefits of HyCoSy. One study reported that the diagnostic accuracy, cost and discomfort of HyCoSy compared unfavourably with HSG.[4] However, this is still subject to debate, and you should discuss the advantages and disadvantages with your doctor.

Laparoscopy and Dye Test

If the HSG or HyCoSy has identified that there is a blockage of some sort or if no blockages have been shown and your specialist feels further investigations are a good idea, you will probably be referred for a laparoscopy. This examination will show up certain conditions or abnormalities that could be affecting your fertility that less invasive tests might not be able to identify.

A laparoscopy is generally accepted by the medical community as the most accurate procedure in evaluating tubal abnormalities and other abdominal causes of infertility.[5]

What Is It?

A laparoscopy is a diagnostic test where a narrow tube with a lens is passed into the abdomen through a small hole in the abdominal wall in order to look at the uterus, fallopian tubes, ovaries and abdominal organs.

The fibre-optic laparoscope used is 0.5–1cm wide and 30cm long, with a small camera on the end. Surgical instruments can be passed down the tube (or another tube placed in your abdomen), such as biopsy instruments, providing a view of, and access to, areas inside the abdominal and pelvic cavities. Do discuss with your surgeon the risks involved. They range from minor risks such as that associated with anaesthetic, or infection to major risks such as damage to the bowel, blood vessels or bladder. This happens very rarely but it must be discussed with your surgeon.

In some cases, the surgeon may discover a minor cause of your symptoms, such as simple ovarian cysts, and may be able to treat it there and then during surgery rather than having to go back and operate a second time. However, the possibilities of this will be discussed with you beforehand.

Because the procedure involves making a small incision just below the belly button, it is performed under a general anaesthetic. Depending on individual circumstances, some couples may choose to wait a while before having this test because of the risks that are involved with any kind of surgery. If your HSG results came back showing up no blockages or obvious abnormalities, this may be all the reassurance you need for the time being. If so, carry on trying as normal, perhaps with a plan to reassess your next step in a few weeks' or months' time.

What Happens?

You'll be told not to eat or take certain medicines about 8–12 hours before the operation. While you are under anaesthetic, the surgeon makes a small incision around your belly button (about a centimetre long), then through a needle carbon dioxide is pumped into the abdominal cavity to lift the abdominal wall like a tent to allow the surgeon to look inside. A further hole is also usually made slightly lower down – around about where the bikini line starts; this is to allow other instruments to be inserted.

The laparoscope is passed through the first incision. The surgeon will look at all the organs in turn, taking biopsies or, in some cases, performing minor procedures such as freeing adhesions, draining cysts and treating endometriosis.

During this process, a dye is generally injected into the cervix (much like the HSG), which then passes through the cervix, uterine cavity and along the fallopian tubes. This also serves to show up any blockages. At the end of the procedure, the laparoscope and instruments are removed and the incisions sutured and dressed.

Once you are awake and have recovered from the anaesthetic, you will generally be allowed home the same day – though you will need someone to be with you. You may feel a little tired afterwards because of the anaesthetic and some women experience pain in the tummy, neck or shoulders – this is nothing to worry about; it's just a side effect of the carbon dioxide in your abdomen. You may also experience some vaginal bleeding. Although the laparoscopy is a minor operation, it's still important that you give yourself time to recover fully. Take it easy for the next couple of days, and if you do experience any cramping or pain, have some painkillers at hand. If things do not improve, contact your doctor.

GOLD STANDARD FOR INVESTIGATION

The laparoscopy and dye test is widely considered a gold standard for investigation of tubal patency. This had led to a recommendation by NICE (National Institute for Health and Clinical Excellence) that women suspected of having endometriosis or pelvic inflammatory disease should undergo a laparoscopy in order to be assessed.[6]

Understanding the Results

The surgeon will send your GP a report detailing what he or she has seen and done. This may say that the laparoscopy has revealed problems that need more extensive surgery or some kind of medical management. Your GP will also receive a report from the pathology lab commenting on any biopsies taken during the test.

Hysteroscopy

These days it is common practice for a clinic or hospital to carry out a hysteroscopy at the same time as the laparoscopy. Having said that, you can also have a hysteroscopy on its own. It requires only mild sedation, local anaesthetic or even no anaesthetic.

What Is It?

A hysteroscopy is a diagnostic procedure in which a lighted scope (called a hysteroscope) is inserted through the cervix in order to view the inside of the uterine cavity. As well as checking for any abnormalities or scarring, this procedure, unlike the previous ones we've looked at, allows the uterus to be 'mapped'. Getting a highly detailed image of the uterine cavity and pelvic organs is a useful reference for any future assisted conception such as in vitro fertilisation. Even though this may not be likely to apply to you, some doctors feel it's a good idea to get the uterus mapped at this stage in order to save time later on, if need be.

What Happens?

The hysteroscope is inserted through the opening of the cervix into the uterine cavity. Sometimes, the cervix may need to be grasped to steady the uterus and a local anaesthetic may be used. Carbon dioxide gas or liquid is introduced to separate the walls of the uterus to make space so that the inside of the uterus can be seen more easily. Usually, the whole procedure can be viewed on a television monitor, and if you are having only a local anaesthetic, you will be able to watch if you like. The doctor may find that there are small polyps inside the uterus, and, in some cases, will be able to remove them during the procedure. At the end of the test, a sample of the lining of the uterus (endometrium) may be taken and sent for pathology examination. The whole procedure shouldn't take much longer than five minutes.

You'll then be allowed home, though it is important that you rest, and, better still, that you have someone with you. Some women may experience period mild cramps afterwards, but a painkiller or anti-inflammatory should help to ease this.

MOVING FORWARD

Once you have undergone one or more of these tests, you will need to take stock and decide on your next move. It may be that the tests have shown that your fallopian tubes are clear and that there are no obvious abnormalities anywhere in the uterine cavity. For many women, this will come as a great relief. Sometimes the very reassurance that this sort of news can bring will result in a pregnancy shortly afterwards. Some women, however, may feel frustrated by the lack of clear answers. This is quite natural and understandable. In both instances you and your partner should take time to discuss what you feel your next few goals are going to be. It may simply be to keep on trying, or you may make an appointment with your GP so that you can discuss other options.

If the tests have shown up any kind of abnormality or scarring, you will probably want to talk to your doctor about your various treatment options and what this means in terms of your fertility.

Whatever the outcome, these tests are an important stage in your information gathering. The more you know and understand, the better equipped you are for making important decisions further down the line – even if the decision is to do nothing.

PART 4

FERTILITY PROBLEMS
AND TREATMENT OPTIONS

As we've already seen, there are many different factors that can affect both male and female fertility, ranging from diet and lifestyle to hormone imbalances and more complex medical problems. In Part 4 I'm going to be describing these key medical problems and the various treatment options available. There are many different options, and this is the stage in which you can find out exactly what's right for you.

Getting a good medical diagnosis is an important step towards finding the best possible treatment – be it conventional, complementary and alternative or both. It can also help to reassure you, as often it is the *not knowing* part of fertility difficulties that can prove to be the most stressful. Once you have a better idea of what might be stopping you from conceiving, you can then make an informed decision about what you would like to do next. Getting as much information as you can is an extremely powerful way of taking charge of your body and your health.

Chapter 20

So What Could Be Wrong?
Fertility Problems Affecting Women

OVULATORY DISORDER

This is a common – if not the most common – cause of female fertility problems and affects about one-fifth of patients attending infertility clinics.[1] This is why when you first go to see your doctor, he or she will want to hear about your menstrual cycle. Simply put, if you are not ovulating, then eggs aren't being released and natural conception can't take place.

OLIGOMENORRHOEA AND AMENORRHOEA

Most women will experience irregular or infrequent periods (oligomenorrhoea) at some time in their lives, and it needn't mean you will then go on to have fertility problems. Women with oligomenorrhoea can still get pregnant; it may just take longer than in women with regular periods, but many will not be ovulating. (See page xxx for advice on predicting ovulation.)

Stress or a poor diet can upset the menstrual cycle, as can coming off the contraceptive pill. By following the guidelines on fertility fitness outlined in Part 2, you can usually rebalance the sex hormones over a matter of months. However, it may be that polycystic ovarian syndrome is affecting your menstrual cycle, so it is worth talking it over with your doctor.

Amenorrhoea is a lack of periods and, like irregular periods, can indicate a hormonal or nutritional imbalance, an underactive thyroid or polycystic ovarian syndrome. Emotional upset can lead to an absence of periods, and it is now widely known that sudden or extreme weight loss or weight gain can cause a temporary failure of the ovaries. One study reported that 12% of ovulatory infertility in the US may be attributable to being underweight and 25% to being overweight.[2] This is why many GPs will recommend a change in diet before going on to consider further medical intervention.

POLYCYSTIC OVARIAN SYNDROME (PCOS)

Polycystic ovarian syndrome is the most common cause of anovulatory infertility in the Western world, with polycystic ovaries estimated to affect 20–33% of the general population[3] and polycystic ovarian syndrome affecting 5–10% of women of reproductive age.[4]

What Is It?

Polycystic ovarian syndrome is a mixed group of different signs and symptoms that form a disorder that has a wide spectrum of presentations from mild to severe. The term 'polycystic ovaries' describes ovaries that contain many small cysts just beneath the surface of the ovaries. These cysts are egg-containing follicles that, due to hormonal imbalances, have not developed properly. These need not cause any problems and are not harmful; however, some women develop additional symptoms, and this is where the term 'polycystic ovarian syndrome' comes in.

What Causes It?

The exact cause is unknown, but it is known to be multi-factorial and related to several genes. People have often asked me why polycystic ovaries are genetic. 5,000 years ago, we were hunters and gatherers and did not know when our next meal was coming. People with polycystic ovaries had a marvellous ability to store food in the form of fat on their bodies. This was ideal because it allowed the individual to store food until they needed it.

However, in modern-day life in the Western world, where there is always an excess of food around, this is not a positive thing as it means individuals with polycystic ovaries find it difficult to maintain their weight.

What Are the Symptoms?

- irregular, infrequent or absent periods
- difficulty in becoming pregnant or recurrent miscarriage
- oily skin or acne
- increased facial and body hair (hirsuitism)
- weight problems, including being overweight, rapid weight gain and difficulty in losing weight
- depression and mood swings

THE BAKED BEAN STORY

If tomorrow it was announced on the radio that no more baked beans were ever going to be sold after 24 hours, there would be a mad panic for people to purchase baked beans. If 12 hours later this threat was removed, you could guarantee that a significant number of people would have a higher number of tins of baked beans in their cupboards than they did before the announcement. I am sure also that this increased number of baked beans would be present for many weeks after the announcement.

In the same way, if patients with polycystic ovaries do not eat regularly, the body begins to believe that they are not going to get any more food and they therefore put on weight.

The symptoms of PCOS are triggered by an imbalance of sex hormones. Women with PCOS may produce higher than normal amounts of the androgen testosterone, and it is this that is responsible for many of the symptoms. The hormone insulin is also a factor. Insulin is produced by the pancreas to regulate the level of glucose in the blood. Women with PCOS – particularly those who are overweight – have been found to have a condition known as insulin resistance, whereby the body has to produce more insulin to compensate. These high levels of insulin affect the ovaries, causing an imbalance of sex hormones.

How Can It Be Treated?

Weight Management

Because the symptoms of PCOS are found to be worst in over-weight women and increase with weight gain, weight loss is always the first recommended treatment. Even moderate obesity is associated with a reduced chance of ovulation.[5] In a study looking at the effect of weight loss on women with anovulatory infertility, in 60 out of 67 subjects, weight loss resulted in spontaneous ovulation with lower than anticipated rates of miscarriage.[6] A low glycaemic index (GI) diet is recommended for weight loss and to balance the blood sugar levels.

Exercise

Exercise is very important in the weight management of patients with polycystic ovaries. By increasing your exercise, you increase your utilisation of carbohydrates, and this will help you to maintain your weight.

It is not difficult to increase your exercise, and indeed one can do it throughout the working day. It is most important that you enjoy your exercise as well as vary it; if necessary, join a gym, speak to a personal trainer or link up with a friend. There is nothing like companionship to help improve one's motivation for exercise.

Set SMART goals (see page 175). Do not be concerned if you do not always reach your targets, but it is important to set them.

THE PARETO PRINCIPLE

In 1906, Vilfredo Pareto, an Italian economist, made an observation that 20% of the population owned 80% of the property in Italy. This was later developed into the 80–20 rule, which can be applied to many different areas of life. Let us look at it in several ways:

20% of your clothes are worn 80% of the time.

20% of your friends are seen 80% of the time.

20% of your carpet is walked on 80% of the time.

When you apply this principle to goals, it is very similar. If you are getting an extension done to your house or are doing up a room, you often realise that you get 80% of it done very quickly. Sadly, the final 20% of any project often takes up to 80% of your time.

Thus, when you are looking at exercise programmes, etc., you must realise that to get to your target, the first 80% may only take 20% of the time, but the final 20% will take 80% of your time. DO NOT get disillusioned by this; remain positive, and even if you only achieve 80% of your target, you are doing extremely well.

Surgical Treatment – Laparoscopic Ovarian Diathermy

See page 282 for information on diathermic laser treatment. This can be useful in patients with anovulation and ovulatory infertility associated with polycystic ovaries.

Prescribed Medication Treatment

Medication can help to treat the symptoms of PCOS, such as reducing the effects of the raised testosterone levels. Ovulation-inducing medication, such as clomifene or gonadotropin therapy, may also be prescribed to help improve fertility. Metformin – a drug that helps insulin resistance – may also have a role.

Complementary and Alternative Medicine (CAM)

Stress can play its part in PCOS, so taking up an activity such as yoga is a good way of asserting your own control over the condition. See Chapter 10 for other ways to reduce stress.

Traditional Chinese medicine, including acupuncture, has long been recommended for the treatment of PCOS and the general rebalancing of the female sex hormones. A recent study carried out found that electro-acupuncture treatments can induce regular ovulation in women with PCOS.[7] See Chapter 13 for more information on the role of CAM.

PREMATURE OVULATION FAILURE (POF)

Premature ovarian failure or a premature menopause occurs when a woman's periods stop before the age of 40. There is often some warning, just as there is at the time of the natural menopause, with periods becoming irregular and more widely spaced. Sometimes, however, periods can just suddenly stop.

What Is It?

The ovaries stop producing oestrogen and so other symptoms of the menopause can occur, including hot flushes and mood swings. The ovaries also stop producing eggs, which is why pregnancy becomes less likely.

What Causes It?

Premature ovulation failure can sometimes run in families; women can have their menopause at a similar age to their mother. Some women have abnormalities of the genes that control ovarian function; others make 'autoantibodies', which prevent the ovaries from working, and a few women can be affected by viral infections of their ovaries. The ovaries can occasionally start working again on their own, although this is the exception rather than the rule. Some women have a long period when the ovaries are slowing down rather than stopping and during which ovulation may occur from time to time.

How Can It Be Treated?

Although women with POF can be prescribed with hormone-replacement therapy (HRT) to protect against osteoporosis and other symptoms, there is as yet no firm evidence that suggests POF can be treated in order to regain fertility. However, it is still possible for women with POF to carry a pregnancy, so egg donation with IVF may be a consideration for couples.

PELVIC INFLAMMATORY DISEASE (PID)

Pelvic inflammatory disease is a general term for a condition that involves infection and inflammation of the upper female genital tract, including the uterus, fallopian tubes and ovaries. Any or all of these parts may be affected. It usually results from an infection in the vagina and the cervix that has passed to the internal reproductive organs.

What Causes It?

The most common infection that causes PID in the UK is chlamydia. When chlamydial infection spreads from the cervix and along the fallopian tubes, it causes inflammation (salpingitis). This causes the lining of the tubes to become red and swollen and makes the already narrow canals even more narrow. Transport is affected. Eggs may not be able to move along the tubes properly; eggs may not reach the sperm, or the embryo may not move to the uterus, causing the development of an ectopic pregnancy. If the infection remains untreated, the inflammation eventually spreads to the whole wall of the tubes causing a build-up of scar tissue.

What Are the Symptoms?

When PID is caused by chlamydial infection, a woman may experience mild symptoms or nothing at all, even though serious damage is being done to her reproductive organs. Because of sometimes vague symptoms, PID can often go unrecognised by women and their healthcare providers until they start trying to conceive.

Women who do have symptoms of PID most commonly experience:

1. lower abdominal pain
2. fever, nausea and vomiting
3. unusual vaginal discharge that may have a foul odour
4. painful intercourse
5. painful urination
6. irregular menstrual bleeding
7. pain around right side of upper abdomen

How Can It Be Treated?

PID can be cured with several types of antibiotics. However, antibiotic treatment does not reverse any damage that has already occurred to the reproductive organs. Any scarring or adhesions caused by the disease may be permanent.

Surgery can help in a few cases. It is my belief that it is often thought that surgery is the answer to everything; surgery has a very important role in the management of pelvic pain, endometriosis, etc., but it is not a total cure. How I often describe it to patients is that if you broke your leg, then putting your leg in plaster would help to mend it, but there is still going to be some scarring where the join is. If you have a big abdominal scar, again, the scar may heal well, but there will still be some scarring.

Prevention is better than cure. It is important that you try to prevent pelvic inflammatory disease. This is done by the following methods:

1. Avoid casual sex.
2. If you do have casual sex, use barrier forms of contraception.
3. If you have any symptoms of infection, including pain or discharge, go to a genitourinary medicine clinic.
4. If you have any concerns, go to a genitourinary medicine clinic or your doctor.
5. If you do have an infection, make sure you are adequately treated and take the tablets for the duration that you are prescribed.
6. Inform any partners if you have contracted chlamydia or other STIs because they will also need to be treated.

ENDOMETRIOSIS

This is a fairly common condition in women of a reproductive age, but because it can often go unrecognised, it's hard to put an estimate against just how many women have it. While it does not directly cause infertility, it can lead to significant problems with ovulation, the movement of the egg along the fallopian tubes and with fertilisation.

What Is It?

Endometriosis is a condition in which the cells lining the inside of the uterus (the endometrium) become established *outside* of the uterus, usually in the pelvic area – the fallopian tubes, ovaries, bladder or bowel – but also sometimes other parts of the body. These implants then behave as though they normally would were they still in the lining of the uterus. So they are stimulated by hormonal changes, build up and bleed monthly. This can lead to inflammation and scarring.

THE GRASS STORY

I often compare endometriosis to grass. The grass growing on your lawn is in the correct place for it to grow. If, however, grass grows on your path, this is the incorrect place. The same is true of endometriosis. The endometrium is growing in your uterus (i.e. the lining of your womb). This is the correct place for it to grow. If the endometrium grows in an incorrect place, then this is endometriosis.

I have a patient who has endometriosis in her nose; therefore every month she actually has a nosebleed. It is difficult to know how this happened, but I believe that on one occasion when she was having a period she had a cut in her nose and may have touched her nose while changing her tampon, causing some of the endometrial tissue to become implanted in her nose.

If you have endometriosis in your abdomen, then you will not only bleed in the form of a period, but you can also bleed into your abdomen. Because there is nowhere for the broken down cells to escape to, however, this can then cause scar tissue, irritation, pain in the pelvic area or adhesions. Scarring within the fallopian tubes can prevent the transportation of the egg after ovulation.

The pain of endometriosis can also be due to the fact that it sticks the ovaries down. During intercourse, the ovaries should move away and not get hit. However, with endometriosis, the ovaries do not move away. The ovaries have the same nerve supply as the testicles, and thus when the ovaries are unable to move away, it can cause significant pain.

What Causes It?

No one is quite sure what causes endometriosis, and there are a number of possible theories. One is that during menstruation some of the menstrual tissue backs up through the fallopian tubes and implants in the abdomen (retrograde menstruation); a second theory is that the endometrial tissue is spread to other parts of the body through the lymph or blood system; and a third theory suggests that the condition is caused by remnants of endometrial cells remaining from the earliest stages of development *before* birth, which then only begin to grow around the time of puberty. It is also possible that some women are genetically predisposed to develop the condition as it appears to run in families. The condition is also linked to the immune system and seems to trigger more severe symptoms during times of illness and stress.

SHOULD YOU USE TAMPONS?

There are conflicting stories regarding whether the use of tampons may increase the likelihood of having endometriosis.

A study conducted with over 2,000 women concluded that women who use tampons during menstruation appear to have a lower rate of endometriosis than women who do not. It's thought that the tampons works to suck the debris out, rather than push the fluid back up as previously thought.[8] However, other schools of thought still believe that tampon use does encourage retrograde flow. Furthermore, up until the mid-1980s the chemical dioxin was commonly used in

---

tampons as a bleaching agent and was believed to cause endometriosis; however, manufacturers no longer use this particular chemical.

Where possible, it is better to use unbleached 100% cotton tampons. If you can, vary this with sanitary towels to allow for a freer flow.

What Are the Symptoms?

Symptoms may vary from hardly any whatsoever to severe pain, and these will again vary throughout the month.

Ten Symptoms of Endometriosis

1. Pain before and during periods
2. Pain during sex
3. Irregular vaginal bleeding
4. Fatigue and low energy levels
5. Painful urination during periods
6. Blood in your bowel movements (you must see your doctor about this)
7. Swelling of the abdomen
8. Painful bowel movements during periods or pain with defecation
9. Diarrhoea, constipation or nausea
10. Generalised lower abdominal pain

How Can It Be Treated?

Surgical Treatment

Remember, this a chronic condition. Treatment depends on the symptoms. Treatment may not improve fertility as damage may have already been done. Or, indeed, no treatment may actually be needed.

It always amazes me that some women can have extensive endometriosis without any problems with fertility or pelvic pain, while other individuals can have very mild endometriosis causing great pain as well as infertility. With regard to pain, I compare it to spots. It is not unknown that you could have an extensive degree of spots on your back and not realise it until you look in the mirror. On another occasion, you could have one tiny little spot on your face that is extremely painful.

You will only be diagnosed with endometriosis once you have been referred for a laparoscopy although a scan may help the diagnosis. It may be that some of the lesions or cysts can be removed surgically at this stage. Sometimes further laser surgery is necessary, depending on the location and severity of the implants, in which the cysts are burnt off. This technique is found to produce better long-term results with fewer recurrent bouts of the condition. If you are considering surgery, it's important to get a good diagnosis and discuss with your specialist the best course of action. As we already know – and as some studies on endometriosis suggest – surgery itself can result in adhesions that may compromise your fertility.[9] If the damage has been done to your tubes and around your ovaries and scarring occurs, surgery will not necessarily improve your chances.

Prescribed Medication Treatment

Endometriosis can also be treated with prescribed medication that work to control the hormones that are stimulating the symptoms. This works a little like the contraceptive pill by stopping ovulation temporarily in order that the growths may shrink.

The main drugs used are danazol, progestogens and synarel. Danazol is a synthetic male hormone that works to stop ovulation, therefore stopping the endometrium from developing. However, the drug can produce serious side effects, including increased blood lipid levels, weight gain, muscle cramps and an increase in male characteristics and therefore it is not used now as much as it was in the past. Danazol offers only a temporary solution: when treatment stops, the symptoms of endometriosis gradually return. Studies show that one year after the end of danazol treatment, 75% of women reported a return of mild symptoms.[10]

Progestogens can help dampen down the endometrium and prevent it from growing – sometimes they can be given in the form of the oral contraceptive pill. Side effects include bloating and premenstrual symptoms.

Gonadotropin-releasing hormone (GnRH) is now regularly used for the treatment of endometriosis. This is taken as a nasal spray or an injection and works to gradually decrease the amount of oestrogen and progesterone produced, effectively suspending ovulation. The treatment usually lasts for six months, after which normal menstruation returns. During this temporary menopause, the endometrium shrinks. Again, there may be side effects that mimic the symptoms of menopause. Because this is a new drug, the jury is still out on its long-term benefits.

Your doctor may also prescribe painkillers such as ibuprofen to deal with the symptoms of pain and inflammation. Any treatment should first be discussed carefully with your GP or specialist, as suspending ovulation may not feel to you to be the ideal solution at this stage.

Complementary and Alternative Medicine

Homeopathy can be used to treat endometriosis at its early stages, reducing the pain associated with it and helping to balance out the sex hormones. As ever, a homeopath will need to take a detailed history from you before prescribing a remedy, as each person will require a different treatment depending on their individual needs.

Scientific research is increasingly showing just how effective traditional Chinese medicine can be in the treatment of conditions affecting the female reproductive system, including endometriosis. TCM convention emphasises the importance of a healthy and balanced blood flow in women for good reproductive health.

Acupuncture has been widely acknowledged in the medical community for its benefits in treating endometriosis by promoting the body's healing responses, stimulating the flow of energy through the body and helping to restore balance.[11] This improved uterine blood flow also has important implications for women who receiving embryo implant treatment.

Clinical evidence has shown that herbal medicine has a significant regulatory effect on the blood circulatory, immune and endocrine systems. One study gave 76 patients, all with endometriosis, a herbal prescription to help remove blood stasis and break down and eliminate the endometrial tissue. The study reported an overall success rate of 80% – 3 out of the 22 women who had previously been diagnosed as infertile became pregnant, and there were significant reductions in nodule size.[12] Herbal remedies should be taken only after consultation with a qualified herbalist. Herbs that are found to balance the hormones, for example chaste tree (*Vitex agnus castus*) may be useful. Yarrow (*Achillea millefolium*) and ginkgo may help improve circulation, while calendula and wild yam (*Dioscorea villosa*) can reduce the inflammation.

Diet

Your diet can also play an important role in managing the condition. A recent study published in the journal *Human Reproduction* found that women who ate beef or other red meat once a day or more were 100% more likely to have endometriosis than women who ate red meat three times a week or less.[13] It also found that women who ate green vegetables twice a day were 70% less likely to have endometriosis than those who ate green vegetables less than six times per week; while women who ate fresh fruit at least twice a day were 40% less likely to have endometriosis than those who ate fruit and vegetables less than once a day.

Look at Chapter 9 to check that you're getting the right amount of good food and limiting the amount of bad. Reduce or eliminate your caffeine, sugar and alcohol intake and try to include foods containing natural phytoestrogens such as pulses, oats, cherries and broccoli. These can help to protect against raised oestrogen levels by balancing the hormones produced.

Chapter 21

So What Could Be Wrong?
Fertility Problems Affecting Men

It is not always possible to get a clear diagnosis of the cause of male infertility, which can be very frustrating both for your partner and you. As your doctor will point out, male factor infertility can often be as a result of a combination of factors, or there may be no apparent cause at all. The good news is that much can be done to tackle the conditions affecting male fertility – which in many cases involve only some of the simple changes we saw in Part 2.

However, the various tests we looked at in Chapter 18 will be looking for one or more of the following main causes of fertility problems in men:

- obstructions (blockages in sperm-carrying tubes)
- testicular disease and injury
- undescended testes
- varicoceles
- sperm disorders
- genetic disorders
- problems with erection and ejaculation
- hormonal problems
- medications that reduce fertility
- environmental toxins and radiation

OBSTRUCTIONS

Just as blockages in the female reproductive tract can lead to fertility problems, so they can in males. A blockage in the sperm-carrying tubes (the vas deferens) may be caused by a number of factors including:

- groin surgery (including hernia repair and fixation of undescended testes)
- trauma (even a fairly minor sporting injury) to the scrotum sac covering the testicles
- inflammation caused by infection (particularly chlamydia and tuberculosis)
- previous vasectomy
- the congenital bilateral absence of the vas deferens (CBVAD)

TESTICULAR DISEASE AND INJURY

A blow to the testes can cause swelling or bleeding in or around them. This can cause the blood supply to the testicles to fail, resulting in permanent damage to the sperm-production mechanism. Torsion of the testicles (twisting of a testicle on its cord) can have a similar effect if it is not treated with surgery.

Viral infections can cause inflammation of the testicles (orchitis, which usually appears as painful swelling of the testicles) and failure to produce sperm. Mumps is the best-known cause; however, it will only affect fertility if it causes orchitis and, even then, only rarely. Other glandular diseases such as thyroid disease or diabetes mellitus can also interfere with the stimulation of the sex hormones and therefore the production of sperm.

UNDESCENDED TESTES

Undescended testes (cryptorchidism) are another common cause of failure of sperm production. It is thought that environmental factors play an important role in causing this. Male infants and children are routinely examined to identify this problem, as future fertility can often be preserved if surgical treatment to fix the testes is performed in early childhood. Men who have one normal testis are more likely to be fertile.

VARICOCELES

Varicoceles are enlarged veins around the testes – similar to varicose veins. Suspending each testis from the abdomen is a spermatic cord. This is made up of arteries, veins, nerves and the tubes that transport sperm from the testes to the penis. When these veins become slack, like any other varicose vein, they become bigger and dilated. The role of this condition in causing infertility is uncertain and controversial.

Varicoceles occur in approximately 10–20% of the male population and account for 30–40% of men with fertility problems.[1] Many men will go through life not knowing they have varicoceles because they often cause no symptoms at all. When they do, the sensation felt is often described as feeling like 'a bag of worms'. They can occur on either or both sides but are far more common on the left because of the way the blood vessels are organised.

It is thought that the varicocele either heats up the testes or impairs their blood supply, which damages sperm production. The coexistence of other risk factors, such as smoking, with varicoceles seems to have a greater effect on the risk of infertility.

Varicoceles can be removed by a surgical procedure called ligation, and some studies show that this can improve the chances of successful conception as well as improving sperm density and motility.[2]

Varicoceles – the Key Points

- Although very common, not all varicoceles require treatment, but do get them checked out.

- Varicoceles are thought to cause sperm defects by raising the temperature in the testes or impairing the blood supply.
- Varicoceles may cause progressive injury to the lining of the seminiferous tubules, but repair can halt this process.
- Varicoceles repair can relieve pain and improve testicular function and semen quality.

SPERM DISORDERS

Disorders of sperm numbers, movement and shape are common in men with infertility. Prolonged abstinence from ejaculation can affect sperm motility. As we saw in Chapter 18, semen analysis can help identify structural and biochemical abnormalities within the individual sperm.

GENETIC DISORDERS

Problems with chromosomes occur in about 2–20% of infertile men and can affect their fertility in two ways:

1. Chromosomal disorders can affect the development of the testes. These are usually disorders of the sex chromosomes, by far the most common being Klinefelter's syndrome (see below).
2. Chromosomal abnormalities such as the carriage of the cystic fibrosis gene, can disrupt cell division and sperm production.

Congenital Bilateral Absence of the Vas Deferens (CBVAD)

CBAVD is a syndrome in which a portion or all of the reproductive ducts (including the epididymis, vas deferens and seminal vesicle) are missing. This causes an obstruction, and while sperm may be produced normally within the testicle, they are in essence 'trapped'.

CBAVD is associated with several diseases including cystic fibrosis (CF) and renal malformation. 65% of men with CBAVD will have a detectable mutation in one of the cystic fibrosis genes, and 15% will have a missing or misplaced kidney. This does not mean that the man has or will develop CF, but it means that he could be a carrier of the gene. If his partner is also a carrier, then there is a 25% chance of a child born to them having CF. It is imperative that all men with CBAVD and/or their partner have genetic screening for CF gene mutations prior to undergoing in vitro fertilisation or ICSI.

Sperm can be successfully harvested from these men for use in assisted conception treatments, mainly ICSI.

Young's Syndrome

This genetic disorder affects the minute hairs, called cilia, that are found along the tubes and ducts of the body. This syndrome results in an inability to produce sperm along with chronic respiratory problems in men.

Klinefelter's Syndrome

Klinefelter's is caused by an abnormal number of sex chromosomes in males. Instead of the normal male XY pattern of 46 chromosomes (46XY), an extra X chromosome is present resulting in XXY (47XXY).

People who have Klinefelter's syndrome tend to have a distinctive physical appearance, although in childhood it may go unnoticed as it is often not until puberty that these features develop. They include:

- a tall thin figure, with long arms
- body shape that looks more female than male, with wide hips and a narrow waist

- breast enlargement at puberty (known as gynaecomastia) while the testes remain small
- little or no facial hair

Because the testes are undeveloped, men with this syndrome either have no sperm or very low sperm counts.

PROBLEMS WITH ERECTION AND EJACULATION

Problems with sex are the principal cause of infertility in about 5% of couples. This can be due to:

- impotence: this is the inability to attain or maintain an erection adequate for intercourse. Impotence can be caused by a number of physical conditions, including diabetes and diseases of the nervous system, which can be treated with hormone treatment or vibratory massage. However, in many cases, the underlying cause is psychological and the stress that can accompany the desire for a baby can often, ironically, exacerbate matters. Fortunately, counselling can be a great help in treating this.
- retrograde ejaculation: this happens when semen, instead of being pumped through the penis, is pushed into the bladder. This may be caused by injury, previous surgery or diabetes. If prescribed medication is unable to help, sperm may still be collected for use in intrauterine insemination (see Chapter 24).
- absence of the vas deferens (see page 260)
- obstruction (see page 258)

HORMONAL PROBLEMS

Testosterone deficiency can reduce fertility and may be caused by problems with testicular testosterone production, the pituitary gland or the hypothalamus, which control testosterone production. This is termed hypogonadotropic hypogonadism and is accompanied by a lack of follicle-stimulating hormone (FSH) and luteinising hormone (LH). Overproduction of prolactin (hyper-prolactinaemia), a hormone produced by the pituitary gland, may also reduce fertility.

Hormonal imbalances may also be due to medical conditions, including liver disease, kidney failure, thyroid disease and diabetes. Diet, exercise and stress will also impact on the balance of hormones.

Just as the menopause is caused by a change in women's sex hormones so, after the age of about 40, men will start to produce less testosterone; this has been labelled the andropause. However, unlike women, most men can continue to father children right up into old age.

Chapter 22

Fertility Treatment – Taking the Next Step

Making the decision to have treatment is an important step in your journey, whether it's medical treatment on the advice of your doctor or specialist or complementary and alternative treatment or perhaps a mixture of both. I encourage the integrated approach.

If you are moving on to getting treatment, then it's likely that you've come to your decision after a number of tests and having spent some time, with your partner, weighing up your options. While you're doing this, it's important to keep in mind the many different factors that will come into play. From the journey to the clinic or hospital, or wherever it is you will need to go, to the amount of time you think you may need to take off from your normal day-to-day responsibilities. You also need to consider how you feel you will be able to cope at an emotional level, too. Everyone is different, so take the time to figure out your own limitations.

THE TEAM APPROACH

The Ten Rules of the Team Approach

1. Discuss at the start who you consider to be important members of the team. This should not only include medical

practitioners but also family, friends, complementary practitioners, etc. There may also be somebody at your work-
place whom you want to inform and who will therefore
become a member of the team.

2. Take time to choose your team members.
3. Get role clarity of the team member.
4. Get role acceptance of the team member.
5. Only once you have got clarity and acceptance can you be
   worried about performance.
6. Feel comfortable with your team member.
7. Review your team every so often.
8. Do not rush to change the team without good reason.
9. Make sure there are good lines of communication with all
   team members.
10. Talk to your team members about any concerns.

This stage can be very exciting – if a little nerve-racking – and
now is definitely the time to keep focused on your goals, stay
positive, and support and encourage each other as a team. There
are others in your team, too – perhaps your GP, your specialist,
the nurse who takes your blood test, your acupuncturist, your
closest friend and anyone else who is helping, informing and
supporting you along the way. Keep the lines of communication
open so that your whole team knows what role it is they need to
play and that they are doing it effectively. If you feel unhappy at
any time about how things are going, you need to let people
know.

It may be that you will have a number of different kinds of
treatments over an extended period of time. That isn't always
easy, and you may feel tired and fed up at points. By reassessing
your goals at frequent intervals and talking things through with
your team, you will be in a better position to make decisions
about your next step. Some couples start along a particular route
of treatment but find it's not quite right for them – whether for
medical, emotional, ethical, financial or practical reasons (think

back to the Dooley equation). Deciding not to proceed with a treatment or to take some time off for a while is just as important as deciding to continue with it. Go at a pace that you feel comfortable with, and keep listening to your own voice.

THE ENGAGEMENT STORY

Sometimes you have got to make a decision in order to realise whether it right or wrong for you. For many, many years, I have never quite understood why individuals got engaged to be married. I now understand the reason why. Courting is rather fun, and there is limited commitment. By being engaged to a particular partner, it suddenly becomes more serious. You start talking about the wedding, where you are going to live, and you start meeting the in-laws. This, therefore, begins to focus the mind, and if you realise now at this stage, having focused the mind, that you are making the wrong decision, you can always pull out.

That is why I think it is important at some stage to engage with a decision, to make a plan and see if you feel comfortable with it. Sometimes it is difficult to make decisions, but not making a decision at all is, in my opinion, the worst thing you can do. Make a decision, try living with it, and see how you feel.

Stick to the guidelines for fertility fitness given in Part 2, keep weighing up your options, and as you embark on this new stage, stay positive!

Chapter 23

Female Treatment Options

THE FIRST OPTION

If you have seen your GP and perhaps also a fertility specialist and the tests have uncovered no obvious reason as to why you haven't been able to conceive, the first option is to do nothing. By nothing I certainly don't mean give up, but rather to keep on having regular unprotected intercourse and simply see what happens. This is sometimes the advice that I give to couples who have no apparent fertility problem. At the same time, I will always arrange a follow-up appointment in a few months' time to see how they're doing. It is also important to continue with the Fit for Fertility Programme.

Often the process of going to see your GP and having some initial tests can be all the reassurance that is needed, and some women find they fall pregnant not long after. It can take healthy couples over a year to conceive so, unless age is a factor, try not to let this become an obsession; let your body relax a bit and see what happens.

If, after having some tests, the results show that there may be some underlying medical conditions that are compromising your fertility, you may want to work out a plan of how to go about doing *your* bit to improve your overall health. This needn't be anything elaborate, but goes back to the idea of 'controlling the controllables' and having goals and mini goals to aim for.

If you feel the time is right and you have decided to explore medical intervention as well as incorporate the Fit for Fertility Programme, there are a number of options open to you, depending on the results of your diagnostic tests.

OVULATION INDUCTION (OI)

If tests have shown that you are not ovulating or you have irregular, infrequent periods or polycystic ovarian syndrome but your fallopian tubes and your partner's sperm are normal, ovulation induction, also called ovarian stimulation, is likely to be the next step.

Simply put, ovulation induction is a drug treatment that works to stimulate ovulation, correct any hormone imbalance and ensure the release of an egg. Anovulatory infertility affects about one-fifth of patients attending an infertility clinic, with approximately 80% caused by PCOS.[1] Once the cause of anovulation has been corrected, good rates of conception can generally be achieved.

Therapies to induce ovulation begin, in most cases, with the anti-oestrogen medication clomifene citrate. If this fails to result in ovulation, the next options tend to be gonadotropin therapy or laparoscopic ovarian diathermy.

Clomifene Citrate

Clomifene citrate, an oral prescription medication, is the most commonly used drug for ovulation induction. Clomifene citrate is used to stimulate FSH, correct irregular ovulation, help increase egg production and correct luteal-phase deficiency. Brand names for this drug include Clomid and Serophene.

How Does Clomifene Work?

Clomifene acts by blocking the ability of cells in the hypothalamus to detect the amount of oestrogen present in the blood. When the hypothalamus senses a deficiency of oestrogen, it responds by releasing more GnRH (gonadotropin-releasing hormone). This in turn prompts the pituitary gland to release high amounts of follicle-stimulating hormone (FSH). The function of FSH is to initiate the growth of the ovarian follicles, which contain the eggs and produce oestrogen. As soon as oestrogen levels rise sufficiently, either in response to clomifene or in natural cycles, there should be a rapid release of luteinising hormone (LH) from the pituitary gland. It is LH that triggers the ovulation process and maturation of the eggs.

How Is Clomifene Taken?

Clomifene is administered for five days during the early menstrual cycle. Some doctors prescribe the drug from days 5–9 of the cycle, while others recommend that the drug be taken from cycle days 2–6 because they believe that the earlier clomifene is administered, the more likely it is to promote the development of the optimal number of follicles. The starting dose is 50mg; this may be increased if there is no response after three cycles.

All women who are prescribed clomifene should be carefully monitored with utltrasound because of the risk of ovarian hyperstimulation (see page 270) and multiple pregnancy. So although some GPs will prescribe the drug, it is on the whole better to be monitored by a fertility clinic.

What Are the Side Effects?

Some women may suffer from one or more of the following:

- headaches
- nausea and vomiting
- hot flushes

- weight gain and bloating
- irritability
- lighter or heavier periods than usual
- breast tenderness
- visual disturbances
- ovarian hyperstimulation syndrome
- abdominal discomfort
- depression
- insomnia
- mid-cycle spotting
- rashes
- dizziness
- hair loss

The side effects are temporary and subside once clomifene is stopped. In some cases, ovarian cysts may develop and remain for four to six weeks following discontinuation of clomifene. These cysts are usually harmless. Very rarely, a large number of cysts will develop in association with very high levels of oestrogen, resulting in accumulation of free fluid in the abdominal area and symptoms such as vomiting, diarrhoea and abdominal distention. This is referred to as Ovarian Hyperstimulation Syndrome (OHSS) and is very rare in association with clomifene.

In the UK, clomifene is only licensed for use for a period of six months, and depending on your doctor or clinic, you may be advised to have a month's break after three months of taking the drug. This is because there have been links reported between the prolonged (that is more than 12 months) use of clomifene and ovarian cancer.[2]

There may be a slight increase in the risk of miscarriage in women who have taken clomifene. This may be due to the fact that women who require the drug for ovulation often have PCOS and this in its own right is associated with a higher risk of miscarriage.[3] There is also a higher multiple birth rate in women who conceive following clomifene citrate therapy (5–10%) than in the rest of the population.

What Are the Success Rates?

Clomifene citrate has been shown to induce ovulation in roughly 80% of women who have trouble ovulating on their own. About half of these women achieve pregnancy during treatment.[4]

Clomifene is generally less effective in older women and in women with a high body mass index (BMI).

CASE STUDY

Mrs A is a 29-year-old shop assistant who is slightly over-weight, with a body mass index of $29kgm^2$. Mr A is a 32-year-old Post Office worker. They have been trying to conceive for a year and are referred to the fertility clinic because Mrs A has irregular periods. Mrs A has a period ranging from every 60–100 days, and she has also noticed a slight increase in spots and hair growth on her face. Her periods are not painful. Neither of them has had children in the past. Otherwise they are well and show no other significant history.

The following preliminary investigations were carried out:

1. *Semen analysis; this was normal.*
2. *Blood tests to look at the hormones, particularly Mrs A's hormones; this demonstrated that she had a slightly raised testosterone level but that the other hormones were normal including normal thyroid function and normal prolactin.*
3. *A transvaginal scan was performed, which demonstrated mild polycystic ovaries.*

There was no history of infection or other abdominal surgery and so it was felt unnecessary to rush into any form of tubal assessment.

During the consultation, it was agreed that we needed to give Mrs A some ovulation-induction medication, and it was decided to use clomifene. In order to explain this, I put the information in a letter to the couple.

Mr and Mrs A
Beech Cottage
104 Woodland Road
Other Place
Anywhere

22 April 2004

Dear Mr and Mrs A,

*It was nice seeing you in the clinic today. I wish to confirm
that you have been trying for just over one year, and from
you history, examination and tests it appears that Mrs A
has polycystic ovaries and is therefore not ovulating
(releasing an egg).*

*In order to help Mrs A ovulate, we agreed that she
would go on drugs. I have discussed with you the risks of
this treatment and this includes the following:*

1. *There may be a slight increased risk of miscarriage.*
2. *There is a slight increased risk of multiple pregnancy.*
3. *There is no guarantee that this will work.*

The side effects that can occur include the following:

1. *You may get visual upsets (problems with your
   eyesight); if this does occur, please stop the
   treatment.*
2. *There is a very small risk of a condition called ovarian
   hyperstimulation, where your ovaries grow large cysts,
   but we will be closely monitoring you by scan.*
3. *You may get hot flushes or abdominal discomfort.*
4. *You may experience occasional nausea and vomiting.*
5. *Some people get mild depression.*
6. *Breast tenderness and headaches.*

7. Occasionally, people find that they get weight gain, have dizzy spells and hair loss.

If you have any concerns about this, please do not hesitate to contact me through my fertility nurse.

We also indicated that there is a very small increased risk of cancer of the ovary if we use this therapy for over six months, but, in your case, I have no doubt that the benefits of a pregnancy are far greater than the risks, and one has also got to remember that a pregnancy would help reduce any increased risk of cancer of the ovary.

We have agreed to do as follows:

1. Mrs A, I would advise you to try to lose some weight because this can have a very beneficial effect on fertility, as we discussed.
2. As you have now not had a period for eight weeks, we have done a pregnancy test, which was negative.
3. I have given you dydrogesterone tablets (10mg to take daily for the next ten days), this is in order to bring on a period. If whilst taking them you have a period, stop taking the tablets and count this as day 1 of your cycle. If you complete the course of the dydrogesterone, you will probably have a period; then I would like you to count the first day you need to use sanitary protection as day 1.
4. On day 1, I would like you to contact the fertility unit and start taking clomifene citrate; 50mg from days 2–6 inclusive (five days).
5. We will then organise for you to have a scan in order to monitor the follicle growth. The purpose of the scan is to make sure that the clomifene is working but also to make sure that we are not getting too many follicles, i.e. increasing the risk of multiple pregnancies (10%). If I find that you are getting too many follicles, then I would advise you to avoid a pregnancy during that cycle.

6. We will organise for you to be scanned using the vaginal probe starting on day 9 of your cycle, then once we have demonstrated that you have ovulated, we will arrange for you to have a blood test for progesterone seven days after ovulation. This will help us to confirm that you have ovulated.

We will obviously encourage you to have intercourse around the time of ovulation.

   If you do have a period after you have ovulated and the blood tests and scans show you have ovulated, then I would like you to continue on the same dose. If you do not have a period, then obviously we will need to do a pregnancy test and we may need to increase the dose of the clomifene, but we will only do this once we have had the results of the test.

   Once we have got the correct dose for you, then I would like you to continue with the clomifene for four months, and I would like you to liaise on a regular basis with our nurse. If after four months you have not conceived, then we need to meet again and discuss whether we need to do some form of tubal assessment.

   I do hope that the above is self-explanatory, and do keep in touch.

All best wishes

Yours sincerely

Mr Michael Dooley
Consultant Obstetrician and Gynaecologist

Cc GP

Gonadotropin Therapy

Gonadotropin stimulation is the next step in treatment for women who are anovulatory and who are clomifene-resistant. (This means the failure to ovulate after clomifene.) It uses injections of hormones to stimulate ovulation. There are two different hormones in common use.

Human Chorionic Gonadotropin (hCG)

If the clomifene by itself has not worked, your doctor may suggest that you have an injection of hCG to help with the final stage of the follicle and the release of the egg. You will be monitored carefully while having the clomifene, and just prior to ovulation, you will have an injection of human chorionic gonadotropin. There are two sorts, one is a preparation of the glycoprotein faction secreted by the placenta and obtained from the urine of pregnant women. There is also one which is slightly purer called Alpha Choriogonadotropin. Intercourse will then need to take place 24–36 hours after the injection to coincide with the egg's release.

Human Menopausal Gonadotropin (hMG)

hMG is a mixture of two hormones: luteinising hormone (LH) and follicle-stimulating hormone (FSH). It directly stimulates the ovaries to produce and mature eggs. Some medication now contains purified FSH, which causes fewer side effects. These medications can be given in conjunction with human chorionic gonadotropin (hCG), which triggers the release of the mature eggs.

How is hMG taken?

A course of injections prompts your ovaries to start developing and maturing egg follicles. After 7–12 days of these injections, an injection of human chorionic gonadotropin (hCG) is given, which tells your ovaries to release the egg or eggs they have developed. Your doctor might show you or your partner how to give the injections so you don't have to journey to the GP's surgery or clinic every day.

During this time, your doctor will monitor you to see when you're likely to ovulate. When the ultrasound indicates that your eggs are mature, an injection of hCG is given to trigger ovulation. Ovulation usually occurs 24–36 hours after the hCG injection. You're either sent home to have sex afterwards or an intrauterine insemination is scheduled for a day later.

Most women go through a maximum of three to six drug cycles. Success rates don't improve if you take the medication for any longer, so if you try three or more times and don't get pregnant, your doctor may increase the dose or suggest another kind of treatment.

Source of Gonadotropins

Gonadotropins are available either from urinary-derived human menopausal gonadotropin (i.e. they are obtained from post-menopausal women and the preparation is purified from urine) or from pure FSH.

More recently, recombinantly derived FSH, hCG and LH are synthesised by transecting the human gonadotropin genes in Chinese hamster ovarian cell lines. They are now widely available for therapeutic use.[5]

What Are the Side Effects?

The possible side effects are the same as those that some women experience with clomifene (see page 269).

What Are the Success Rates?

About 80% of women will ovulate using them. If this is the only cause of infertility then the chance of a pregnancy if under 35 is up to 80% in a year.

Other Gonadotropin Therapies

Gonadotropin-releasing Hormone (GnRH)

GnRH is released from the hypothalmus in small amounts at intervals of about 90 minutes, a little like a pulse. This in turn stimulates the pituitary gland to release FSH and LH. A lack of GnRH consequently means these two important sex hormones aren't being released. GnRH deficiency may be caused by being underweight, a systemic illness or by excess exercise. And it's important that the underlying cause is addressed, particularly as pregnancy will call for good health.

GnRH treatment needs to mimic the body's natural production, which means an automatic pump must be worn 24 hours a day. Every 90 minutes, the pump releases the GnRH into the bloodstream.

What Are the Side Effects?

Side effects may include nausea and headaches. This treatment is rarely used now because much simpler treatments are available.

What Are the Success Rates?

Many women, understandably, may feel unhappy using this sort of equipment. However, this treatment does limit the chances of ovarian hyperstimulation and multiple pregnancy and shows good results, with 80% of selected patients conceiving within six months.[6]

Gonadotropin-releasing Hormone (GnRH) Agonist

This is more commonly used in IVF treatment, in what is called superovulation – we'll be coming to that shortly. Rather than releasing an amount of GnRH every 90 minutes, this hormone is prescribed as an injection or nasal spray and gives a constant dose. This 'overdose' saturates the hormone receptors so that the pituitary gland stops producing LH and FSH. This causes oestrogen levels to drop. This stops the follicles from releasing the egg until it's more mature – and so more 'ready' for fertilisation.

GnRH analogues are also often used to treat endometriosis and uterine fibroids.

Other Drug Treatments

Bromocriptine

This drug is prescribed if a woman is secreting too much prolactin. The name of this condition is hyperprolactaemia. Raised levels of prolactin happen naturally during pregnancy and while a woman is breastfeeding – it is the hormone that stimulates breast milk. It also stops ovulation because it inhibits the release of FSH and LH. Hyperprolactaemia can be caused by stress and, surprisingly, running. One research study compared the levels of prolactin in runners and swimmers. The prolactin was much higher in the runners due to the fact that their breasts were moving up and down as they ran. A good reason to wear a support bra while jogging!

Too much prolactin can also be related to problems in the pituitary gland such as small benign tumours, so it's important to get this checked out. Medication taken to treat depression and certain blood pressure medication can also lead to excess prolactin.

The most common symptoms experienced by women with this particular hormone imbalance are lack of periods, vaginal dryness, reduced libido, pain during intercourse, visual field defects and milk coming from the breasts. However, the last two symptoms are far less common than the others.

The drug bromocriptine inhibits the release of prolactin allowing the other hormones to return to the normal levels required for ovulation and regular menstruation.

What Are the Side Effects?

Some women experience rather unpleasant side effects from the drug including nausea, vomiting, low blood pressure, dizziness and headaches and occasionally spasms of the fingers and toes. In very rare cases, if high doses are prescribed, women can become confused and have problems with their lungs, but this is only in high doses. Long-term side effects include Raynaud's disease, constipation and, very rarely, psychiatric changes. Carbergoline is a more recent drug that works in much the same way as bromocriptine but has fewer side effects.

CASE STUDY

Martin is a 34-year-old farmer who has had two children by a previous relationship. Linda is a 28-year-old shop assistant who has never had any children. They have been trying to conceive for a year. The main problem apparent from the history is that Linda has not had a period for six months. She is not overweight, and she is on no medication, but she is complaining of milk coming from her breasts. A general examination of both Martin and Linda proved normal, and it was decided to do certain investigations. These investigations included the following:

1. semen analysis on Martin, which was normal
2. a thyroid function test on Linda, which was normal
3. a prolactin level on Linda, which was raised
4. other endocrinology tests on Linda, which were normal

The prolactin level was raised to level of 3,500mu/l. The test was repeated, and the next level was found to be 3,650mu/l.

Armed with these results, the findings were clearly described to Martin and Linda, and we arranged for Linda to have a MRI scan of her pituitary gland. The reason for this is that we needed to make sure that there was no significant *tumour in the pituitary or the hypothalamus. This was duly performed and a small micro adenoma of the pituitary measuring 4mm in diameter was noted in the right lobe of the pituitary.*

The results were carefully discussed with Martin and Linda, and it was explained that she did have a small benign growth in her pituitary. We discussed different forms of treatment, and it was decided to put Linda on bromocriptine. Bromocriptine is used for the treatment of milk coming from the breasts and breast pain as well as the treatment of tumours in the pituitary.

In Linda's case, I started her off on 1.25mg daily at night. I measured the prolactin four weeks later, and it had only gone down to 1500mu/l; therefore I increased the dosage gradually to 2.5mg three times a day. I advised Linda to start her treatment at night for the first three days and take the tablets in the middle of a mouthful of food.

Following the reduction of prolactin, I am delighted to say that Linda's periods returned to normal, and I reviewed her in the clinic three months later. I tested her progesterone in the luteal phase, and this confirmed that she was ovulating. I therefore encouraged her to continue to try to conceive naturally for the next six months.

I am glad to say that, after five months of trying, they conceived and went on to have a normal, healthy baby boy.

Metformin

A relatively new method of inducing ovulation in women with polycystic ovarian syndrome is to use an oral medication called metformin.

Metformin has been used in the past as an oral agent to help control diabetes by reducing insulin levels. Recently, it has been found to facilitate ovulation in *some* women with PCOS. Some women who do not ovulate after taking metformin will be able to ovulate when taking metformin in combination with clomifene. This drug is not an ovulation-induction agent but rather it normalises the hormones, encouraging regular periods.

CASE STUDY

When Tim and Susie, both 32 year-old teachers, came to see me, they had both been extensively investigated and Susie had been found to have polycystic ovaries. Her periods were very irregular, occurring about four times a year. Susie was very overweight, with a body mass index of 34kg per m^2 and when I talked to her, I established that her over-eating was related to comfort eating due to stress at work. Susie started a weight loss and stress reduction, which had a very positive influence. Over 12 months she lost 10kg, which brought her body mass index down to 30. During this time, it was interesting that her periods did begin to occur more frequently and occasionally she actually had a 28-day cycle but at other times she still went 8–14 weeks without a period.

Susie was very positive about the lifestyle programme and understood the fact that this in its own right was treatment. However, six weeks after stabilising at a body mass index of 29 it was felt that we needed to add another element of treatment, so I prescribed metformin. Unfortunately, Susie did develop significant side effects including bloatedness, some nausea, flatulence and diarrhoea, however as we took things very slowly in increasing the dose, these side effects were minimised and eventually she was well able to tolerate the drug. After six months of treatment, Susie's periods became regular with a cycle range of between 28–35 days and after nine months of treatment with metformin, Susie did conceive. Very sadly, after nine weeks, she had a miscarriage. Following a time for recovery, she has lost more weight, is back on the metformin and is having regular periods and awaiting, hopefully, a successful outcome.

Using metformin benefits some women with PCOS who would rather not run the risk of ovarian hyperstimulation and multiple pregnancy. It also avoids the inconvenient daily injections and trips to the clinic for monitoring that comes with taking gonadotropins.

What Are the Side Effects?
Side effects include bloatedness, nausea and diarrhoea.

Laparoscopic Ovarian Diathermy (LOD)

If after trying the drug treatment described above and keeping your weight within a healthy range, you are still not ovulating regularly, your doctor may suggest ovarian diathermy.

Also, somewhat off-puttingly, known as 'ovarian drilling', this is a surgical treatment that can trigger ovulation. The laparoscopy is usually carried out with a short general anaesthetic, and you will be in and out of the hospital within the same day.

A small incision is made in the abdomen just below the belly button. A laparoscope (like a small telescope) is then inserted into the abdomen so that the surgeon can look at the internal organs. The ovaries are identified, and several small holes are made in each ovary, either with a fine hot diathermy probe or via laser. It is not entirely clear how this works, but it can restore ovulation or make the ovary more sensitive to clomifene.

After the surgery, make sure you have someone to take you home and be with you. You should recover very quickly and be back to you normal activities within a few days to a week.

What Are the Side Effects?
As with any kind of surgery, there is a small risk of infection. You may experience some cramp-like feelings in the abdomen after the surgery. This is due to the small amount of carbon dioxide gas that is used to inflate the abdomen during the surgery. You might also feel a little groggy after the anaesthetic.

The main concern to bear in mind when considering LOD, is that there is a very small risk that the procedure itself can damage the ovary, leading to ovarian failure. However, this is very uncommon (less than 1%).

How Successful Is It?

Remember, this is only suitable for women with normal tubes, polycystic ovaries and where the partner's sperm is normal.

Reports based on studies looking at around 1,000 women suggest that by 12 months after LOD the average pregnancy rate is around 60–80% (though this does not represent the live birth rates).[7] The greatest success rates are in women with a shorter length of infertility (less than three years) and a higher level of the luteinising hormone (LH).

The advantages of LOD include the fact that it may improve other symptoms of PCOS such as menstrual irregularity and infrequency, as well as avoiding the need for stimulatory drugs and their known side effects, including the increased risk of overstimulation and multiple pregnancy.

TUBAL SURGERY

Fallopian-tube obstruction is thought to play a role in 12–33% of subfertile couples.[8] If your tests have come back showing that you are ovulating but that there are blocks or adhesions in the fallopian tubes that are preventing the passage of the egg, you may be offered tubal surgery. As we saw in Part 3, sometimes the surgeon will remove the adhesions during the investigative procedure (the laparoscopy). However, this isn't always possible and so you may need some more surgery. Your doctor should help you to weigh up the pros and cons of this surgery. It is also terribly important that your partner has been properly tested *before* you embark on any kind of surgery – or indeed any kind of treatment.

The specific type of surgery depends on the location and extent of the fallopian-tube blockage, but the most common tubal surgery procedures are outlined below:

Tubal Reanastomosis

This is typically used to repair a portion of the fallopian tube damaged by disease. The blocked or diseased portion of the tube is removed, and the two healthy ends of the tube are then joined. This procedure is usually done through an abdominal incision (laparotomy).

Salpingectomy

Salpingectomy, or removal of part of a fallopian tube, is done to improve IVF success when a tube has developed a build-up of fluid (hydrosalpinx). Hydrosalpinx makes it half as likely that an IVF procedure will succeed.[9] This procedure is preferred to a salpingostomy (see below).

Salpingostomy

Salpingostomy is also done when the end of the fallopian tube is blocked by a build-up of fluid (hydrosalpinx). This procedure creates a new opening in the part of the tube closest to the ovary. However, it is common for scar tissue to regrow after a salpingostomy, reblocking the tube.

Fimbrioplasty

This procedure may be done when the part of the tube closest to the ovary is partially blocked or has scar tissue preventing normal egg pick-up. This procedure rebuilds the fringed ends of the fallopian tube.

Selective Tubal Cannulation

For a tubal blockage next to the uterus, this non-surgical procedure is the first treatment of choice. Using hysteroscopy (see page 235) to guide the instruments, a doctor inserts a catheter through the cervix and the uterus and into the fallopian tube.

What Are the Side Effects?

As with any surgery, there is some risk of infection and there may be an increased risk of ectopic pregnancy.

You will need to think about your recovery time. After abdominal surgery, there is usually a five-day hospital stay, and it could be up to six weeks until you're able to return to work. If you're having laparoscopic surgery, there is usually only a brief hospital stay, and you will be able to return to your normal activities within a few days to a week.

Take time to consider your options and how you think you will be able to manage. It's very important that you have your partner's full support – at a practical and an emotional level.

What Are the Success Rates?

The success of a fallopian-tube procedure depends in part on the location and extent of the blockage, as well as the presence or absence of other fertility problems. Age has a huge influence as well.

- Clearing a blockage in the part of the tube closest to the uterus (termed 'proximal occlusion') is more likely to be successful. These blockages often are functional (such as a mucus plug) rather than structural (such as scarring or other obstruction). Up to 60% of women with proximal occlusion have been reported to have successful pregnancies after tubal surgery.[10]
- 20–30% of women with a blockage near the end of the fallopian tube have had successful pregnancies after tubal surgery.[11]

- The amount of fallopian tube that remains after surgery will affect the function of the tube. If a large part of the tube has to be removed to eliminate blockage, the likelihood of pregnancy after surgery is reduced.

Your doctor should take you through the risks associated with these procedures prior to you making a decision. The more information that you can get, the better. Don't be afraid to ask as many questions as you like.

Chapter 24

Assisted Conception – the Main Options

If your and your partner's tests have come back and the results suggest that diet and lifestyle changes, drug treatment or minor surgery are not going to offer you the best chances of getting pregnant, then, for many couples, the next stage will be assisted conception.

You may have come to this conclusion after many months of tests and waiting, or it may be that your initial tests made it clear early on that this was a probable option, perhaps because your partner's sperm levels are very low or you are not ovulating. This is an important milestone in your journey and is likely to be a major decision for you both.

This chapter will cover the different options available to you. The kind of treatment you decide to have will depend on lots of different factors, not least waiting times and money. But as well as the practical implications, you must also take into account the physical and emotional strain that any treatment can place on a couple.

If you have been on a course of ovulation-inducing medication, you may be feeling fine and looking forward to having lots of sex with your partner at the time of ovulation, but you may also be suffering from the side effects of the treatment. Only you and your partner can decide – with the advice of your doctor – what you are prepared to do in order to maximise your chances of having a baby.

Some couples who come to me are only interested in getting pregnant and are not concerned about *why* they are not conceiving. In these instances, tests or investigations are of less interest, and the couple will want to proceed as quickly as they can to the stage of assisted conception. Other couples, however, want to get pregnant but they also want to understand why they are having difficulty. This may involve more investigative procedures and preliminary treatments before, perhaps, moving on to IVF.

You need to work out a package of care and treatment that suits your particular needs. The more information you have regarding procedures, waiting lists, success rates and costs, the better equipped you will be to make these decisions.

Remember to keep focused on your goals, amending and revising them if necessary. Stay positive and keep the lines of communication between you and your partner open. Treatment and worries over what the next stage may involve can be very stressful, and these stresses are often taken out on those nearest to us. Be aware that emotions can be volatile at times – this is to be expected – so try not to blame or lash out at your partner. Give each other space, take time to listen to each other's hopes and fears, and work together as a loving team.

WHAT DOES ASSISTED CONCEPTION MEAN?

If you think back to Part 1, in which the process of fertilisation was described, the key points in amongst the various complex processes that occur are the meeting of a sperm and an egg, the fertilisation of the egg, its safe journey along the fallopian tube to the uterus and its subsequent implantation into the wall of the uterus. If one or more aspects of this journey are, for whatever reason, failing to happen and if drug treatment has failed to allow the entire journey to be completed, then this is where assisted conception can be of use. Quite literally, it helps bring together the egg and the sperm to enable fertilisation, and, in some cases, it will help to get the fertilised egg into the right place for pregnancy to occur safely.

There are a number of different procedures, which are described below, that can assist in some or all of these aspects of the 'journey'. Depending on your unique set of circumstances, you will be advised which of the procedures is most likely to be right for you and your partner.

WEIGHING UP YOUR OPTIONS

Embarking on fertility treatment can be a nerve-racking experience for most people, particularly as there are no guarantees of a successful outcome. It's important to take time to talk over your concerns and any questions you may have with your team. This should include your partner first and foremost, your doctor or specialist, your complementary and alternative medicine practitioner, family and friends and also your work, as you're likely to need time off.

Look back at the Dooley equation (see page 7) and try to consider your options from a number of different viewpoints. These should include the following:

- Medical procedures – find out exactly what is likely to be involved.
- Ethical implications – weigh up any ethical issues you may have with the proposed procedure.
- Emotional – it isn't always easy to assess how you're going to feel once the treatment has started, but think about what you feel able to cope with. What is your support system like? Are there ways of offloading some of your other responsibilities temporarily to reduce the strain? Are you certain this is what you want? Will there be long journeys to the hospital? How will this affect your daily routine? Can you find ways of reducing your stress levels?
- Financial – this can play a very important part in the decision-making process as many couples choose to pay for the treat-

ment themselves to avoid long waiting lists. Do your homework and find out how much it is likely to cost. Don't forget to include any hidden costs such as petrol money to and from the hospital, time taken off work and so on. Chapter 16 gives you lots of advice on costs and choosing a clinic.

- Legal – lots of legislation now surrounds the area of fertility treatment. This is there to protect you but also the welfare of any child born. In cases where you are using donated sperm, you will need to be aware that donors are no longer anonymous.
- CAM – do explore the different treatment options available to you that can be used concurrently with your medical treatment (see Chapter 13), but remember to always let your doctor or specialist know of any complementary and alternative treatment you are receiving. Remember the cooperation card (see page 159).
- Family – for many couples, the support and blessing of their family and friends is really crucial in their decision making. This might mean relying on a parent for transport or taking into account the feelings of children you may already have.

THE HORSE RACE STORY

It is very important to plan ahead and keep many options open. A patient recently said to me that it's a bit like asking a horse to win a race. If your aim is for your horse to win a race and you have eight races for which he can be entered, you don't just enter and run one race and then decide what to do next. You plan your journey; you look at the different races; you may even enter the races way ahead in order to make sure that you don't miss the closing date. You prepare things ahead of time even though you may not actually have to go to that fourth or fifth race because the horse may win the first race.

Once you've decided to go ahead with a treatment, it's a good idea to work out a plan of action. This is much like the goal setting described in Chapter 14 can be as detailed as you like.

Here's an example:

CASE STUDY

Mrs S. is a 43-year-old lady who has been trying to conceive for 12 months. Mrs S. came to see me to discuss her fertility. She was generally fit and healthy and has been trying to conceive with a new partner for one year. Having done the preliminary investigations, the options for treatment included:

1. Following the Fit for Fertility Programme.
2. Keep trying to conceive naturally.
3. Although it might seem premature, at 43, one hasn't got much time in order to conceive and therefore IVF would be a very viable option with possibly pre-implantation genetic diagnosis.
4. I also would advise them that an early stage to get their name down for egg donation. Sadly, egg donation programmes often have long waiting lists.

I often ask people whether they want to consider egg donation. If the answer is 'no' then that is fine. If, however, the answer is 'yes' or 'maybe', it is important to get their name down because there may be a long delay.

CASE STUDY

Mr and Mrs S. T. are both 25 and have only been trying for six months. To date, the reason for not conceiving is unexplained. The options for treatment for this couple include the following:
1. Get fit for fertility.

2. *Maximise natural conception.*
3. *Keep trying for another six months.*
4. *Have basic re-investigations.*
5. *Then keep trying for another six months.*
6. *Then consider intrauterine insemination for three to six cycles.*
7. *Then to consider IVF.*

In the end, it is a concept of mixing and matching different forms of treatment.

In some ways, conceiving is a three-pronged approach. This includes:

1. the Fit for Fertility Programme
2. maximising natural conception
3. the journey of assisted conception

IS IT SUITABLE FOR ME?							
	Clomifene	IUI	GIFT	IVF	ICSI	Egg Donation	Donor Insemination
Normal sperm	√	√	√	√	N/A	√	N/A
Abnormal sperm	X	Possible	X	X (depend on level)	√	√	√
Not ovulating but able to with drugs	√	√	√	√	√	N/A	
Premature menopause	X	X	X	X	X	√	X
Blocked tubes	X	X	X	√	√	√	X

The main assisted conception treatment options are:

- intrauterine insemination (IUI)
- in vitro fertilisation (IVF)
- gamete intra-fallopian transfer (GIFT)
- intra-cytoplasmic sperm injection (ICSI)
- percutaneous epididymal sperm aspiration (PESA)

INTRAUTERINE INSEMINATION (IUI)

IUI is a method of inserting sperm directly into the uterus to coincide with ovulation, using a very fine catheter, to enhance the chances of fertilisation. The purpose of IUI is to increase the number of sperm that reach the fallopian tubes. The woman often takes fertility drugs to boost ovulation.

Who Is It Suitable For?

IUI is typically only used if the woman is known to have healthy, unblocked fallopian tubes. It is often used for couples who have been trying to conceive for at least two years but who have unexplained fertility. It may also be recommended in cases where the male partner has a slightly low sperm count or where there are conditions that make it difficult for the sperm to reach the egg (such as hostile cervical mucus).

It can also be used if there are problems with intercourse (e.g. impotence or premature ejaculation).

IUI can be used with women who have ovulatory problems in conjunction with stimulating drugs such as clomifene.

Because IUI requires the sperm to reach and fertilise the egg on its own, it is important that the sperm is known to be healthy and motile. IUI basically gives the sperm a head start, but it still has to seek out the egg on its own, i.e. helping the two to get together.

IUI may also be used with donor sperm. This is an option if your partner is infertile or has a genetic disorder that could be passed on to any offspring. Donor insemination is not something to embark on lightly as it may have significant long-term emotional consequences for both you and your partner and also for your child. Clinics should always offer counselling to couples considering embarking on donor insemination. Talking over your concerns and feelings with someone impartial can be extremely beneficial and can help to work through the difficult issues the procedure might raise.

There are many advantages for doing IUI because it also provides diagnostic information. Medically, one learns about the cycle in more detail as well as what the sperm is like after preparation. The insemination is very much like an embryo transfer in IVF and thus one can see whether this is possible. The other diagnostic area is whether one can cope with going through invasive infertility treatments. If a couple cannot with IUI, then IVF is unlikely to be for them.

To summarise, IUI is suitable for:

1. mild sperm problems
2. unexplained fertility
3. problems with intercourse – e.g. impotence or premature ejaculation

What Happens?

The procedure itself is relatively simple, which can make it an attractive and less costly option to many couples.

It can be performed whether or not you are receiving clomifene or other ovulation stimulants; I think ideally some stimulation should be used. This decision will depend on your cycle and will be something to discuss with your doctor, but the stimulation of the ovaries to increase egg production does increase the odds of success with IUI .[4] You will need to be ready to go to the clinic at the time of your ovulation, as there is a relatively small window of time in which the procedure can be successfully carried out – 12 to 24 hours either side of ovulation. Again, this is something you can work out with your doctor in advance.

The procedure begins by monitoring the woman using ultrasound in order to measure the size of her follicles. You may then be given human chorionic gonadotropin (hCG), causing the egg to be released from the follicle 34–40 hours after it is administered.

Your partner will then provide the clinic with a fresh semen sample. (If a donor is used, the sample is already in the laboratory frozen.) The semen is washed in order to filter out the sperm from the seminal fluid and to remove any malformed sperm. Around ovulation, the prepared sperm (less than a ¼ of a teaspoon) is inserted directly into the uterus by placing a thin, flexible catheter through the cervix. The process takes no more than a few minutes; it shouldn't be at all painful and doesn't require any anaesthetic. Once the catheter has been withdrawn, the woman will be asked to rest for a few minutes to allow time for the cervical mucus to seal off the passage leading to her cervix. It's then fine to go home. There is no reason why you cannot have natural intercourse after this – indeed, I would encourage it.

You will usually be offered a pregnancy blood test two weeks later.

What Are the Success Rates?

The average success rate for IUI ranges from (in a young age group) 10–15% in one cycle, however this increases by approximately 5% when used in conjunction with ovulation-stimulating drugs such as clomifene.

IUI has the advantage of being relatively non-invasive, with no surgery necessary. Because the procedure takes a very short time to carry out, it will have less of an impact on your daily routine and will be less costly than other treatments. However, as insemination must be performed within a very specific timeframe, you need to make sure that a) you are going to be available and b) that your clinic has adequate and flexible opening hours.

Does It Hurt?

Usually not. Occasionally, you may get cramps – like period pains. The actual insemination can on occasion cause discomfort as the catheter enters the cervix.

IN VITRO FERTILISATION (IVF)

The birth of Louise Brown on 25 July 1978, the first ever 'test-tube baby' was no doubt one of the most important medical achievements of the last century and has since changed the lives of literally thousands of couples. IVF was the first assisted reproductive technology (ART) to be developed and remains the most commonly performed ART procedure.

In its simplest term, IVF is the uniting of an egg and sperm in vitro (in the laboratory). The fertilised egg is then placed back into the uterus. Chapter 25 looks at the process of IVF in more detail, but here is a brief overview:

Who Is It Suitable For?

IVF is not a procedure to undertake lightly: it's costly, time-consuming and invasive and therefore can be very stressful for couples. It is often a last resort for those who have tried other means of assisted conception without success.

IVF is specifically recommended for women with absent, blocked or damaged fallopian tubes. It is also often used in cases of unexplained infertility, in some cases of male factor infertility and can be used in combination with ICSI (intra-cytoplasmic sperm injection) in cases of severe male factor infertility. It is also an option for older women and for women using donated eggs.

What Happens?

Once the body has been prepared for superovulation and the follicles have matured, the eggs are collected. The number varies depending on your age and drugs used but will be between one and twenty – many more than that could run the risk of ovarian hyperstimulation syndrome. These are mixed with a sample of your partner's sperm (or, depending on your circumstances, a donor's). Those eggs that are successfully fertilised and have begun to mature into embryos are then transferred back into the uterus (up to a maximum of two embryos or three if you are over forty). Progesterone or HCG is prescribed to increase the chances of the embryo implanting.

What Are the Success Rates?

As with all assisted conception treatments, the success rate of IVF will vary from clinic to clinic and will depend on a number of factors, including the number of embryos transferred, your age and your overall health. However, according to the latest report produced by the HFEA the average success rates are:[1]

WOMAN'S AGE	SUCCESS RATE (%)
<35	27.6
35–37	22.3
38–39	18.3
40–42	10
42<	less than 10

Talk It Through First

Before embarking on IVF treatment, it's terribly important that you discuss all the pros and cons with your partner and with other members of your 'team'. IVF treatment can involve major upheaval and will have a big impact on your body, your day-to-day life and possibly your relationships. You need to ask yourself a number of questions and get as much information as you can, before you make your decision. Don't lose sight of the wonderful and exciting possibilities that IVF can offer, but do make yourself aware of the whole picture.

Ten Reasons Why Your IVF/ICSI Cycle May Have to Be Cancelled

1. At the baseline scan, an ovarian cyst is found.
2. At the down-regulation scan, an endometrial polyp is found.
3. You do not get down-regulated.
4. The ovaries do not respond to the drugs.
5. The ovaries over-respond and there is a great risk of ovarian hyperstimulation syndrome.
6. No eggs are found.
7. Your partner does not produce sperm.
8. The eggs collected fail to fertilise.
9. The eggs, once fertilised, fail to divide.
10. You cannot cope with the course and want to pull out.

Side Effects and Risks Involved with IVF/ICSI

As with any medical procedure, there are a number of possible side effects and risks involved.

Fortunately, side effects to the fertility drugs you'll be given are not too common. You may have local reactions to the injections themselves such as mild bruises and soreness at the site of injections. There is also a small risk of a generalised allergic reaction.

Other drugs, such as the GnRH agonit, may cause headaches, mood changes, hot flushes and vaginal dryness in some women. However, these are usually short-lived and are no cause for concern.

Approximately 15% of patients will develop functional cysts while on GnRH agonists regimes. These cysts may produce oestrogen and *sometimes* are associated with a poor IVF outcome. If this happens, the patient will be advised to continue taking GnRH agonist drugs until the cysts resolve by themselves. In some cases, aspiration of the cyst may be required.

Ovarian Cancer

Some studies have made a link between ovarian-stimulation drugs and ovarian cancer. The evidence is observational, and there are significant problems in many of these studies, particularly in the inability to control for other cancer-confounding factors. Some research has shown that infertile women who use infertility drugs but still never achieve pregnancy had a significantly increased risk of ovarian cancer compared to women who had no infertility problem.[2] Do talk to your consultant about this.

Ovarian Hyperstimulation Syndrome (OHSS)

Some women respond very sensitively to the fertility drugs given to stimulate their follicles and, as a result, produce too many. This can cause the ovaries to enlarge and blood oestrogen levels to rise. Your blood protein level drops, which causes fluid to leak into the abdominal cavity or around the lungs. This can result in problems producing urine, mineral imbalances in the blood and clotting problems. Development of OHSS is not always predictable or avoidable, though it is more common in younger women and women with PCOS.

Symptoms of OHSS are most common around the time of egg collection to about ten days after embryo transfer. You may find that things improve only to worsen again nearer the time of your pregnancy test. Symptoms include:

- abdominal pain
- swollen abdomen
- passing small amounts of concentrated urine
- thirst, nausea and vomiting
- diarrhoea and dizziness
- shortness of breath
- weight gain

You should contact your doctor immediately if you experience any of these symptoms; however, careful and frequent ultrasound monitoring should also help to identify any problems. The overall risk is about 4%, and severe cases occur in about 0.25%.

In some cases, your doctor will recommend that you do not take the hCG injection and wait until the oestrogen levels go back down before proceeding to egg collection. Or you may be advised to have a reduced dose of hCG. It may be that the eggs are not collected and you continue to take the down-regulation medication until your symptoms improve. If eggs are collected, your doctor might recommend that any embryos created are frozen for replacement in a future cycle. A frozen embryo-replacement cycle will not cause OHSS, as the ovaries are not stimulated. If the embryos are replaced in a fresh cycle and you become pregnant, your blood oestrogen level will start to rise again and make your condition worse. This is a potentially very serious condition; you must get a 24-hour helpline number from your clinic – if you are worried and cannot contact your clinic, go to accident and emergency immediately.

Egg collection

Any kind of surgery comes with its own risks. Before having your eggs retrieved your doctor will warn you of the following associated risks:

- pain and discomfort following the procedure
- bleeding
- infection – although you will be given an antibiotic to help reduce this risk
- a very small risk of bowel damage or bladder damage

Multiple Pregnancy

The chances of a multiple pregnancy (twins or triplets – or more) is more likely with assisted conception because up to three eggs or embryos are returned to the fallopian tubes.

Currently, 0.5% of IVF births are triplets – down from almost 4% in the early 1990s – while 20% of IVF births are twins.[3] Multiple pregnancies carry an increased risk of complications for the mother and baby – not to mention increased emotional, physical and financial demands.

Ectopic Pregnancy

This is when a pregnancy develops outside of the womb, usually in the fallopian tube. There is a slight increased risk in IVF/ICSI cycles, especially if you have blocked tubes. Symptoms include:

- vaginal bleeding
- abdominal pain
- shoulder-tip pain

If you have any concerns, call your clinic.

Recurrent IVF Treatment Failure: What Can Be Done?

IVF success is dependent on the development of the embryo and the endometrium (the lining of the womb). Persistent abnormalities in either can lead to recurrent treatment failure. Most clinics define recurrent IVF failure as four or five failed cycles. There are different reasons as to why repeated implantation failure occurs: it may be that the quality of egg, sperm or embryo is poor or that there is a failure of implantation which might be due to blood clotting problems, lupus anticoagulant, Anticardiolipin or Natural Killer Cells. The shape of the uterus may also be a factor and should be looked into.

NATURAL CYCLE IVF

Using no drugs to stimulate the ovaries, one egg is collected from you during your normal monthly cycle. This is very attractive in many ways as there are no drugs and thus no side effects. The risk of multiple pregnancy is also reduced. The downside is that the success rate is low, about 5–8% per cycle (i.e. you need to have three to four cycles of natural IVF to equalise the success rate of conventional IVF). Also, the success rate is severely reduced as one gets older and is probably best to consider in women under the age of 35.

With time, this technique may become more successful. Watch this space.

GAMETE INTRA-FALLOPIAN TRANSFER (GIFT)

This technique was popular in the 1980s but is less commonly used in clinics these days, as it tends to be more expensive and more invasive than IVF.

GIFT is an assisted reproductive procedure that involves removing a woman's eggs, placing them in a test tube with sperm and immediately replacing them back into the fallopian tube. The main difference between GIFT and IVF is that the fertilisation process takes place *inside* the fallopian tubes rather than in the laboratory.

This procedure can be carried out using donated eggs and/or donated sperm. Depending on your own circumstances, this may be an option that you'll want to consider. Again, counselling should always be offered to any couples planning on embarking on this particular route, as using a donor can, for many reasons, be an emotive and complex decision.

Who Is It Suitable For?

GIFT is only suitable for women with healthy, unblocked fallopian tubes and no intrauterine adhesions. In general, IVF is a better approach for couples with male factor infertility. As fertilisation takes place inside the body GIFT may be more appropriate for certain religious groups.

What Happens?

The management of a patient in a GIFT treatment cycle is usually exactly the same as for an IVF cycle up until the point at which the eggs have been recovered.

You will be given a prescription of ovulation stimulants to encourage the development of more than one egg (superovulation); this is so that up to three eggs can be placed into the fallopian tube to improve chances of fertilisation. Your doctor will discuss with you which drugs are likely to be best for you.

The growth of the ovarian follicles in which the eggs are developing will then be traced by ultrasound and sometimes blood or urine tests. When the follicles are considered to be mature enough, you will be given an injection of human chorionic gonadotropin (hCG) to prepare the eggs for collection, which will occur 34–36 hours later.

Most clinics will recover the eggs using an aspirational needle guided by ultrasound (transvaginal ultrasound-directed technique); this is the same technique that's used for IVF. Some clinics will, however, recover the eggs laparoscopically, which will involve making a small incision in the abdomen (see page 233). If they are being collected this way, you'll need to have a general anaesthetic.

Once the eggs have been collected and identified, the best two or three are then selected. Then, under a microscope, a preparation of sperm – your partner's or the donor's – is drawn into a fine catheter, followed by a small pocket of air and a small drop of fluid containing up to three eggs. The tube is gently inserted through a laparoscope into the outer ends of one or both fallopian tubes, and the egg and sperm are released into the tube/s to mix together. This does require a general anaesthetic.

Once the procedure is over, you'll be returned to the ward to recover. In almost all cases you'll be able to return home the same day.

Most patients are given either injections or pessaries of progesterone, and, 15 days later, a pregnancy test is carried out to determine whether there is early evidence of a pregnancy.

What Are the Success Rates?

GIFT is generally found to be slightly more successful than IVF in most clinics. This is probably because the fallopian tube is the natural environment for fertilisation to occur as opposed to laboratory conditions. However, the procedure does require a laparoscopy for the insertion of the sperm and eggs, and most clinics are not convinced that the extra inconvenience and potential discomfort and danger of a laparoscopy justifies the slightly increased pregnancy rates. If a clinic is achieving good results with IVF, then they will generally not do GIFT.

INTRA-CYTOPLASMIC SPERM INJECTION (ICSI)

ICSI is a relatively new laboratory technique that has been embraced as a breakthrough in treating male factor infertility. It involves the direct injection of a selected individual sperm into the egg for fertilisation. The fertilised egg is then implanted in the womb.

Who Is It Suitable For?

ICSI may be an option if your partner's sperm count is too low or has poor motility, making IVF unviable. It may also be used if your partner has an obstruction preventing sperm from being released, if he is unable to ejaculate, if there appear to be problems with his sperm binding to and penetrating your egg or if antisperm antibodies are thought to be the cause of the infertility.

What Happens?

As with IVF treatment, you will be given drugs to stimulate your ovaries to develop several mature eggs for fertilisation. Once the eggs are ready for retrieval (this will be monitored by ultra sound), you and your partner will each undergo separate procedures.

For men unable to ejaculate or with obstructions, sperm samples can be taken directly from the testes or the epididymis using a fine needle under anaesthetic (percutaneous epididymal sperm aspiration). If this technique doesn't remove enough sperm, the doctor will take a biopsy of testicular tissue, which sometimes has sperm attached.

You will then be given a local or general anaesthetic and, using a fine catheter guided by ultrasound, the doctor will remove the mature eggs just as with IVF.

An embryologist then isolates an individual sperm and injects them into individual eggs. The sperm is immobilised – usually by fracturing its tail – to prevent it from swimming back out of the egg. The process of inserting the sperm into the nucleus of the egg is very delicate, and even with an experienced embryologist, about 1 in 20 eggs will be damaged during this part of the procedure.

Two days later, the fertilised eggs become embryos. The doctor will transplant two or three embryos into the uterus through your cervix using a thin catheter. (Extra embryos, if there are any, may be frozen in case this cycle isn't successful.) After about two weeks, you'll be able to take a pregnancy test.

What Are the Success Rates?

Fertilisation occurs in 50–80% of injected eggs.[5] However, the fertilised egg may fail to divide or the embryo may arrest at an early stage in development. Studies carried out in the US show that approximately 30% of ICSI cycles result in live births;[6]

however, this will vary from clinic to clinic and will also depend on factors including a woman's age and egg quality. The success rate under the age of 35 is in the order of 30%, between 35 and 40 about 20% and 10% above 40 i.e. very similar to IVF. It's also important to know why your partner is infertile. If there are chromosomal abnormalities, it may mean an increased risk of miscarriage.

What Are the Risks?

Concerns have been raised about the risks to children born through ICSI. It has been suggested that there is a slight increase in the incidence of gene mutations such as cystic fibrosis and in birth defects such as cleft palate. However the evidence is by no means conclusive and further studies are required.

PERCUTANEOUS EPIDIDYMAL SPERM ASPIRATION (PESA)

Much like the initial stage of ICSI, PESA is a non-invasive method of sperm recovery.

Who Is It Suitable For?

PESA is usually offered to couples where the man has almost no sperm count due to an obstruction or has had a vasectomy and does not wish to undergo a reversal. It can also be used for men who have had an attempted vasectomy reversal which has failed. This technique is also applicable for men with congenital absence of the vas deferens (see page 260), who have had a previous infection that has resulted in blockages in the epididymis, or men with ejaculatory dysfunction due to multiple sclerosis or diabetes.

What Happens?

PESA is a relatively simple technique, requiring only a local anaesthetic. The surgeon uses a small needle to aspirate sperm from the epididymis or directly from the seminiferous tubules. The sperm is then taken to the laboratory to be frozen and used at a later date or, in some cases, used immediately during an ICSI cycle.

What Are the Success Rates?

In one study, an analysis of 181 ICSI treatment cycles following PESA revealed a successful epididymal sperm retrieval rate of 83%. The study confirmed that PESA is an effective sperm-retrieval method and the associated ICSI pregnancy rate (35% per embryo transfer) compared favourably with that of other sperm-retrieval methods, including ejaculated sperm.[7]

Infertility is the most common reason for women aged 20–45 to see their GP, after pregnancy itself.[8]

Chapter 25

IVF Treatment – Understanding the Process

A WALK THROUGH AN IVF CYCLE

There are a number of stages in an IVF cycle, all with their own procedures and protocols. By familiarising yourselves with these different steps along the way, you and your partner will get a better sense of how your lives will be (temporarily) affected and be able to make provisions for this. Looking at the different stages can also make the whole procedure seem less daunting. You can only take things one day at a time, while keeping your mind focused on your ultimate goal.

There are four main steps involved in an IVF cycle:

1. stimulation of the ovaries to encourage development and maturation of the eggs
2. retrieval of the eggs
3. fertilisation of the eggs and culture of the embryos
4. transfer of the embryos back into the uterus

Step 1: Stimulation of the Ovaries

Also called controlled ovulation or superovulation, this is the first stage in IVF. If your hormones are at the right levels and you have a regular cycle, you may follow what is termed the long protocol. If, however, you have high levels of FSH (follicle-stimulating hormone) or have responded poorly to ovulation stimulants in the past, you may follow the short protocol. This is just a rule of thumb, and all clinics may vary their stimulation programmes. Indeed, some clinics put you on the oral contraceptive pill for the cycle prior to stimulation and others may give you progestegens. Do not worry about the protocol that you are given, but I do think it is important to ask questions: Are there any different protocols that can be arranged? What are the associated risks and benefits of different protocols? Here I'm going to be concentrating on the long protocol, but we will come back to the short protocol.

THE SMARTIE STORY

I have often thought of the ovarian cycle like the Smartie story. Each month your ovaries are able to produce a certain number of eggs. Some of these eggs are good-quality eggs, and others are not such good-quality eggs. In some ways, there is very little that one can do to change the numbers of eggs that are produced, nor can you change the quality of these eggs. I look at it as a tube of Smarties. Consider each month that your ovaries are willing to produce a tube of Smarties. Each month there may be a different number of Smarties in the tube. The blue Smarties are the good Smarties, and the other Smarties are not so good. The number of blue Smarties in each tube will vary. Some months, there are lots of Smarties (lots of eggs) but few blue ones (i.e. a lot of poor-quality eggs). Another month, you may have fewer Smarties than usual but of those a lot of them are blue. A lot of patients get frustrated that they haven't had the right stimulation, but the amount of stimulation may be slightly academic; it may purely be that there aren't enough eggs available.

In order that your body's own natural rhythm doesn't upset the IVF cycle, you will be given an injection or nasal spray of GnRH (see page 277); this will put your body into a temporary menopausal state so that you are no longer producing sex hormones and so that an egg is not released early. This stage is called 'down regulation' and usually takes around 14 days. Generally a scan is done before down regulation to make sure there are no cysts present. You will then have another scan and a blood test for oestradiol make sure that you are adequately down-regulated. You will need to go to your clinic during this time so that they can monitor how well your hormones have been suppressed. The timing, dosage and administration of the hormonal medications are critical to the success of the cycle.

Once your doctor is happy that you are in the down-regulation phase, you will be given injections of FSH or hMG (human menopausal gonadotropin) to stimulate the development of the follicles in the ovaries. Excessive amounts of these medications may result in hyperstimulation of the ovaries (see page 270), whereas insufficient quantities of the drugs may result in an unsuccessful cycle, leading to cancellation. Therefore, careful physician monitoring is necessary to adjust dosages and ensure an optimal stimulation period. These follicles are monitored, using ultrasound and sometimes also blood tests. You will also continue to take the suppression drugs to prevent the ovulation occurring before the eggs are ready to be retrieved.

By around day 10 of your injections, assuming that your doctor is happy with the size and development of the follicles, you will be given an injection of human chorionic gonadotropin (hCG). This triggers the final stages of egg development. Once you have had the hCG injection, you may be advised to stop taking the suppressant (GnRH). You may be given additional progesterone at this stage to help keep the lining of your uterus receptive for pregnancy.

Short Protocol

This is also sometimes called the flare protocol. The short protocol generally mirrors your normal cycle and so takes approximately four weeks (rather than six weeks for the long protocol). The short protocol is usually used when a woman has not produced many eggs under the long protocol or when she is a bit older than average.

The main difference between the two protocols is that the short protocol doesn't wait for you to be down-regulated. It also takes advantage of your body's natural rise in FSH and LH levels around day 3 of your cycle, which stimulates the follicles to grow. On day 3 of your cycle, you start the stimulation injections described above and at the same time start to take the down-regulating nasal spray or injection. You will then be asked to return to the clinic after a few days and thereafter will have regular scans and blood tests until you're ready for egg collection. From then on the process is exactly the same as the long protocol.

The advantages of the short protocol are that there are fewer drugs to take as you miss out the initial down-regulating stage, and it's also a faster treatment cycle. Some women who have not had a very good response under the long protocol find that they produce more eggs under the short protocol, but this is not always the case. Remember that there are many different protocols and your unit will offer the best one for you

Step 2: Retrieval of the Eggs

The eggs will be ready for retrieval 34–36 hours after your hCG injection. This is timed just before ovulation.

In almost all cases, egg retrieval is accomplished non-surgically through the vagina using an ultrasound scanner to guide a needle into each of the follicles in the ovaries. The procedure may not require general anaesthetic and is carried out under light sedation. However, some units do give a general anaesthetic. I think it is important for you to consider what anaesthetic you require, discuss it with the unit and also the anaesthetist who may be present. It should take only 20–40 minutes. In some cases, eggs will be retrieved by a laparoscopy (see page 233).

The needle passes down a hollow guide tube through the vagina and into the ovaries. The ultrasound image allows more accurate aspiration attempts because the doctor can guide the needle into each follicle in order to withdraw the egg. After recovering the eggs, they are transferred to a sterile container containing nutrient-rich fluid and are placed in an incubator to await fertilisation in the laboratory. Not all of the eggs retrieved will be used in the current IVF cycle. Unhealthy eggs are abandoned.

This can be a particularly anxious time, but you should remember that the number of eggs retrieved doesn't necessarily indicate how many embryos you will have after their fertilisation.

ACUPUNCTURE AND IVF

Extensive scientific studies have been carried out on the role of acupuncture in the treatment of health in general, and there has been much research on how it can be used in conjunction with IVF.

A study conducted by researchers reported a 50% increase in IVF success rates when carried out alongside acupuncture.[1] Of 160 women undergoing IVF, half received standard in vitro fertilisation, and half were given acupuncture treatments before and after. The report found the pregnancy rate in the group receiving acupuncture was 42.5%, while the group that did not receive the therapy had a rate of 26.3%.

The researchers chose acupuncture points that traditional Chinese medicine believes relax the uterus. They also used needles to stimulate meridians involving the spleen, stomach and colon, to improve blood flow and create more energy in the uterus. Acupuncture affects the autonomic nervous system, which is involved in the control of muscles and glands, and can therefore make the lining of the uterus more receptive to receiving an embryo.

If you can, make some time to fit in a few acupuncture sessions. You may also find it helps ease some of the side effects you may be experiencing due to the drugs you have to take.

Remember to talk over any extra treatment you're considering having with your doctor first and bear in mind that not everyone is convinced about the role of acupuncture and further studies are required to produce a clear evidence base for its use.

Step 3: Fertilisation of the Eggs and Culture of the Embryos

While the egg-retrieval stage is proceeding, your partner will be asked to produce a semen sample early the same day. He will be advised to abstain from sex for two days leading up to this point. See page 213 for more information on providing a sperm sample.

The sample is then taken to the laboratory, where a concentrated preparation of the best motile sperm is extracted. The sperm preparation will contain approximately 150,000 sperm. The sperm is added to the dishes containing the eggs, and they are incubated together overnight at a temperature identical to that of the woman's body (37°C).

On the morning after egg retrieval, the eggs are examined to see which have fertilised. Fertilised eggs (zygotes) are then routinely cultured in the IVF laboratory until days 2–3, at which time the best one to two embryos are selected. (In exceptional circumstances and if you are over the age of 40, you may be allowed to have three embryos put back after adequate counselling and signing the appropriate consent forms.) Clinics grade embryos according to the evenness of cell division and the number of cells counted. Try not to get too hung up on the grading as it does not automatically predict the outcome of implantation.

BLASTOCYSTS AND BLASTOCYST CULTURE

A blastocyst is an embryo that is developed five to six days after fertilisation. For some patients, a blastocyst-transfer cycle may have been recommended, in which case embryo culture is extended to day 5. This is the stage of development that the embryo must reach before it can implant in the uterus.

It is known that some embryos will arrest at early stages, so extended culture allows the embryologist to identify which (if any) of a group of embryos have the best potential for implantation by identifying those which form a normal blastocyst in culture.

Transferring embryos at the blastocyst stage provides a better coordination between the embryo and the uterus by putting the embryo back in the right place (the uterus) at the right time (blastocyst stage). However, the chances of having no embryos for transfer at all are also higher, and it is less likely there will be spare embryos left over for freezing.

WHO WILL BENEFIT MOST FROM A BLASTOCYST CYCLE?

If your IVF did not work, despite the fact that you had embryos for replacement on day 2 or 3, blastocyst culture could help your doctor determine whether your embryos develop beyond day 3 at all (even very good-quality day-3 embryos may not form blastocysts), and if so, which of those embryos would be the best ones to transfer.

As blastocyst culture can help to determine which embryos have the best chance of being able to implant, your doctor can potentially reduce the number of embryos that are replaced into the uterus and thereby reduce the risk of a multiple pregnancy.

DOES IT INCREASE MY SUCCESS RATE?

In some couples the success rate may be increased, but equally you may have no embryos to transfer back. Please discuss this with your doctor.

Step 4: Transfer of the Embryos Back Into the Uterus

Embryo transfer usually takes place two to five days (blastocyst culture) after fertilisation depending on your own set of circumstances. It is not a complicated procedure and is performed without anaesthetic. Indeed, it is a little bit more than having a cervical smear. UK law rules that a maximum of two (unless you are older than 40) embryos may be implanted back in the uterus. This is in order to reduce the risk of multiple pregnancy. The embryos are placed in a fine plastic catheter, which is inserted through the vagina and cervix into the uterus. Most clinics will use ultrasound to guide the catheter. Once the catheter has released the embryos into the uterus, it is carefully removed. The catheter is then checked to ensure the embryos have been implanted.

PREIMPLANTATION GENETIC DIAGNOSIS (PGD) AND PREIMPLANTATION GENETIC SCREENING (PGS)

Preimplantation genetic diagnosis and screening allow genetic analysis to be performed on early embryos *prior* to implantation and pregnancy. This is particularly beneficial to parents who have a significant risk of conceiving a baby affected by a known recurrent genetic disorder or a disease. PGD means that only embryos found not to be carrying the disorder will be transferred to the womb.

At the time of writing, about 3,000 IVF babies have been accompanied by PGD, resulting in about 700 births.[2] Soon, virtually any genetically inherited disease that is diagnosable in humans can be identified in a single cell. A further potential application of PGD will be a prediction of disease susceptibility.

In order for PGD to be performed, a single cell is removed from the embryo using a very fine glass needle. This is examined under a microscope and tested for any molecular or chromosomal abnormalities.

By looking for these chromosomal problems and only transferring the embryos that were chromosomally normal, investigators were able to reduce the pregnancy loss rates in women over 35 from the 36% which had been expected to only 17%.[3]

In the UK, this procedure is regulated by the HFEA, which rules that an embryo may only be tested for genetic conditions and not simply for social reasons – such as selecting an embryo for its sex.

Although PGD does provide a huge advance in reproductive technology, it opens up a Pandora's box of ethical conundrums.

'Medicine was in history, first of all curative, then preventative and finally predicted. Whereas today, the order is reversed; initially predictive, then preventative and finally, only in desperation, curative.'

John Dausset[4]

You'll then be given some time to just lie still and recover. It's a good idea to have your partner with you at this stage. Not only is it a vital step in the IVF procedure and one that he will probably want to be present at, but it is also a very nerve-racking time for most women. Having your partner or a close friend by your side will help to calm your nerves and limit the stress you may be experiencing.

This is a really good time to practise your deep-breathing techniques (see page 133) and some positive visualisation. Focus your mind on your healthy growing embryos implanting securely and snugly in the lining of your womb where they have all the good nutrients and rich blood supply to mature and develop.

After the Cycle

After implantation, I encourage plenty of rest. The evidence for this is limited, but I believe it is good to take things easy. What I often say is go down a gear or two. You've been through a difficult and stressful time and your body – and mind – needs time to recover. Also, it makes good sense that the calmer and more rested you are, the more your body can concentrate its energies on taking care of those embryos.

'It's like the end of an exam – all the revision and exams are over. I felt tired, drained but positive.'

After implantation, I advise the following precautions:

- AVOID caffeine, smoking, alcohol and drugs.
- AVOID heavy lifting.
- AVOID strenuous exercising and housework (including vacuuming).
- AVOID bouncing activities (horseback riding, aerobics, etc.).
- AVOID sunbathing, saunas, hot tubs and Jacuzzis.
- AVOID swimming and baths.

Get your partner to spoil you a bit, and don't rush back to your normal routine. Keep to the Fit for Fertility Programme, remembering to eat healthily and avoid alcohol. Take some time each day to practise your deep-breathing exercises and positive visualisations. You may find that burning essential oils at bedtime helps you to relax and prepare for sleep. Lavender is particularly soothing. If you're not sure whether you should do something, don't. There is probably very little you can do to cause harm, but I never want my patients to blame themselves. Thus my mantra is 'If in doubt, leave it out.'

MAKING A COMPLAINT

Sadly, you may not be happy with your treatment. Be careful not to shoot the messenger. If you do have a complaint/ worry, it is very important to express your feelings. Often these can be resolved by talking to the clinical team. All clinics will have a complaint procedure, and do ask to see a copy of these. If you are not happy with your reply, then within the NHS you can write to the Chief Executive and ask for an independent review. Private clinics are regulated by the Healthcare Commission and you can write to them or to the HFEA.

The Waiting Stage

Known as the two-week wait, this is the period after implantation and before your clinic asks you in for a pregnancy test. It is not a particularly fun couple of weeks; all the couples I see agree on that point. You are likely to feel a mixture of emotions – from hopeful and upbeat one minute to discouraged and despairing the next. This is perfectly natural. Not only have you been through an emotionally and physically demanding procedure, but you also have to cope with knowing that there is no guarantee of a successful outcome.

Some women start to look for signs of pregnancy or interpret their body's every symptom. Again, this is perfectly understandable, but do try not to work yourself up into a state of anxiety. You may find it helps to see friends or read a good book – to take your mind off things. It can be a terribly frustrating time for you both, so try not to take it out on each other. Emotions can run high, and it's important that you try to keep your stress levels down.

Try to stay positive throughout this time and, if you can, keep planning and weighing up all your options. For some couples who receive a non-positive result, it helps to have had a back-up plan – whether that was the decision to try another cycle or to leave it for six months. Remember, this is a journey.

During this two week wait, you may be given progesterone pessaries to take or have additional injections of HGC. Both can help to maintain the lining of the womb, to encourage the embryo to stay safely implanted in the womb.

After the two weeks are up, you'll need to go to your clinic or surgery to have a pregnancy test. If you want to, you can do a home pregnancy test on your urine. The kits you can buy over the counter are reasonably accurate.

The Outcome

Remember, you are on a journey. Whatever the outcome, it can and should be positive. Each result leads to a different action plan. You do not stop, you move on. I have often said that life is a game of snakes and ladders, ups and downs, but remember you never win. If you do, the game is over!

A Positive Pregnancy Test?

If your pregnancy test results come back positive, then that's wonderful news! Congratulate yourselves! You've done a brave and difficult thing. You may want to tell everyone immediately or keep it to yourselves while the news gradually sinks in. Savour this moment, it's what you've been dreaming of for a long time.

Your emotions will be up and down. These mixed emotions are common, do not worry – it is the beginning of another journey. On the practical side, call your clinic and discuss whether you need to stay on or start any other treatment. Such things include further progesterone suppositories, aspirin or even heparin. They will also arrange for you to have a scan to confirm that all is going well and also to see if you have twins. Once you have had this, you need to get booked into the antenatal clinic.

You're going to need to carry on looking after yourself – and your new precious cargo. So look back over the Fit for Fertility Programme, and make sure you're getting a good and balanced diet.

Physically, your pregnancy will be no different to any other, but emotionally, you may be challenged. Any pregnancy carries a 15% risk of miscarriage. Following fertility treatment, the risk is around 15–20%. This is because the pregnancy tests are done so much earlier in the preganancy when it is even more vulnerable.

Ectopic Pregnancy

This is when a pregnancy grows outside the uterus, usually in the fallopian tube. Just because you have had the embryo placed in your uterus, there is still a risk of an ectopic – this risk is increased if you have had damaged tubes or a previous ectopic. The diagnosis can be difficult, but there are important signs to be aware of including bleeding and pain (see page 248).

A Non-positive Pregnancy Test?

As you can see, I have called this 'a non-positive pregnancy test'. I am trying to avoid the term 'negative' because negative thoughts lead to negative results.

A non-positive result can be one of the hardest things you've had to cope with, and you're bound to feel desperately sad and upset. Try to allow yourself to express these feelings; it's better to feel your emotions and not bottle them up. You may decide you can't face telling people and that you'd rather take some time to process your feelings before getting back into your daily routine. Take some time off work and look after yourself. Some women find that at this stage it helps to talk to a counsellor about how they're feeling rather than friends and family, who will have their own emotions to deal with. Your doctor will be able to refer you if necessary.

Reasons why the embryo may fail to grow in the womb include:

1. chromosomal problems with the embryos
2. poor-quality embryos
3. poor blood flow to the uterus

4. poor lifestyle issues
5. unknown

Make an appointment to see your specialist – even if you have a non-positive pregnancy result, there may be a lot you can learn. Just staying the course is positive, getting eggs can be positive. If you have failed fertilisation, you may decide to have ICSI. If you get no eggs, then egg donation or adoption may be options. Or you may decide to give up and move on to new challenges.

Feelings of failure, guilt and blame are common. Don't torture yourself with what ifs, IVF is a difficult and complex process, and there are lots of reasons why it doesn't always work – and none of them are your or your partner's fault.

'In time of difficulties, we must not lose sight of our achievements.'

Mao Tse-Tung

Try to think about how far you've come. You now know what IVF involves – and you have done it, be proud of yourself. Some women are keen to try again almost straightaway and feel they want to put this result behind them and move on. For others, it will take longer. You may decide to have a break from the treatment and reconsider it in another six months or so. Some couples feel they can't go through the process again and will want to find out about the other options open to them. Remember that you can always change your mind. You may be thinking 'never again', but in a year from now, you could be in a very different frame of mind and feel it's time for another shot at it.

> Do tell your clinic of any change of address because communication needs to continue for many years.

Future Plans and Difficult Decisions

Deciding to go along a journey and where to go can be difficult, and I think it is important to look through your options. Remember DR AID: diagnose, review, agree the plan, implement and demonstrate. This is a continuous cycle even after a non-positive result. Review your treatment journey, learn from it, possibly change your medication regimes, etc., and then move on.

CASE STUDY – HOW A NON-POSITIVE RESULT CAN BECOME POSITIVE

A couple came into my clinic recently whom I had not seen for five years. I remembered them well. They had had four attempts at IVF, but sadly, each attempt had resulted in a non-positive pregnancy test. At the last consultation, they had been extremely distressed. Indeed, during the last IVF cycle, only one egg was obtained from the lady despite maximum drugs to stimulate her ovaries, and no fertilisation occurred. They were hugely disappointed and made the difficult decision to stop having IVF cycles and to move on. They pursued the course of adoption.

Five years later, when I saw them in my clinic, they had two young children with them, James and John, aged three and two. I enquired about these children and they told me that they had adopted them and were now blissfully happy.

I asked them if they recalled the last time we had met when they were devastated about the lack of success of IVF. They replied that this was a dark time in their lives, but now they were delighted that the IVF had not succeeded because if it had been successful, they would never have had the privilege of adopting their two children.

To me, this demonstrated a lovely outcome. It proved that whatever the outcome, it can be positive. You never go forward by looking back, but you can learn from the past.

Chapter 26

Assisted Conception – a Closer Look at the Options

If the investigations described in Part 3 indicate that you are not producing eggs or your partner is not producing sperm, or either of you have a genetic disorder that could be dangerous to pass on, you still have options to enable you to become parents.

However, there are important emotional and ethical factors linked to these options. You'll need to ask yourselves some important questions and think very hard about the answers.

SPERM DONATION

Reasons for sperm donation include if your partner has had a vasectomy or a failed vasectomy reversal. Single women or lesbian couples may consider sperm donation.

Donor sperm has been used in assisted conception treatments for many years. An estimated 7,000 patients receive treatment with donated eggs and sperm, known as gametes, every year, and, as a result, 2,000 children are born.[1]

All donors are carefully screened for infectious diseases and cystic fibrosis, and they have to be aged 18–45.

A donor will also be matched, as far as possible, to your partner's own physical characteristics, including race, eye colour, build and blood group. They are usually anonymous to you. If you want to use known donation, you can discuss this with your clinic.

Until 2005, the identity of the donors was strictly confidential. The law has now changed and rules that once a child conceived in this way has reached the age of 18, he or she may be able to identify their genetic parents. However, the donor will not be able to trace the child. This is a rather controversial ruling, and many doctors and donors feel this will deter potential donors.

All donors are counselled, and the sperm is frozen for six months. This incubation period allows for retesting of HIV and hepatitis. Usually, the donor comes from the UK, although sperm can be imported with HFEA approval.

How Is It Done?

After adequate counselling, you will be given time to consider your options. If you have any doubts, delay treatment and talk it through.

The clinic may do some tests on your tubes to see if they are open. I often advise starting treatment for three cycles and then, if it is not successful, to have your tubes tested. You will be asked to monitor your urine to detect pre-ovulation, then insemination will take place on one or two occasions, 24 hours apart.

On many occasions, you will also be given fertility drugs to improve your chances and combine this with an intrauterine insemination (see page 299), talk this through with your clinic.

The insemination takes place in the clinic, and sperm is placed around the cervix or sometimes into the uterus, as in an IUI. Donated sperm is used in assisted conception in exactly the same way either for ICSI or IVF.

What Are the Success Rates?

According to the HFEA, the success rates are:

WOMAN'S AGE	SUCCESS RATE PER CYCLE OF DONOR INSEMINATION (%)
>30	13.5
35–39	9
>40	2.5

In your journey, I would consider six cycles and then review.

EGG DONATION

If your body is not producing eggs, for whatever reason – be it due to an absence of ovaries (from birth or due to surgery) or as a result of an early menopause – you still may be able to conceive and carry a child. This is often an option for older women whose egg quality has naturally declined or for couples who know they are at risk of passing on a genetic disorder.

As with sperm donations, egg donors are screened so that they closely match your own physical characteristics. All egg donors are rigorously tested for HIV and other infections. Once the donor has been selected, she will be given the drugs required for a standard IVF treatment and then will undergo the egg-retrieval surgery described on page 311. Once the eggs have been collected, the donor's involvement is over, and she won't need to take any further medication.

Eggs from a donor are used fresh because, unlike sperm, they do not survive freezing terribly well. Once the egg has been fertilised with your partner's sperm, the fresh embryo will then be transferred to your uterus just as it would be for IVF. Your doctor will have prescribed you with oestrogen and progesterone in order to prepare the lining of the uterus for the transfer. You'll need to continue to take some medication after the embryo has been transferred to help maintain the pregnancy in the early weeks.

Spare embryos may also be frozen at this stage in case they're needed later on. This is particularly important for couples who go on to have another child and are anxious to have the same genetic parents for both children.

Some couples who have successfully received IVF or have decided not to follow this route any longer choose to donate any additional (frozen) embryos that they stored at the time of their fertility treatment.

The law states that all couples using donors must be offered professional counselling. Talking over the implications of donor treatment is very important. Not only are there emotional issues of your own that need to be considered but you also need to take into account your unborn baby and how this might affect their future.

After 2008 (when children born after 1 August 1991 reach 16), donor children intending to marry can contact the HFEA to find out if they are related to their partner.

What Are the Success Rates?

Results produced by the HFEA in 2001 show that 1,783 cycles of IVF were carried out using donated eggs in the UK, and 189 cycles of IVF using donated embryos. In that year, there were 465 live births resulting from IVF with donated eggs or embryos.[3]

EGG SHARING

Some clinics have introduced an egg-sharing programme. This allows women who cannot afford IVF to go through a treatment programme of IVF at a reduced cost if they share their eggs with a third party. Egg sharing is regulated in the UK by the HFEA.

EMBRYO FREEZING

Following embryo transfer, any remaining viable embryos may be frozen for later transfer (this process is called cyropreservation). The sperm could come from either her partner or a donor. In the UK, the embryos can be frozen for up to ten years with the intent of thawing and transferring them at a later date.

Embryos may be stored from the following situations:

1. Surplus embryos are produced at timed IVF/ICSI cycles.
2. If you are at great risk of ovarian hyperstimulation, the clinic may decide to freeze them all.
3. If there are medical reasons why at present you should not have the embryos replaced (e.g. if you are about to undergo chemotherapy or radiotherapy).

Having embryos stored means that you do not have to go through another full IVF/ICSI treatment cycle. If, at some future stage, you did not want to use frozen embryos for yourself then they could either be destroyed, donated or used for research e.g. stem cell studies.

Embryos are stored in liquid nitrogen. Before freezing, more consent forms will need to be completed, and you will be asked to decide what to do with them if you or your partner die or separate.

The maximum time allowed to store embryos is usually five years but in certain circumstances this can be increased to ten years. Charges in clinics vary according to length of stay. Very rarely (e.g. following cancer treatment), you may be allowed to store embryos up until you are 55 years of age.

When one is undergoing treatment for the first occasion, freezing may be an ideal solution. Indeed, I often see couples who are extremely disappointed if they do not have freezing available. However, on many occasions, I have come across situations where couples, having had successful treatment, find that freezing can create a dilemma. The example below is very typical.

CASE STUDY – THE DILEMMA OF FREEZING

Mr and Mrs S. G. had been trying for three years to conceive and were both aged 34. They had had one child in the past, and sadly, after this pregnancy, Mrs S. G. had had two ectopic pregnancies and both tubes had been removed. In view of this, they went on and had an IVF cycle. I am delighted to say that the first cycle was successful and twins were conceived and eventually delivered. During this IVF cycle, they had another six embryos, which were stored.

Three years later, they came to discuss the options for the embryos with me. They had now completed the family and did not want to have further children. The options were as follows: 1. destroy the embryos, 2. use the embryos themselves, 3. offer the embryos for research, 4. donate the embryos. They were not comfortable with any of the options, but having discussed them and seen different counsellors, they eventually agreed to destroy the embryos. They were, however, concerned that their twins would realise their would-be siblings had been destroyed.

What Are the Success Rates?

In most IVF clinics, the transfer of frozen embryos results in a lower pregnancy and live birth rates than fresh embryo transfer. The risk of multiple pregnancy is also lower. The success rate does not depend on the length of time they have been stored. It is usually about half that of a fresh transfer.

Not all embryos are suitable for freezing; overall, about 50% of frozen embryos survive the thawing process, and there may be difficulties in fertilising the thawed eggs.

BREAKING NEWS!

A mother has given birth to what are believed to be the first twins to be born in the UK from frozen eggs. The two girls, Isabella and Anna Fahey, were born from eggs that had been kept in deep-freeze storage for two years. Their mother's own eggs were fertilised by her partner's sperm.

OVARY TRANSPLANT – BREAKING NEWS

A woman who became infertile during her teens gave birth to a baby girl in 2005 after receiving healthy ovary tissue from her identical twin sister. The woman had gone through a very early menopause at the age of 14, but her twin sister had not and had had three children of her own. After unsuccessfully trying to conceive using eggs donated by her sister, doctors decided to try to graft some of her sister's ovarian tissue onto each of her ovaries. Because the twins have the same genes, there was a decreased chance of organ rejection. Soon after the procedure, the previously infertile woman started having periods and was able to conceive.

The success of this treatment may have far-reaching implications for women who want to preserve their fertility before having to have potentially sterilising cancer treatment. Doctors may be able to graft back a piece of a woman's ovary that was frozen before her cancer treatment.[4]

CONCLUSION

By now you will have gathered together lots of information from many different sources. Often it can feel as though there is a minefield of detail to navigate your way through. As you reassess and update your goals and mini goals, questions and insights will occur to you. It's a good idea to write these down – organising your thoughts in this way can bring clarity and help you to work out your own personal preferences, limitations and motivations.

There a number of different routes and options in the area of fertility, and finding a way of integrating these can feel a bit like putting together a 1,000-piece jigsaw. That's why it's so important to work out your own bespoke package of treatment. This means looking at the options and suggestions given here – from diet and lifestyle to the different types of assisted conception techniques – deciding which seem best suited to you and your partner *at this time* and putting them together in an easy-to-follow plan.

Remember, communication is important. If different practitioners are involved, get them to communicate with each other using the cooperation card on page 159.

There is no one set of rules or guidelines that I give to each of the couples that I see. What might be right for one couple may not be right for another. Each couple's needs, fears, limitations (emotional, physical, financial and so on) and priorities will differ wildly from the next; that's why I believe it is so important to find a plan that fits *you*.

One of the most important elements in your bespoke package – and one that I advise all of my patients to follow – is the Fit for Fertility Programme outlined in Part 2. Fill in the Fit for Fertility Checklist on page 55. The programme really is the bedrock of your programme and so, to recap, let's go over its main elements one last time.

FIT FOR FERTILITY PRE-CONCEPTION PROGRAMME

Getting your body ready for conception and pregnancy can be one of the most useful and effective steps you take. And don't forget: this applies to your partner, too! Give yourselves three months to really boost your overall health, to eliminate toxins and to clear up any infections. You can also use this time to explore the complementary and alternative measures described in Chapter 13 and to find ways of reducing your stress levels.

If you and your partner are planning to have IVF or another kind of assisted conception treatment, it is just as important that you get yourself into good health. Studies show that this can affect the outcome of fertility treatment.

Here's a fertility fitness reminder to help you kick-start your package of treatment:

- **Stay positive.** Positive thoughts are so important. Keep this at the forefront of your mind – you are a winner. I use positive thoughts as reinforcements. Write your mantra and keep it in your diary. Stick to it. Stick it on your wall. On my mobile phone, the logo I used to have was 'Positive thoughts lead to positive results.' I now have 'Adversity is an inspirational leader.' Remember to use your visualisation technique.
- **Diet.** Make sure you and your partner are getting enough good foods and limiting the amount of bad foods in your diet. Stock up on fresh fruit and vegetables, preferably organic. Try to

include foods rich in zinc, folic acid and essential fatty acids. Check that your weight is within the recommended range. Eat enough protein and stay well hydrated.

- **Alcohol.** Cut back on your drinking or, even better, stop drinking alcohol altogether. You'll probably feel much better for it, and reducing your alcohol intake will help balance out those all-important hormones. This is particularly important for your partner.

- **Smoking.** Stop! I'm afraid there's no halfway house with smoking. Whether you are trying to conceive naturally or going on to have IVF treatment, it is vital that you kick the habit. Chemicals in cigarettes not only rob the body of important nutrients but they severely affect both male and female hormones and can seriously put your fertility at risk.

- **Screening.** Make an appointment with your GP so that you can both be screened for any underlying medical conditions or infections that could be compromising your fertility.

- **Supplements.** Make sure you are both getting at least a good multivitamin each day. There is lots of research to suggest that taking certain vitamin and mineral supplements can improve your fertility fitness. Refer back to Chapter 9 to see which ones you should be taking.

- **CAM.** CAM therapy has an important role, and I believe this role increases as more and more evidence develops. Look into acupuncture, medical herbalism, homeopathy and hypnotherapy. At the Poundbury Clinic and Westover House, we are working together as a team in an integrated way to get the best results for you.

- **See your GP.** If you have been trying to get pregnant for some time and are over 35, it might be a good idea to start the ball rolling by making an appointment with your GP during this three-month programme. There is no harm in getting a medical assessment sooner rather than later and, for many women, having an appointment in place can help to clarify what decisions need to be made. This is particularly relevant for older women who may go on to have fertility treatment where there can be long waiting lists to contend with.

'To accomplish great things, we must not only act, but also dream; not only plan, but also believe.'

Anatole France

THE NEXT STEP – KEEP SEVERAL OPTIONS OPEN AT ONCE

After your three-month pre-conception programme, depending on your age, you may decide to just keep trying naturally. Good health and balanced hormones can mean you'll conceive surprisingly quickly.

Most couples I see, however, prefer to have a plan mapped out with more than one option.

This plan could simply be: make an appointment to see my doctor in six months and in the meantime keep trying. Or it could be: make an appointment now for some initial fertility tests and in the meantime keep trying and stick to the Fit for Fertility Programme. Or the plan may be: make an appointment now for some fertility tests, stick to the Fit for Fertility Programme and visit some fertility clinics to see which might be best suited to me for any future fertility treatment.

Or if you have already had fertility investigations and know the cause of your fertility problem: put my name on the IVF waiting list and in the meantime have six sessions of acupuncture, work out whether we can afford to pay for private IVF treatment and visit some clinics and compare their prices and success rates on the HFEA website (see Useful Contacts and Websites).

DON'T THINK MONTH TO MONTH

'We live each month under the tyranny of her cycle.'[1] This powerful, and, for many, recognisable, statement is the voice of a

334

clearly despondent man trying to conceive with his partner. Thinking month to month can put a terrible strain on you both and on your relationship. Rather than focusing on goals over which you can assert your control, the agonising guessing game of waiting 'to see' each month can dramatically undermine your confidence, positivity and hope.

Create long- and short-term goals that are achievable. You don't have to get pregnant *this* month, but you could speak to your doctor about ovulation induction, and next month, you could plan to start a course of ovulation-induction medication, and the month after that, you could see a fertility specialist about having IUI treatment.

> 'Be of good cheer. Do not think of today's failures but of the success that may come tomorrow. You have set yourselves a difficult task, but you will succeed if you persevere; and you will find a joy in overcoming obstacles. Remember, no effort that we make to attain something beautiful is ever lost.'
>
> *Helen Keller*

DON'T WAIT FOR 'FAILURE'

Remember, this is a journey – plan as much as you can, but you can always change it with new information that you get.

So then perhaps you will plan to ask about IVF, the month after you plan to see about IUI. Even though you won't yet know the outcome of the ovulation induction or indeed the outcome of IUI, you are nonetheless keeping several options open at once and therefore maximising your chances of finding one that works for you. Don't wait for one route to 'fail' before exploring another. Stagger your treatment options over time but have them in place if it helps to keep you focused and motivated.

I count it as hedging your bets, do not forget certain options take time to put into action. Egg donation has up to an 18-month waiting list, so get your name on the list early; you can always take it off. Adoption can also be a slow process, so get the ball rolling early. You may not eventually go down this line but explore all the options.

Each success is something to feel proud of, whether it's having those six sessions of acupuncture that you promised yourself, or losing the 10lb that needed to be lost or beginning your first IVF treatment cycle. This is a difficult journey and you need to acknowledge that, and at the same time, congratulate and reward yourselves for taking each important step.

DON'T TURN YOUR DESIRE INTO AN OBSESSION

While I strongly advocate the need for a plan and for careful goal setting, trying for a baby should not take over your entire lives. This isn't good for you, your partner or your relationships.

Make time out for activities or breaks that are not about your fertility or conceiving. Allow your mind to focus on other areas:

- See your friends –find out what's going on with them.
- Enjoy your work – get your teeth into a new project.
- Spend time with your partner *not* discussing treatment or temperature charts.
- Have sex at the *wrong* time of the month, just because you feel like it.
- Take advantage of the freedom of not having a child right now.

COPING WITH YOUR EMOTIONS

Going through fertility treatment can bring up all sorts of emotions from excitement and hope to anger and frustration. You will need to find ways of coping with this, whether through talking over your worries and concerns with your partner or a counsellor or having some complementary and alternative therapy to help manage your stress levels.

Treatment can put a great strain on your relationship, and you both may need to remind yourselves from time to time that you're on the same side. Try not to blame each other for what is happening to you. This is nobody's fault, and there are no guilty parties. Some men express feelings of guilt that their partner is having to go through invasive treatment because of something that is wrong with *them*. Remember that there are two of you in the relationship and any decisions you make are because it is what you have *both* agreed. Support each other through this time; after all, you are both striving for the same result.

Talking things through and trying to see the situation from the other's perspective can bring a new level of mutual respect and understanding that can only deepen your relationship.

There may be days when you feel cut off from the rest of world and alone in your situation. Talking to other women going through the same experience can be very rewarding and reassuring. Ask you doctor about being put in touch with groups and organisations that can offer this support (see Useful Contacts and Websites).

Don't put yourself into situations that add to your pain. It's perfectly all right to decline invitations to baby-focused gatherings or celebrations. Your friends and family will understand.

Equally, you are likely to feel pretty tired a lot of the time, especially if you are going through IVF treatment. Don't feel pressured into attending social events or taking on more work. Be firm about the time you need for yourself.

WORK OUT YOUR LIMITS

We all have different limits with different factors influencing our choices. Our family backgrounds, the work we do, the beliefs we hold, the money we have and the lives we choose to lead are all what make us so unique and what will help to form the decisions we make.

When I see couples who have been trying to conceive for many years without success, I sometimes hear them say, 'I'll do anything to have a baby.' But often when we explore this statement together, a different message emerges. Some couples *will* do just about anything for a baby, but for most, there is a limit.

We all have limits – this could be financial, age or the age gap between other children. What I look at is creating this journey to give you the best chance for you with your unique circumstances. With this, whatever the outcome, you can at least say, 'We have tried our best; we have no regrets.'

If you have had three rounds of unsuccessful IVF treatment, your desire for a baby may not have diminished, but the cost – emotionally and physically as well as financially – may now seem to you to be too great. At this point, I might suggest adoption or surrogacy as an alternative route. Some couples will decide to pursue this, but others may strongly feel that this is not going to be an option for them – even if this means not having a baby.

WHAT TO TELL YOUR CHILD

You will also want to think about how the decision you make now will affect you, your partner and your child in the future. This is particularly relevant when considering egg or sperm donation. You both need be sure this is something you feel committed to. Many couples are delighted to be having a child and the genetics are not felt to be important, but others feel concerned that they will feel and be seen as less of a parent. Before you make your decision, you should be offered counselling, this is a good way of understanding and articulating your feelings and concerns.

Parents will also need to decide whether and when to tell their child/children about the way in which they were conceived. There are arguments for and against disclosure. Some will say that by not telling their child the couple themselves and their child will be protected from negative social attitudes and that the relationship between the child and the non-genetic parent will not be put under difficult psychological strain. The other side of the argument favours openness and uses the example of adoptive parents and their children, where it's widely acknowledged that adopted children benefit from knowing about their genetic parents. A more obvious argument, of course, is that to maintain this sort of secrecy within a family can be detrimental to the different relationships. Any kind of revelatory outburst from either parent later on in the child's life could be extremely damaging.[2]

Because of the new HFEA ruling, children born of donors will be able to trace their biological parent when they turn 18. This is also something you need be prepared for if you are deciding to pursue this particular treatment option.

> 'The bond that links your true family is not one of blood,
> but of respect and joy in each other's life.'
>
> *Richard Bach*

KNOWING WHEN TO STOP

Infertility is an experience that continually changes in intensity, so at different stages, you will have different feelings, needs and concerns. Staying positive and focused is an important way of dealing with these difficult feelings and keeping you motivated when nothing seems to be working for you. Recognising when you have had enough is terribly important, too.

Sometimes, I see couples who have tried just about every treatment and who have a very limited chance of success carrying on regardless month after month year after year. Deciding to end treatment is a painful process, especially in situations where there is no conclusive diagnosis.

For some couples, there simply comes a time when they feel they have reached the end of the road. This can be a gradual realisation or more sudden. It may be that one of you reaches this conclusion before the other. Counselling can help you both to deal with this and talk through your feelings together.

The idea of stopping treatment is a frightening one – what lies beyond the treatment that has become so integral to daily life? Having to deal with the grief and sense of loss that comes with not being able to have a child can be delayed, to some extent, while treatment is still ongoing. Deciding to stop means having to address difficult feelings that can often seem overwhelming. People who have successfully dealt with challenges in other areas of their lives can feel that 'giving up' after so much investment and struggle is almost unthinkable.

Deciding to take a break from treatment can often be a compromise for weary couples. By planning to reassess where you are in six months' time, you give yourselves time out without having to make a final decision. Often this break will give you time to really think about how much further you're prepared to go. Or you may use the time to consider other options, such as adoption or fostering. Some couples say that having a break allows them to feel what it's like to have their lives back, and this sense of relief is enough to help them decide to stop treatment altogether.

It's important to talk things through with your doctor, too. Sometimes there can be a sense that by stopping treatment you are in some way letting your doctor and clinic down. Please be reassured that this is never the case; you will not be disappointing your doctor. Their role is as much about helping you to stop as it is about encouraging you to continue.

Here are some questions that may help you and your partner come to a decision:[3]

- Do you feel you have explored all the medical options you wish to?
- Would it help you to get another medical opinion?
- Do you feel resentment or excitement when you go to speak to your doctor about your treatment plan?
- Are you continuing treatment to avoid disappointing someone else?

- Is getting pregnant more important than being a parent?
- Have you started to consider other family-building options that you wouldn't have considered this time last year?
- How would you feel if your doctor told you there was nothing more he or she could do for you?
- Do you feel you have begun to let go of the dream of having your own biological child?

This decision will probably be one of the hardest you will ever have to make. Once you have made it, it's likely you will experience an onslaught of conflicting feelings. Couples describe feeling a range of emotions that change daily. Here are some of the most common emotions you might be dealing with:

- Grief – for the child you won't have.
- Anger – with yourself, your partner, the medical profession for not being able to make your dream come true.
- Relief – that you can now leave behind the difficult medical procedures and return to your life again.
- Loss – that there is no longer the routine of medical treatment and with that the hope of something at the end of it.
- Exhaustion – both physical and emotional.
- Pride – that you have been able to survive such a difficult process, that your relationship has weathered this experience and brought you closer together.
- Optimism – for what the future holds for you both, without the stress and anxiety that trying for a baby brought with it.

It may take some time for these feelings to subside and for you to really be able to feel that you have moved on. That's perfectly natural, and you shouldn't try to rush back into your normal routine if you're not ready. Tell people if you want, but do this in your own time. Support each other through this difficult stage and seek professional counselling if you feel talking about it with someone less involved may help.

Take time to be kind to yourself, you have been through a lot, and you're going to need plenty of love and care. Make plans for the future if that helps, but give yourself time and space to fully recover.

STAYING POSITIVE

Whatever your unique set of circumstances happen to be, dealing with fertility problems can be a challenging and demanding experience. It can be an experience that makes you stronger, braver and more self-aware. And it can bring new understanding to your relationship, deepening your love and respect for your partner and strengthening the bond between you.

Learning to stay positive in the face of setbacks and disappointment is a remarkable achievement and one that you should feel very proud of. Being positive is about seeing beyond the difficulties and finding the hope and opportunities that can often be shadowed.

Set your goals and congratulate yourself for achieving them. Every step of this journey, whatever the outcome, is a significant one and deserves to be acknowledged as such. Don't be afraid to try new things or change tack if you feel the route you are on is no longer the right one for you. Listen to your own inner voice and let that guide you.

Keep communicating, with your partner, your friends and family, and your doctors and therapists. Let them know how you're feeling; they are there to help you. Talking things through can help unravel the confusing knots that are bound to crop up.

Above all, remember who you are! You are not defined by your fertility or by whether or not you have a child. Family means much more than having children; it's about forming and sustaining caring relationships with people you love and who love you, and that is something we can all achieve.

Remember, keep positive and good luck.

Hospital No.:   Registration Date:

Woman's FIRST NAME: LAST NAME:

D.O.B: /   /   AGE:

Man's FIRST NAME: LAST NAME:

D.O.B: /   /   AGE:

Who referred you?

    1.   Consultant   (name)

    2.   G.P.   (name)

    3.   Self referred

How long have you and your partner been together?:   since . . . . . . (specify year)

When did you first start trying for a baby?:   since . . . . . . (specify year)
    (i.e.: when did you stop using any form of contraception)

PREVIOUS PREGNANCIES

A. WOMAN

How many pregnancies have you had with your partner? (if none please state)

How many pregnancies have you had with any previous partners? (if none please state)

YEAR AND OUTCOME OF ANY PREGNANCIES

Year	Outcome (live birth, miscarriage, ectopic, termination)	Type (Natural / IVF / Donor)

B. MAN

How many pregnancies have you fathered with previous partners? (if none please state)

FEMALE HISTORY

MENSTRUAL HISTORY

How old were you when your period started?   years

Are your periods regular?   YES / NO

How many days do you bleed for?   days

If your periods are regular, how many days are there usually
between the first day of one period and the first day of the next?   days

If your periods are not regular, what are the shortest and
longest times between periods in the last 12 months?

When did your last period start?   /   /

Are your periods painful?   YES / NO

How many times do you have sexual intercourse?   / week

Do you bleed during or after sexual intercourse? YES / NO

Do you experience pain during intercourse? YES / NO

Do your breasts ever secrete fluid? YES / NO

Do you have a problem with body hair? YES / NO

Have you started your menopause? YES / NO

If so, when?

Do you take hormone replacement therapy? YES / NO

If so, when started?

What form of HRT do you take?

PREVIOUS CONTRACEPTION: (please tick)

	years (from/to)	problems
The pill (brand:) ( )		
IUCD (coil) ( )		
Barrier (condom/cap) ( )		
Intra-muscular injection ( )		

PREVIOUS SURGICAL HISTORY (please tick if you have had any of the following)

( ) Wedge Resection of ovaries ( ) Removal of right ovary

( ) Laparoscopic Ovarian Diathermy ( ) Removal of left ovary

( ) Tubal Surgery ( ) Removal of ovarian cyst

( ) Appendectomy ( ) Surgery on cervix

( ) Separation of adhesions ( ) Sterilisation

( ) Removal of fibroids (myomectomy) ( ) Reversal of sterilisation

Other abdominal or pelvic operations:

PREVIOUS MEDICAL HISTORY (please tick if you have had any of the following)

( ) Rheumatic Fever ( ) Radiotherapy

( ) TB ( ) Chemotherapy

( ) Diabetes ( ) Thyroid

( ) Jaundice ( ) Asthma

( ) Hypertension ( ) Myocardial Infraction

( ) CVA ( ) Epilepsy

Do you have any inherited conditions? YES / NO
If yes, please give details

Do you have immunity to rubella? YES / NO

Do you have   Sickle cell anaemia or trait   YES / NO
                 Thalassaemia   YES / NO

Are you on any long-term medication? YES / NO
If yes, please give details

Do you have any allergies? YES / NO
If yes, please give details

GYNAECOLOGICAL HISTORY

Any vaginal discharge requiring treatment by a doctor (excluding thrush)? YES / NO

STD (e.g.: chlamydia, syphilis, gonorrhoea, genital herpes or genital warts? YES / NO

Pelvic inflammatory disease? YES / NO

When was your last cervical smear? / /

Have you ever had an abnormal smear? YES / NO
If yes, please give details (repeat smear, colposcopy only, cone biopsy, laser treatment)

GENERAL HEALTH

How tall are you?

What is your weight? BMI:

Is your weight steady / increasing / decreasing?

Do you smoke? YES / NO
if yes, cigarettes/day

Do you drink? YES / NO
if yes, units/week

Do you take any social drugs? YES / NO

Do you have any relevant family history? (particularly any history of breast
or gynaecological cancer on your mother's side of the family) YES / NO
If yes, please give details

Have you had any hospital admissions for any other illnesses? YES / NO

Have you had any problems with anaesthetic in the past? YES / NO

Have you ever used any form of complementary therapy? YES / NO
If yes, what and when
If yes, please give names of practitioners
If yes, consent to contact practitioners? YES / NO

What is your occupation?

PREVIOUS INVESTIGATIONS *Please indicate if you have ever had any of the following*

	Carried out	Year	Place
Laparoscopy	( )		
Hysteroscopy	( )		
Hysterosalpingogram	( )		

MALE HISTORY Have you ever had any of the following?

Undescended testicle	YES / NO
Surgery for hernia	YES / NO
Surgery for prostate enlargement	YES / NO
Surgery for twisted testicle (torsion)	YES / NO
Testicular tumour	YES / NO
Accident involving your genitalia	YES / NO
Varicocele	YES / NO
Diagnosed sexually transmitted disease	YES / NO

Inflammation of the testicle or epididymis	YES / NO
Mumps (age)	YES / NO
Cystoscopy	YES / NO
Vasectomy	YES / NO
Vasectomy reversal	YES / NO
Previous radiotherapy	YES / NO
Previous chemotherapy	YES / NO
Congenital Vas Aplasia	YES / NO

SEXUAL HISTORY

Do you have any problems with sex?	YES / NO
Are you able to produce a semen sample by masturbation?	YES / NO
How many times do you have sexual intercourse?	/ week

GENERAL HEALTH

Have you had any serious illnesses in the past? If yes, please give details	YES / NO
Are you on long term medication?	YES / NO
Do you smoke? if yes,	YES / NO cigarettes/day
Do you drink? if yes,	YES / NO units/week
Do you take any social drugs?	YES / NO
Do you have any inherited conditions? If yes, please give details	YES / NO
Have you ever used any form of complementary therapy? If yes, what and when If yes, please give names of practitioners If yes, consent to contact practitioners?	YES / NO YES / NO
What is your occupation?	
Has the male partner ever had a semen test? If Yes, when	YES / NO

PREVIOUS FERTILITY TREATMENT *(To be filled by the Couple)*

Have you had any fertility treatment in the past? If so, states how many cycles. If Yes:	YES / NO
Did you receive treatment with Clomid?	YES / NO
Did you have artificial insemination (IUI)?	YES / NO
Did you have previous attempts at (IVF)?	YES / NO
Did you have previous attempts at (GIFT)?	YES / NO
Did you have previous attempts at (ICSI)?	YES / NO
Did you have previous attempts at (Frozen ET)?	YES / NO
Did you have previous attempts at (Egg Donation)?	YES / NO

GLOSSARY

abandoned cycle
: An IVF treatment cycle stopped after drug administration has begun but before the collection of eggs.

assisted hatching
: The laser or mechanical breaking of the outer layer of the egg (the zona pellucida).

assisted reproductive technology (ART)
: The collective name for all artificial techniques used to assist conception.

azoospermia
: The absence of sperm in male ejaculate.

blastocyst
: A five- to six-day-old embryo.

CAM
: Complementary and alternative medicine.

cervical mucus
: Secretions in the cervical canal, which alter in consistency during ovulation.

cervix
: The narrow neck at the lower end of the uterus or womb that joins the vagina.

chlamydia
: A sexually transmitted disease that can remain undetected for some time. The disease can damage the male and female reproductive systems.

clomid	A drug used to induce ovulation.
clomifene	A drug used to stimulate the production of follicles.
corpus luteum	This is what remains from the follicle once the egg has been released.
cryopreservation	The freezing of gametes or embryos.
cyst	A cyst in an ovary is a fluid-filled structure that does not contain an egg.
DFI	DNA fragmentation index.
donor insemination (DI)	The introduction of donor sperm into the cervix or womb.
egg	The female gamete released during each monthly menstrual cycle.
egg collection	The collection of eggs from a woman's ovary using either a laparoscope or an ultrasound-guided needle.
egg donation	The donation of eggs by a fertile woman for use in fertility treatment.
egg sharing	A relatively new arrangement in which, during the course of IVF treatment, a woman uses some of her eggs but also donates some for others to use.
embryo	A fertilised egg that has the potential to develop into a foetus.
embryo freezing	A process in which 'spare' embryos are frozen and stored for future use.
embryo transfer	The transfer of embryos into the female patient.
endometriosis	A female condition in which parts of the lining of the womb (endometrium) grow outside of the womb, leading to pain during intercourse and possible infertility.

endometrium	The lining of the womb, which sheds during menstruation and which supports a foetus when pregnancy occurs.
epididymis	A coiled tube, around 7m in length, that connects the testes to the vas deferens and through which sperm travels.
fallopian tube(s)	The tube where the egg and sperm meet that connects the ovaries and the womb.
fertilisation	The penetration of an egg by a sperm resulting in the formation of an embryo. Natural fertilisation takes place within a woman's body, but it can also occur in laboratory conditions (in vitro).
fibroid	A non-cancerous growth in the muscular wall of the uterus.
foetus	The term given to an embryo after eight weeks of development up until birth.
follicle	A small sac-like structure in the ovary in which the egg develops.
follicle-stimulating hormone (FSH)	A pituitary-released hormone that stimulates follicle production. It is also used in assisted conception to stimulate the production of several follicles.
gamete	The male sperm or the female egg.
gamete intra-fallopian transfer (GIFT)	An assisted-conception procedure in which eggs are retrieved, mixed with sperm and replaced back into the fallopian tube for fertilisation to occur.
gonadotropins	Hormones (FSH and LH) released from the pituitary gland that stimulate the ovaries.

hormones	Chemical messengers produced by different glands that run our minds, brains and bodies.
human chorionic gonadotropin (hGC)	The presence of this hormone in female blood or urine indicates a pregnancy.
HFEA	Human Fertilisation and Embryology Authority.
hysterosalpingogram (HSG)	An X-ray of the fallopian tubes to ascertain any obstructions.
implantation	Where an embryo embeds itself in the lining of the uterus, having passed through the fallopian tube.
impotence	A man's inability to gain an erection.
insemination	The artificial placing of sperm in the female reproductive tract.
intra-cytoplasmic sperm injection (ICSI)	A procedure in which a single sperm is injected into an egg.
intrauterine insemination (IUI)	Insemination of sperm into the woman's uterus.
in vitro fertilisation (IVF)	Process in which eggs and sperm are mixed together in the laboratory. Any embryos that develop are then transferred into the female or frozen.
laparoscopy	An internal examination of the abdomen and pelvic organs using a telescope. Usually carried out under a general anaesthetic.
luteinising hormone (LH)	Hormone released by the pituitary gland. Essential for the development of eggs and sperm.
menstrual cycle	A woman's monthly cycle where an egg is released from the ovary, the lining of the womb develops and then

	sheds via the vagina, unless pregnancy occurs.
mixed agglutination reaction test (MAR)	The test for antisperm antibodies.
multiple birth	When a multiple pregnancy results in the birth of two or babies.
multiple pregnancy	Where two or more foetuses develop at one time in the womb.
oestrogen	A group of female hormones produced by the ovaries. The levels of the hormone change during the menstrual cycle.
oligozoospermia	Low sperm count.
oocyte	The female egg (gamete).
ovarian failure	When the ovary stops producing eggs.
ovarian hyper-stimulation syndrome (OHSS)	A serious complication following the stimulation of the ovaries with ovulation induction drugs.
ovary	The female reproductive organ that contain and release eggs.
ovulation	The monthly release of an egg.
pelvic inflammatory disease (PID)	The infection of the organs within the pelvis.
percutaneous epididy-mal sperm aspiration (PESA)	A technique for sperm removal in which a fine needle is passed into the coiled tubing surrounding the testicles that store the sperm and sperm are recovered through suction.
polycystic ovaries (PCO)	A common condition where ovaries increase slightly in size with small cysts. PCOs may lead to polycystic ovarian syndrome (PCOS).
polycystic ovarian syndrome (PCOS)	This may result in irregular periods, infertility, excessive hair growth, acne or obesity.

preimplantation genetic diagnosis (PGD)	The removal of one or two cells from an embryo to test for genetic disorders.
premature menopause	Ovarian failure before the age of 40–45.
progesterone	A hormone produced by the ovary and corpus luteum after ovulation to encourage the growth of the lining of the uterus.
prostate gland	The gland that secretes a solution that makes up the major part of the ejaculate.
seminiferous tubules	Long and convoluted tubes that make up the bulk of the testicles. It is here that sperm are produced.
sperm	Male gametes. A single sperm is called a spermatozoon.
spermatid	An immature sperm cell.
stimulated cycle	A treatment cycle in which drugs are administered to produce more eggs than usual during a woman's monthly cycle.
superovulation	The stimulation of the ovary with drugs to induce the production of multiple follicles in a single cycle.
testis	A testicle or male gonad.
testosterone	The male hormone (woman have a smaller amount of this hormone).
transvaginal aspiration	Method of egg recovery in which a needle is inserted into the ovary.
transvaginal oocyte recovery	Method in which a needle is passed through the vagina using ultrasound guidance in order to retrieve eggs.
treatment cycle	One complete treatment. The cycle begins with the administering of drugs or first insemination.

unstimulated cycle	A natural cycle, without ovulation-stimulating drugs.
uterus	The womb, where the embryo develops.
varicocele	A varicose vein on the testicle.
vas deferens	A pair of tubes that connect the epididymis to the urethra and transport the sperm.
zona pellucida	The membrane surrounding the female's egg.
zygote	The fertilised egg.

USEFUL CONTACTS AND WEBSITES

CLINICS AND FERTILITY PRACTITIONERS

The Hale Clinic
Complementary therapists who deal with fertility issues using herbalism, Ayurveda, homeopathy, acupuncture and nutrition.
Tel: 0207 6310156
Web: www.haleclinic.com

Marilyn Glenville
Nutritionist and psychologist specialising in women's natural health.
Tel: 0870 5329244
Web: www.marilynglenville.com

The Poundbury Clinic
Women's integrated health clinic directed by Michael Dooley.
Tel: 01305 262626
Web: www.thepoundburyclinic.co.uk
www.fitforfertility.co.uk

Viveka
London-based clinic offering a range of medical services and complementary therapies.
Tel: 0207 4830099
Web: www.viveka.co.uk

Zita West
NHS-trained midwife who runs a private clinic offering fertility, ante- and post-natal services.
Tel: 0207 5802169
Web: www.zitawest.com

Westover House
Private general practitioners and visiting consultant specialists working alongside traditional and complementary therapists for an integrated approach to healthcare.
Tel: 0208 8771877
Web: www.westoverhouse.com

The Zhai Clinic
Fertility treatment using traditional Chinese herbal medicine and acupuncture.
Web: www.zhaiclinic.com

FERTILITY ORGANISATIONS

Human Fertilisation and Embryology Authority (HFEA)
Regulates fertility clinic, produces guidelines and provides useful information including a list of UK clinics. *The HFEA Guide to Infertility and Directory of Clinics* can be ordered by phone or downloaded from the website.
Tel: 0207 2918200
Web: www.hfea.gov.uk

Royal College of Obstetricians and Gynaecologists
Provides information including FAQs and links to support groups.
Tel: 0207 7726200
Web: www.rcog.org.uk

HELPLINES AND SUPPORT NETWORKS

British Association for Counselling and Psychotherapy (BCAP)
Tel: 0870 443 5252
Web: www.bacp.co.uk

Cruse Bereavement Care
An organisation offering counselling, advice and support for people suffering from grief and bereavement.
Helpline: 0870 1671677
Web: www.crusebereavementcare.org.uk

Endometriosis.org
A global platform for news in the field of endometriosis. It facilitates the exchange of current information and evidence-based research between clinicians, scientists and support groups worldwide.
Web: www.endometriosis.org

Fertility UK
An educational service that provides information and free downloadable fertility charts.
Web: www.fertilityuk.org

The FPA
Formerly the Family Planning Association, the FPA can provide a list of trained NHS fertility-awareness practitioners.
Helpline: 0845 3101344
Web: www.fpa.org.uk

Infertility Network UK
A national charity offering support and information to those experiencing fertility problems.
Tel: 0870 1188088
Web: www.infertilitynetworkuk.com

International Stress Management Association (ISMA)
Tel: 07000 780430
Web: www.isma.org.uk

London Bereavement Network
A charity offering information about bereavement services in London.
Tel: 0207 2471209
Web: www.bereavement.org.uk

NHS Stop Smoking Programme
Helpline: 0800 1690169
Web: www.giveupsmoking.co.uk

NUTRITION

British Association for Nutritional Therapy (BANT)
Tel: 08706 061284
Web: www.bant.org.uk

Institute of Optimum Nutrition (ION)
Tel: 0208 8779993
Web: www.ion.ac.uk

Natural Health Advisory Service
Formerly the Women's Nutritional Advisory Service.
Tel: 09062 556615
Web: www.naturalhealthas.com

Victoria Health
For advice on what supplements you should be taking.
Web: www.victoriahealth.com

COMPLEMENTARY AND ALTERNATIVE MEDICINE

Aromatherapy and Allied Practitioners' Association (AAPA)
Tel: 0208 6539152
Web: www.aromatherapyuk.net

Alliance of Registered Homeopaths
Tel: 08700 739339
Web: www.a-r-h.org

British Acupuncture Council
Tel: 0208 7350400
Web: www.acupuncture.org.uk

British Complementary Medical Association (BCMA)
Tel: 0845 3455977
Web: www.bcma.co.uk

Brahma Kumaris
World spiritual organisation (for meditation and prayer)
Tel: 0208 7273350
Web: www.bkwsu.org.uk

British Medical Acupuncture Society
Tel: 01753 743348
Web: www.medicalacupuncture.co.uk

British Osteopathic Association
Tel: 01582 488455
Web: www.osteopathy.org

British Reflexology Association
Tel: 01866 821207
Web: www.britreflex.co.uk

The British Wheel of Yoga (BMY)
Tel: 01529 306851
Web: www.bwy.org.uk

Central Register of Advanced Hypnotherapists (CRAH)
Tel: 0207 3549938

Confederation of Healing Organisations (CHO)
A government-recognised body for healing practitioners.
Tel: 0239 2713607
Web: www.confederation-of-healing-organisations.org

Institute of Complementary Medicine (ICM)
Tel: 0207 2375165
Web: www.icmedicine.co.uk

Integrated Medical Centre
Directed by Dr Ali and Dr Wendy Denning
Web: www.dr-ali.co.uk

International Federation of Qualified Aromatherapists (IFPA)
Tel: 01455 637987
Web: www.ifparoma.org

International Register of Consultant Herbalists
Tel: 01792 655886
Web: www.irch.org

Massage Therapy UK
Web: www.massagetherapy.co.uk

National Institute of Medical Herbalists
Tel: 01392 426022
Web: www.nimh.org.uk

Register of Chinese Herbal Medicine
Tel: 01603 623994
Web: www.rchm.co.uk

UK Homeopathy Medical Association
Tel: 01474 560336
Web: www.homeopathy.org

Yoga Therapy Centre
Tel: 0207 6893040
Web: www.yogatherapy.org

REFERENCES

INTRODUCTION

1. K. J. Thomas, P. Coleman and J. P. Nicholl, 'Trends in access to complementary and alternative medicine via primary care in England: 1995–2001' (results from a follow-up national survey), *Family Practice* (2003), vol. 20, pp. 575–7.
2. Simon Parry, *South China Morning Post*, 12 March 2005.
3. 'Fertility: assessment and treatment for people with fertility problems', NICE, developed by the National Collaborating Centre for Women's and Children's Health Clinical Guideline (11 February 2004).
4. 'Tomorrow's Children: a consultation on guidance to licensed fertility clinics on taking into account the welfare of children to be born of assisted conception treatment', HFEA (February 2005).
5. K. Thomas and P. Coleman, 'Use of complementary or alternative medicine in a general population in Great Britain' (results from the National Omnibus Survey), *Journal of Public Health* (2004), vol. 26, no. 2, pp. 152–7.
6. Alice D. Donmar, Michelle M. Seibel and Herbert Benson, 'The mind/body program for infertility: a new behavioural treatment approach for women with infertility'.
7. Prof. Michael Hull, 'Infertility Treatment: Needs and Effectiveness' (report from the University of Bristol, Department of Obstetrics and Gynaecology), *Journal of Human Reproduction* (November 1992).

CHAPTER 1

1. 'Sexual Positions and Fertility' (from www.fertility.com).

CHAPTER 2

1. 'Greater risk for children of mothers over 40 to die in the womb or as a newborn', *Journal of Obstetrics and Gynaecology* (2004), vol. 104, pp. 727–33.
2. 'Guideline for Practice: Age-related Infertility', American Society for Reproductive Medicine.
3. Hull, 'Infertility Treatment: Needs and Effectiveness'.
4. Adam Balen and Anthony Rutherford, 'Age and the geographical lottery', *Pathways to Pregnancy* (autumn 1999), iss. 1, p. 27.
5. *Ibid.*
6. *Ibid.*
7. *Human Reproduction* (2000), vol. 15, no. 8, pp. 1703–8.
8. Nicky Bradford, *Natural Fertility* (Hamlyn, 2002).

CHAPTER 3

1. Hull, 'Infertility Treatment: Needs and Effectiveness'.
2. 'Infertility: an Introduction' (from www.fertility.com).
3. Herbert Reiss (ed.), *Reproductive Medicine from A–Z* (Oxford University Press, 1998).
4. E. Norwitz and J. Schorge, 'The infertile couple', *Obstetrics and Gynaecology at a Glance* (Blackwell Science, 2001).
5. C. H. Wu, and B. Gocial, *International Journal of Fertility* (1988), vol. 33, no. 5, p. 341.
6. J. Menken, J. Turssell and U. Larsen, 'Age in Infertility', *Science* (1986), vol. 23, p. 1389.

CHAPTER 6

1. Zita West, *Fertility and Conception: the complete guide to getting pregnant* (Dorling Kindersley, 2003).
2. *Ibid.*
3. Adam Balen and Howard Jacobs, *Infertility in Practice* (Churchill Livingstone).

References

4. A. P. Streissguth, H. M. Barr, P. D. Sampson, F. L. Bookstein and B. L. Darby, 'Neurobehavioral effects on prenatal alcohol' (Part 1, Research Strategy, Review of the Literature), *Neurotoxicology and Teratology* (1989), vol. 11, pp. 461–76.

5. D. W. Smith, *Mothering your Unborn Baby* (W.B. Saunders Co., Philadelphia, 1979).

6. Z. West, *Fertility and Conception*.

7. D. H. Van Thiel, R. Lester and R. J. Sherins, 'Hypogonadism in alcoholic liver disease: evidence for a double defect', *Gastroenterology* (1974), vol. 67, pp. 1188–99.

8. D. H. Van Thiel, J. S. Gavaler, R. Lester and M. D. Goodman, 'Alcohol-induced testicular atrophy: an experimental model for hypogonadism occurring in chronic alcoholic man', *Gastroenterology* (1975), vol. 69, pp. 326–32.

9. H. S. Bennet, A. H. Baggenstgors and H. R. Butt, 'The testes, breast and prostate in men who die of cirrhosis of liver', *American Journal of Clinical Pathology* (1950), vol. 20, pp. 814–28.

10. A. Brzek, 'Alcohol and male fertility'(preliminary report), *Andrologia* (1987), vol. 19, pp. 32–6.

11. Balen and Jacobs, *Infertility in Practice.*

12. West, *Fertility and Conception.*

13. *Independent* (7 April 2005).

14. *Pathways to Pregnancy*, p.22.

15. 'Smoking and Pregnancy: a survey of knowledge, attitudes and behaviour 1992–1999', Health Education Authority.

16. K. M. Curtis, D. A. Savitz and T. E. Arbuckle, 'Effects of cigarette smoking, caffeine consumption, and alcohol intake on fecundability', *American Journal of Epidemiology* (1997), vol. 146, pp. 32–41.

17. J. Olsen, 'Cigarette smoking, tea and coffee drinking, and subfecundity', *American Journal of Epidemiology* (1991), vol. 133, pp. 734–9.

18. M. G. Hull et al., 'Delayed conception and active and passive smoking', *Fertility and Sterility* (2000), vol. 74, pp. 725–33.

19. C. R. Weinberg, A. J. Wilcox and D. D. Baird, 'Reduced fecundability in women with prenatal exposure to cigarette smoking', *American Journal of Epidemiology* (1989), vol. 129, pp. 1072–8.

20. D. Poswillo and E. Ablerman, *Effects of Smoking on the Fetus, Neonate, and Child* (Oxford University Press, 1992).

21. M. Saraiya et al., 'Cigarette smoking and the risk factor for ectopic pregnancy', *American Journal of Epidemiology* (1998), vol. 178, pp. 493–8.
22. 'What to do when miscarriage strikes', *PDR Family Guide to Women's Health and Prescription Drugs*.
23. M. Wynn and A. Wynn, 'The prevention of handicap of early pregnancy origin', Foundation for Education and Research in Childbearing (1981), pp. 28–33.
24. R. L. Naeye and E. C. Peters, 'Mental development of children whose mothers smoked during pregnancy', *Journal of Obstetrics and Gynaecology* (1984), vol. 64, no. 5, pp. 601–7.
25. M. L. Rantala and A. I. Koskimies, 'Semen quality of infertile couples – comparison between smokers and non-smokers', *Andrologia* (1986), vol. 19, pp. 420–46.
26. M. H. Briggs, 'Cigarette smoking and infertility in men', *Medical Journal of Australia* (1973), vol. 1, p. 616.
27. V. Kulikauskas, D. Blausutein, R. J. Ablin, 'Cigarette smoking and its possible effect on sperm', *Fertility and Sterility* (1985), vol. 44, pp. 526–8.
28. *Ibid.*
29. L. Wichmann, 'The value of semen analysis in predicting pregnancy', *Acta Universitatis Tamperensis* (1992), series A, vol. 346.
30. *Independent* (from a study in *Human Reproduction*, 7 April 2005).
31. 'Passive smoke link to miscarriage', BBC News (30 April 2004).
32. T. Sorahan et al., 'Childhood cancer and parental use of tobacco: deaths from 1971 to 1976', *British Journal of Cancer* (1997), vol. 76, no. 11, pp. 1525–31.
33. International Food Information Council (IFIC), (2002).
34. Alison Palkhivala, 'BMI linked with changes that may affect fertility', *Urology Times* (Feb 1 2006).
35. American Society for Reproductive Medicine (ASRAM) (Oct 2003).
36. European Society of Human Reproduction and Ebryology (June 2004).

CHAPTER 7

1. E. C. G. Grant, 'Allergies, smoking and the contraceptive pill', *Biological Aspects of Schizophrenia* (G. Hemmings, ed., G. John Wiley and Sons, 1982).

2. D. D. Lewis, 'Alcohol and pregnancy outcome', *Midwives Chronicle and Nursing Notes* (December 1983), pp. 420–3.

CHAPTER 8

1. Ofra Kalter-Leibovici, MD, et al for the Israel Diabetes Research Group (IDRG), 'Clinical, Socioeconomic, and Lifestyle Parameters Associated With Erectile Dysfunction Among Diabetic Men', *Diabetes Care* (2005), vol. 28, pp. 1739–1744.
2. Dua AA, Vaidya SR. 'Sperm motility and morphology as changing parameters linked to sperm count variations.' *J Postgrad Med* 1996;42:93–6.
3. American Fertility Association, (2004).
4. Fertility and IBD, NACC, (July 2001).
5. Gutierrez MJ et al, 'Pregnancy in renal transplant recipients' *Transplant Proct.* (2005 Nov) 37 (9):3721–2.
6. Ajay Kumar Gupta, 'Sex and drug effect', Indmedica, 2005.
7. 'Male Fertility'. Atlanta Reproductive Health Center, June 2005.
8. *Pathways to Pregnancy*, p.22.
9. Balen and Jacobs, *Infertility in Practice*.
10. 'Chlamydia Trachomatis PCR/Antigen (lower tract) and Serum Antibody (upper tract)', *The Doctors' Laboratory* (spring 2005).
11. Bradford, *Natural Fertility*.
12. Peter Chen, MD, 'Early Miscarriage' (review dated 29 June 2001), Obstetrics and Gynecology, University of Pennsylvania School of Medicine.
13. C. E. Swenseon et al., 'Ureaplasma urealyticum and human fertility: the effect of antibiotic therapy on semen quality', *Fertility and Sterility* (1979), vol. 31, pp. 660–5
14. 'Cytomegalovirus (CMV) Infection', National Centre for Infectious Diseases.
15. M. W. Alder, *ABC of Sexually Transmitted Diseases*, British Medical Association (1984).
16. 'Toxoplasmosis', American Pregnancy Association.

CHAPTER 9

1. Food Standards Agency (FSA).
2. Leslie Kenton, *The X-Factor Diet* (Vermillion, 2002).
3. *Dietary Reference Values for Food Energy and Nutrients for the United Kingdom*, Department of Health (1991).
4. FSA.
5. Kenton, *The X-Factor Diet*.
6. 'High Protein Diet, Low Fertility?' *New Scientist* (3 July 2004).
7. Department of Health (25 March 2003).
8. 'Date Production in Namibia', Agriculture and Rural Development in the South.
9. 'Nutrients and Supplements for Fertility and IVF', Infertility Health Information Organization (from www.infertility.health-info.org).
10. 'Infertility', *The Green Pharmacy Herbal Handbook* (Rodale).
11. 'Fertility Diet and Supplements' (from www.infertility.health-info.org).
12. 'Dietary Recommendations for Estrogen Progesterone Balance' (from www.infertility.health-info.org).
13. 'Infertility' (from www.holistic-online.com).
14. C. R. Kennedy, Y. Zhang, S. Brandon, Y. Guan et al., 'Salt-sensitive hypertension and reduced fertility in mice lacking the prostaglandin EP2 receptor', *Nature Medicine* (February 1999), vol. 5, no. 2, pp. 217–20.
15. H. Ohguro, H. Katsushima, I. Maruyama, T. Maeda, S. Yanagihashi, T. Metoki and M. Nakazawa, 'A high dietary intake of sodium glutamate as flavoring (ajinomoto) causes gross changes in retinal morphology and function', *Experimental Eye Research* (September 2002), vol. 75, no. 3, pp. 307–15.
16. L. Russell and M. D. Blaylock, *Excitoxins: The Taste that Kills* (Health Press, 1994).
17. Drs William J. Pizzi, June E. Barnhart et al., 'MSG greatly reduces pregnancy success', *Neurobehavioral Toxicology* (1979), vol. 2, pp. 1–4.
18. Dr Joseph Mercola, NutraSweet Scandal (from www.mercola.com).
19. Richard W. Pressinger and Wayne Sinclair, 'Environmental Causes of Infertility', (report, August 1998).

20. 'Guide to Food Additives', SPI (from www.cspinet.org).

21. 'Acrylamide in staple food: a summary of the April 2002 alert in Sweden, Elisabeth Borch', SIK– the Swedish Institute for Food and Biotechnology (25 April 2002).

22. 'Dietary dangers for fertility and IVF', Infertility Health Information Organization (from www.infertility.health-info.org).

23. *Dorland's Medical Dictionary* (W. B. Saunders, 2000).

24. 'Nutrients and Supplements for Fertility and IVF', Infertility Health Information Organization (from www.infertility.health-info.org).

25. Rotham et al., *New England Journal of Medicine* (1995), vol. 333, no. 221, pp. 157–9.

26. 'Nutrients and Supplements for Fertility and IVF', Infertility Health Information Organization.

27. NHS Direct recommendations.

28. West, *Fertility and Conception*.

29. G. S. Kidd et al., 'The effects of pyridoxine on pituitary hormone secretion in amenorrhea-galactorrhea syndromes', *Journal of Clinical Endocrinology and Metabolism* (1982), vol. 54, no. 4, pp. 872–5.

30. Balen and Jacobs, *Infertility in Practice*.

31. R. Isoyama, Y. Baba, H. Harada et al., 'Clinical experience of methyl-cobalamin (CH3-B12)/clomifene citrate combined treatment in male infertility', *Hinyokika Kiyo* (1986), vol. 32, pp. 1177–83.

32. Jack Forem, *The Complete Book of Men's Health* (Mitchell Beazley, 2004).

33. I. Igarashi, 'Augmentative effects of ascorbic acid upon induction of human ovulation in clomiphen-ineffective anovulatory women', *International Journal of Fertility* (1977), vol. 22, no. 3, pp. 68–73.

34. R. Bayer, 'Treatment of infertility with vitamin E', *International Journal of Infertility* (1960), vol. 5, pp. 70–80.

35. J. Tarin et al., 'Effects of maternal ageing and dietary antioxidant supplementation on ovulation, fertilisation and embryo development in vitro in the mouse', *Reproduction, Nutrition, Development* (1998), vol. 38, no. 5, pp. 499–508.

36. E. Geva et al., 'The effect of anti-oxidant treatment on human spermatozoa and ferilisation rate in an in vitro fertilisation program', *Fertility and Sterility* (1996), vol. 66, no. 3, pp. 430–4.

37. Miscarriage Association newsletter (1992).

38. J. M. Howard, S. Davies and A. Hunnisett, 'Red cell magnesium and glutathione peroxidase in infertile women: effects of oral supplementation with magnesium and selenium', *Magnes Res.*, (1994), vol. 7, no. 1, pp. 49–57.

39. E. A. Doisy, 'Trace Substances in Environmental Health. Proceedings of the University of Missouri's 6th Annual Conference' (1972), p.193, in *Trace Element Metabolism in Animals* (W.G. Hoekstra et al, eds, Univer Park Press, Maryland, 1974), vol. 2, p. 664.

40. G. Saner et al., 'Hair manganese concentrations in newborns and their mothers', *American Journal of Clinical Nutrition* (1985), vol. 41, pp. 1042–4.

41. A. S. Al-Kunani, R. Knight, S. J. Haswell, J. W. Thompson and S. W. Lindow, 'The selenium status of women with a history of recurrent miscarriage', *BJOG: An International Journal of Obstetrics and Gynaecology* (2001), vol. 108, no. 10, pp. 1094–7.

42. R. Scott et al., 'The effect of oral selenium supplementation on human sperm motility', *British Journal of Urology* (1988), vol. 82, pp. 76–80.

43. S. Jameson, 'Effects of zinc deficiency on human reproduction', *Acta Medica Scandinavica* (1976), suppl. 539, pp. 3–82.

44. A. E. Omu, H. Dashti and S. Al-Othman, 'Treatment of asthenozoospermia with zinc sulphate: andrological, immunological and obstetric outcome', *European Journal of Obstetrics and Gynaecology and Reproductive Biology* (1998), vol. 79, pp. 179–84.

45. Horrobin, *Journal of Reproductive Medicine*, (vol 28, 1983).

46. Sijur Olsen, Niels Jurgen Secher, 'Low consumption of seafood in early pregnancy as a risk factor for preterm delivery: A prospective cohort study', *Int J Epidemiol* 1990;19:9717.

47. Hampton, 'Male Fertility', *Journal of the American Medical Association* (JAMA).2005; 294: 2829–2831.

CHAPTER 10

1. Z. West, *Fertility and Conception*.

2. E. Sheiner, E. K. Sheiner, G. Postashnik, R. Carel and I. Shoham-Vardi,

'The relationship between occupational psychological stress and female fertility', *Occupational Medicine* (2003), vol. 53, pp. 265–9.

3. A. Donmar, PhD, *Self-Nurture* (Viking, 2000).
4. 'Bottling it up could reduce fertility', BBC News (2 September 1999).

CHAPTER 12

1. 'Smoking and Infertility', the American Society for Reproductive Medicine.
2. BBC News (31 March 2004).
3. Dr John Dean, Fertility Problems (from wwww.netdoctor.co.uk 1998–2005)
4. *Human Reproduction* (DOI: 10. 1093/humrep/deh616).
5. *The Complete Book of Men's Health*.
6. *Journal of Human Reproduction* (29 April 2004).
7. Drs Hurst, St John, Barratt, Bao and Williamson, 'Selenium and Male Fertility' (reported at the May 1999 annual meeting of the Federation of American Societies for Experimental Biology).
8. R. Bayer, 'Treatment of infertility with vitamin E', *International Journal of Fertility* (1960), vol. 5, pp. 70–8.
9. M. Scibona, P. Meschini, S. Capparelli et al., 'L-arginine and male infertility', *Minerva Urologica e Nefrologica* (1994), vol. 46, pp. 251–3.
10. G. Vitali, R. Parente and C. Melotti, 'Carnitine supplementation in human idiopathic asthenospermia: clinical results', *Drugs Under Experimental and Clinical Research* (1995), vol. 21, pp. 157–9.
11. R. Isoyama, Y. Baba, H. Harada et al., 'Clinical experience of methyl-cobalamin (CH3-B12)/clomifene citrate combined treatment in male infertility', *Hinyokika Kiyo* (1986), vol. 32, pp. 1177–83.

CHAPTER 13

1. Thomas and Coleman, 'Use of complementary or alternative medicine in a general population in Great Britain'.
2. Thomas and Coleman, 'Trends in access to complementary and alternative medicine via primary care in England: 1995–2001'.
3. Bradford, *Natural Fertility*.

4. *Healthy Way,* iss. 24, article 9.
5. 'Herbs for Fertility', from Conceiving Concepts, Inc.
6. David L. Hoffmann, 'M.N.I.M.H. False Unicorn Root', *Herbal Materia Medica.*
7. David Bellamy, *The Bellamy Herbal* (Century, 2003).
8. 'Herbs for Fertility', from Conceiving Concepts, Inc.
9. 'Supplements' (from www.wholehealthmd.com).
10. Bellamy, *The Bellamy Herbal.*
11. Raymond Chang, MD, Pak H. Chung, MD, Zev Rosenwaks, MD, 'Role of acupuncture in the treatment of female infertility' *Fertility and Sterility* (December 2002), vol. 78, no. 6.
12. 'Can reflexology help overcome fertility?' (from www.bbc.co.uk).
13. 'Infertility Research: Alternative and Complementary Therapies', Internet Health Library.

CHAPTER 15

1. D. Cahill and P. Wardle, *Understanding Infertility* (British Medical Association, 2000).

CHAPTER 16

1. 'New NHS guidelines for fertility treatment', National Institute for Excellence press release, (25 February 2004).

CHAPTER 17

1. Balen and Jacobs, *Infertility in Practice.*
2. P. B. Miller and M. R. Soules, 'The usefulness of a urinary LH kit for ovulation prediction during menstrual cycles of normal women', *Obstetrics and Gynecology* (1996), vol. 87, pp. 13–17 (1996 by The American College of Obstetricians and Gynecologists).

CHAPTER 18

1. Terri Yablonsky, 'Male Fertility Testing', *Laboratory Medicine* (June 1996), pp. 379–82.

2. D. P. Evenson, L. K. Jost, M. J. Zinaman, E. Clegg, K. Purvis, P. de Angelis and O. P. Clausen, 'Utility of the sperm chromatin structure assay (SCSA) as a diagnostic and prognostic tool in the human fertility clinic', *Human Reproduction* (2000), vol. 14, pp. 1039–49.
3. *Ibid.*

CHAPTER 19

1. V. A. Akande, L. P. Hunt, D. J. Cahill, E. O. Caul, W. C. L. Ford, J. M. Jenkins, 'Tubal damage in infertile women: prediction using chlamydia serology', *Human Reproduction* (2003), vol. 18, no. 9, pp. 1841–7.
2. *Ibid.*
3. D. W. Cramer, I. Schiff, S. C. Schoenbaum, M. Gibson, S. Belisle, B. Albrecht, R. J. Stillman, M. J. Berger, E. Wilson, B. V. Stadel et al., 'Tubal infertility and the intrauterine device', *New England Journal of Medicine* (11 April 1985), vol. 312, no. 15, pp. 941–7.
4. C. Stacey, C. Bown, A. Manhire and D. Rose, 'HyCoSy – as good as claimed?' *The British Journal of Radiology*, vol. 73, iss. 866, pp. 133–6 (© 2000 British Institute of Radiology).
5. Sandra J. Tanahotoe, MD, Peter G. A. Hompes, PhD, and Cornelis B. Lambalk, PhD, 'Accuracy of diagnostic laparoscopy in the infertility work-up before intrauterine insemination', *Fertility and Sterility* (February 2003), vol. 79, no. 2.
6. 'NHS Fertility: Assessment and Treatment for People with Fertility Problems – Full Guideline', National Institute for Clinical Excellence (RCOG Press, 2004).

CHAPTER 20

1. Adam Balen, 'Ovulation induction – optimising results and minimizing risks', *Human Fertility* (2003), vol. 6, supp. 42–51.
2. J. W. Rich-Edwards, D. Spiegelman, M. Garland, E. Hertzmark, D. J. Hunter, G. A. Colditz, W. C. Willett and J. E. Manson, 'Physical activity, body mass index, and ovulatory disorder infertility', *Epidemiology* (March 2002), vol. 13, no. 2, pp. 184–90.

3. Balen, 'Ovulation induction – optimising results and minimizing risks'.

4. E. S. Knochenhauer, T. J. Key, M. Kahsar-Miller et al., 'Prevalence of the polycystic ovary syndrome in unselected black and white women of the southeastern United States: a prospective study', *Journal of Clinical Endocrinology and Metabolism* (1998), vol. 83, pp. 3078–82.

5. F. Grodstein, M. B. Goldman and D. W. Cramer, 'Body mass index and ovulatory infertility', *Epidemiology* (December 1983), vol. 5, pp. 247–50.

6. A. M. Clark, W. Ledger, C. Aglletly, L. Tomlinson, F. Blaney, X. Wang and R. J. Norman, 'Weight loss results in significant improvement in pregnancy and ovulation rates in anovulatory obese women', *Human Reproduction* (1995), vol. 10, pp. 2705–12.

7. E. Stener-Victorian, U. Waldenstrom, U. Tagnfors, T. Lundeberg, G. Lindstedt and P. O. Janson, *Acta Obstetricia et Gynecolgica* (Scandinavia, 2000), vol. 79, pp. 180–8.

8. Dr Harvey Kliman, *Gynecologic and Obstetrical Investigation* (June 2002).

9. M. Canis, G. Mage, A. Wattiez, C. Chapron, J. L. Pouly and S. Bassil, 'Second-look laparoscopy after laparscopic cystectomy of large ovarian endometriosmas', *Fertility and Sterility* (1992), vol. 58, pp. 617–19.

10. D. R. Mishell, Jr, et al., 'Endometriosis and adenomyosis', *Comprehensive – Gynecology* (St Louis: Mosby, 2001), pp. 531–64.

11. Chang, Chung and Rosenwaks, 'Role of acupuncture in the treatment of female infertility'.

12. Xian Xu, Hang Yin, Daiyi Tang, Li Zhang and Roger G. Gosden, 'Application of traditional Chinese medicine in the treatment of infertility', *Human Fertility* (2003) vol. 6, pp. 161–8.

13. F. Parazzini et al., 'Selected food intake and risk of endometriosis', *Human Reproduction* (2004), vol. 19, no. 8.

CHAPTER 21

1. Balen and Jacobs, *Infertility in Practice*.

2. M. Yamamoto, H. Hibi, Y. Tsuji, K. Miyake, 'The effect of

varicocele ligation on oocyte fertilization and pregnancy after failure of fertilization in in vitro fertilization-embryo transfer', *Hinyokika Kiyo* (August 1994), vol. 40, no. 8, pp. 683–7.

CHAPTER 23

1. Balen, 'Ovulation induction – optimising results and minimizing risks'.
2. M. A. Rossing et al., 'Ovarian tumours in a cohort of infertile women', *New England Journal of Medicine* (1994), vol. 331, pp. 771–6.
3. Z. Shoham, R. Borenstein, B. Lunenfeld and C. Pariente, 'Hormonal Profiles following Clomifene Citrate Therapy in Conception and Non-Conception Cycles', *Journal of Clinical Endocrinology* (1990), vol. 33, pp. 271–8.
4. 'Female infertility: treatment options for complicated cases' (ESHRE Capri Workshop), *Human Reproduction* (1997), vol. 12, pp. 1191–6.
5. Balen and Jacobs, *Infertility in Practice*.
6. Balen, 'Ovulation induction – optimising results and minimizing risks'.
7. 'Management of infertility caused by ovulatory dysfunction', ACOG practice bulletin, American College of Obstetricians and Gynaecologists (2002), no. 34.
8. J. A. Collins, E. A. Burrows and A. R. Wian, 'The prognosis for live birth among untreated infertile couples', *Fertility and Sterility* (1995), vol. 64, pp. 22–8.
9. 'Salpingectomy for hydrosalpinx prior to IVF', *Practice Committee Report*, American Society for Reproductive Medicine (2001), pp. 1–4.
10. K. Duckitt, 'Infertility and subfertility', *Clinical Evidence* (2003), vol. 9, pp. 2044–73.
11. *Ibid.*

CHAPTER 24

1. HFEA (May 2005).
2. Rossing et al. (1991, 2004); Shushen et al. (1996); Gaathier et al. (2004); Kashvap et al. (2004); Brinton et al. (2005)
3. HFEA (May 2005).

4. Drs Aniruddha Malpani and Anjali Malpani, *A Guide for the Infertile Couple*, UBS (1994).
5. ICSI fact sheet from American Society for Reproductive Medicine (August 2001).
6. *Ibid.*
7. HFEA (May 2005).
8. *Ibid.*

CHAPTER 25

1. Chang, Chung and Rosenwaks, 'Role of acupuncture in the treatment of female infertility'.
2. HFEA (May 2005).
3. *Fertility and Sterility* (August 2005), vol. 84, no. 2.
4. John Dausset, *Journal of Bio Medicine and Bio Technology* (2001), vol. 1, pp. 1–2.

CHAPTER 26

1. HFEA (May 2005).
2. *Ibid.*
3. *Ibid.*
4. BBC News (6 July 2005).

CONCLUSION

1. Joan Raphael-Leff, *Inconceivable Conceptions and Psychological Aspects of Infertility and Reproductive Technology* (Jane Haines and Juliet Miller, eds, Brunner-Rutledge).
2. Clare Murray and Susan Golombok, 'To tell or not to tell: the decision-making process of egg-donation parents', *Human Fertility* (2003), vol. 6, pp. 89–95.
3. Diane N. Clapp, 'Helping patients know when "enough is enough"', *Sexuality, Reproduction and Menopause* (September 2004), vol. 2, no. 3.

INDEX

test 222–3
anxiety 1, 19, 54, 64, 78, 110, 129, 341
aphrodisiacs 164–5
aromatase inhibitors 246
aromatherapy 137
ART *see* assisted reproductive technology
artificial insemination 33
artificial sweeteners 103
aspartame 101
aspermia 216
aspirin 319
assisted conception 287–307, 323–9
  egg donation 325–6
  egg freezing 327–8
  egg sharing 326
  gamete intra-fallopian transfer 302–4
  intra-cytoplasmic sperm injection 304–6
  intrauterine insemination 299–302
  natural cycle 299
  percutaneous epidydmal sperm aspiration 306–7
  sperm donation 323–5
  in vitro fertilisation 293–9
  weighing up your options 289–92
  what it means 288–9
assisted reproductive technology (ART) 293
asthenozoospermia 216
athletes 18, 20, 53, 172
autoantibodies 247
autonomic nervous system 150, 312–13
Ayurvedic medicine 13, 164
azoospermia 42, 216

bad foods 100–102, 154, 220, 256, 332
balding 199
basal body temperature 30, 32
baths 147, 317
beans 88, 94, 103
behavioral treatment 19
bergamot 170
beta carotene 107, 108, 109, 120
Billings, John 31

bisphenol A 149
blame 143
blastocyst culture 314, 315
blastocysts 314
blindness 83
blood clotting abnormalities 48
blood clotting problems 298
blood pressure
  high 66, 75–6, 89, 100, 150
  reduction of 170
blood sugar 76, 88, 89, 99, 101, 118, 244
blood tests 201–4
  androgens 202
  antimullerian factor 203
  follice-stimulating hormone (FSH) 202, 221
  full blood count 201–2
  luteinising hormone (LH) 202, 221
  prolactin 203
  rubella 204
  testosterone 221
  thyroid function tests 204
body mass index (BMI) 56, 65, 66, 67, 186, 271
botanical medicine *see* herbal medicine
box schemes 96
brain
  calification 84
  hypothalamus region 24
brazil nuts 98, 120
breads 88, 89, 100
breakfast 103–4
breasts: discharge of milk 36, 199
breathing 133–4, 316
British Equestrian Federation 18
British Psychological Society 140
broccoli 98, 256
bromocriptine 278–80
brucella 102
brucellosis 102
Bull, Dr Stephen J. 173, 174

cadmium 72
caffeine 48, 58, 64–5, 103, 132, 317, 2565
calcium 64, 114